I0529250

LIFELIKE

SELF-AWARENESS
ENLIGHTENMENT
LIFESTYLE

TAPUWA SHEREKETE RUSHESHA

Copyright @2022 by Tapuwa Sherekete Rushesha

All rights reserved. No part of this book may be reproduced in any form or by any electronic or mechanical means, including information storage and retrieval systems, without permission in writing from the publisher, except by reviewers, who may quote brief passages in a review.

This publication contains the opinions and ideas of its author. It is intended to provide helpful and informative material on the subjects addressed in the publication. The author and publisher specifically disclaim all responsibility for any liability, loss or risk, personal or otherwise, which is incurred as a consequence, directly or indirectly, of the use and application of any of the contents of this book.

WORKBOOK PRESS LLC
187 E Warm Springs Rd,
Suite B285, Las Vegas, NV 89119, USA

Website: https://workbookpress.com/
Hotline: 1-888-818-4856
Email: admin@workbookpress.com

Ordering Information:
Quantity sales. Special discounts are available on quantity purchases by corporations, associations, and others.
For details, contact the publisher at the address above.

Library of Congress Control Number:
ISBN-13:   978-1-957618-22-7 (Paperback Version)
                978-1-957618-75-3 (Hardcover Version)
                978-1-957618-23-4 (Digital Version)

REV. DATE: 22/02/2022

LIFELIKE

By Tapuwa Sherekete Rushesha

To my daughters

Tanya-Rozina
Clara-Nakai
Natasha-Tawanna
Chidochemoyo-Nelia

"Who am I", especially when nobody is watching.

Contents

Preface

As we progressively go through the days of our adult lives, we increasingly realise the nagging need that has constantly stayed at the back of our minds, to try and unbound ourselves and escape from both our historicity and the ferocity of a dominant society. We feel an awareness of its contribution towards limiting our realm of inner experience. How have we dealt with the demands of our inner selves? How have we faired with the more demanding and continuously competing diverse environments and their accompanying inevitable backlashes?

The ability to develop coping mechanisms comes at a great cost to us. These external demands, on the most part, require us to progressively acquire competent knowledge, all forms of intelligences, wisdoms and insights, stimulating and bringing about greater consciousness. If transformative, these tool us to craft desirable innovations that manifest self-in praxis. For innumerable reasons and excuses, we have limited success at achieving our inner desires and objectives. How were we successful at some and faired not so great at others? Can we evaluate those we were successful at? How particular and peculiar were they to us, to our related families, communities, organisations and societies?

A significant number of us thrive to escape into a global transcultural relevance that defuses our immediate and imposing communities' expectations. Unfortunately, regardless of where and who we are, an insatiable demand exists at all levels of complexity, of maximal commitment of our great minds. Greatness that manifests in the form of higher dimensions of consciousness, appropriately tooled to confront the inherent challenges that reciprocate our advancements towards our desires.

We may need to effectively start with revealing our challenges through digging deep into our missing depths. It necessarily ventures into those of our families, communities and inherent natural environment, highlighting the divides we must attempt to bridge. impacting on our roles in them? How can this be shared without prejudice, mutilation and exclusion on a daily basis? How do we precipitate most of the knowledge we acquire into relevant and usable formats propagated as structured concepts? They essentially translate what is universal to the particular.

We then engage with it at an operational level transforming it into apparatus of production and control. This limits advancement of the process of individuation we journey through from birth. Limitations we experience and confront objectifies a life worth living! It defines our role in it, thus contributing to the outer self and the global society at its fullest extent. It simultaneously commits our abilities in the best way we know how as an ultimate. It puts us on a life trajectory that continuously strives to create internal capacities to navigate towards the creation of free time to use as we desire.

It enables us lifestyles that are lifelike on the basis that most of our primary and vital needs are met. Welfare of our families, shelter, food, clean water, a green world and freedom of the mind to dream, ideate, conceptualise and draw realizations as we please. To live lives experiencing minimum prejudice, minimum exclusion, minimum muzzling and minimum mutilation.

How can this be achieved without reducing ourselves to the dictates and direction of others? How can our lives realize its fullest intensity as we desire it on our terms without following pre-conceived paths carved for us by others? How can we minimize our reduction to conform to a strongly and externally crafted structured formulaic existence at home, at work and in our social life?

One view perceives the process of individuation as that which effectively tools us to genuinely conscientise our bodies, minds, hearts, souls and spirits. Those transformative processes equip us with the requisite consciousness and capacities to truly unchain and unbound ourselves. At times, the responsibility on self is overwhelming that we advance all kinds of discourses to justify our staying bound and chained to the tried and tested formulaic forms of lifestyles and existence. Self extrication requires us to journey through development of personalized and integrated life designs.

We engage the Dreams to their Realisation Continuum. We first develop necessary consciences that can dream, ideate, conceptualise and finally have the ability to effect these into transformative and practically realisable processes. It necessarily must result in objectifying our transcendence individually and collectively into being lifelike.

Our design roots itself in Lessem and Schieffer's thinking in their Integral World's philosophy. It attempts a humanistic, holistic, rational, pragmatic and practical approach. It draws from knowledge systems that evolved over centuries peculiar and particular to clearly identifiable four world views.

The Integral Worlds approach captures the wisdoms of four major world philosophies simultaneously and integratively building on the works of many others like Carl Jung, Polanyi and Ken Wilber. The idea here is to balance our senses of being, becoming, knowing and doing for them to complementarily work inclusively. In the process, it comprehensively embraces maximally relevant knowledge both existing and newly created.

It makes sense to first consider the closest one, most sensitive to nature and our collective being of cultures. In essence, it is strongly related to relational ways of highly rooted local communities, like Africa and South America.

We engage this as an originating and grounding process that releases related latent energies through venturing into nature's sustainable ways and tapping on the energy inherent in the collective. Our individual being gets connected to nature's creativeness enabling us in the process to articulate its hidden knowledge and knowing processes. Nature and its quintessential nurturing ways offer ecologically balanced green systems our thinking processes can adopt to function as its archetype. Our quests drive the inner selves and senses of being to meet with what the world hungrily demands of us in our lifestyles and lifetimes conscientised through it.

Simultaneously, we manage to uncover, differentiate and alleviate our original and grounded imbalances existing in us. These result in fully integrated approaches that since became part of us. Already evident in technological innovations and advancements are its basis and primal origination and grounding in epistemic and ontologic platforms simulating nature and culture.

The first stage of origination and grounding defines our states of being that are static needing to engage renewing and dynamic views. These are well pronounced in their deep sense rooted in inclusive cultural and spiritual knowledge systems. They are well developed, founded and relate strongly to the Eastern Asian and Arabic life practices.

How does all this consider, relate and impact our bodies, hearts, minds, souls and spirits to further define our senses of being? As we will progressively realise, this journey ultimately tools us with capacities to push forward transformation of our inner most desires and visions into realities. They cohesively process synthesisation of all the parts we gathered over the years to articulate our life stories towards our ultimate legacies. It is through this philosophy and others that we start to shift our inner static states of being to more universal outer transformative journeys. They interface with and are reinforced by our societal objectives in particular and our enterprising in general.

We are thus exposed to the need for us to implicitly, explicitly and tacitly know as much as possible how we are wired. It includes our need for the best educative, learning and training models that work for us. Through creation of a clear understanding of the respective analytical and transformative navigation paths that work for us, we realise our normative renewal's greatest potential. Easier said than done! How do we even start to try and actualise this?

Who are we, especially when nobody is watching?

A good place to start is by attempting to define the present state of our being. The first iteration may prove to be mission impossible!! We can start with what we know for a fact and what we are comfortable emphasising to define our past and present. The next process of normative renewal, manages to bring it together organically. The objective is to emerge our futures that can confront our increasingly complex and chaotic selves and the world around us.

Our construction requires us to transcend to higher levels with ability to handle emergent complexities of competing magnitude. We are pushed to draw on the synthesis of our ontological makeup and epistemologies of our ecosystems.

We discover that our prevailing mindsets die first to be reborn in the disguise of norms and practices that do not stifle unmutilated creative thinking with originality and contextual relevance. Is it not through our past and present we were psychologically conditioned into mindsets lesser than our true selves and subservient to prewritten scripts authored and edited by others?

We critically first explore who we are, the *I am* that reveals the extent of our present capacities and weaknesses to be rooted in sync with our cultures, families fully lodged in our societies. It is difficult to extricate the self from own nature, community and culture and still be able to function optimally. These appear to be intertwined and inseparable at first. The evolution of one part triggers that of the other.

How do we intend to rise above it all? How can we realign, redefine and reorient their emergence without each compromising the other? How can we cultivate the necessary self control, self planning and self organizing demands of our endeavor?

We are empowered further through acquisition of necessary tools that capacitate us to tap into our hidden depths. We manage to find our paths of renewal through the unfolding awareness of our being. We necessarily and pragmatically consider how to rationalise these new discoveries with emerging new capacities we were unconscious ever existed. Can we at best pragmatically rationalise the renewed dynamic selves without risking the safe familiar and that which is generally acceptable to our peers?

We now integratively engage the third worldview renowned as most able at pragmatically rationalising new creations and re-births. It considers in detail our static state of being and its dynamic renewal. In the process, it emerges the recognizable and desirable new. Further emancipation draws out the new into a format that is universally acceptable.

How do we now collate, consolidate, synthesize and rationalise the new for its consumption by everyone standing in waiting to adjudicate on who we have become only to nail us back into the ground?

Ironically, this new found consciousness is an inclusive result derived from convergence of diverse narratives revealed at different levels and from various sectors. Dialectical and dialogical inclusivity relevantly brings out our renewed stories relevantly. Are we able to identify with our renewed stories and remain calm enough to keep transcending our renewal paths to new and unchartered levels?

Dichotomies and parallels revealed this far indicate a nexus in our struggles with relationships between the self and other, tradition and modernity, local practice and global integrity, indigenous and exogenous knowledge systems and that which we know from explicit learning (academia) and business praxis. Self validation may genetically require the approval of dialectics on their terms, content, rules of interaction and cooperation. It defines the domain of our existence in a way simplified to mechanical behavior. It mutilates the vision of our horizons of life.

How do we manage to engage created tensions to our advantage to enhance our balance we now view as our inner desires or callings? Did we reveal any internalized psychological, metaphysical tendencies and mutilations? Are they inhibitive to our process of growing our abilities towards consciousness of the authentic selves? Was this a manifest of the dialect created between the self and the origins of formidable barriers we now perceive to exist in us?

Critiquing of our discoveries so far require an empirical whole approach to consider observable facts of the context rather than the tendency of a Newtonian approach that mostly distinguish and isolates parts of the overall consciousness. Our context focuses on facts that expose the level of our imbeddedness and how we fit into the context structure to effectively function in it. We realise and integrate our unconscious imbedded in our shadows bringing them forward into our conscious thus realising the unknown to the known- unknown. Venturing into those dark areas of the unknown greatly enhances our processes of individuation.

Our challenge is to come up with an integrated approach (design) that is holistically inclusive to dream, ideate, conceptualise and realize our aspirations. Our partially informed approaches lack in full information and fully independent conscious consideration. The approach here, from the onset attempts to clearly demonstrate how a personalized approach can be designed and applied in making critical life decisions.

It is trans-sectorally inclusive of all major global philosophies and knowledge systems that originate and ground us through sustainable nature and its collective ways. It then emerges the revealed imbalances through culture and spirituality. As these two are generally considered as a mixed bag of subjectivity and objectivity, we emancipate what emerged in science and technological intelligence globally revered as the house of pragmatism and rationality. Finally, we critically ensure that our integral design is complete enough to result in the renewed us. We become the best at what we do buoyed in full self-awareness of who we are. It includes our abilities to effectively apply and practice in a way that brings the world a step closer to resolving its imbalances especially those existing in our humanity and preservation of our earth for future generations to come. As *lifelike lifestyles* intend!

The Dreams Continuum framework coupled with the ingenious Integral Worlds philosophy conscientise us to learn to be and to fully bring out our *I am* first. It then reveals emancipatory paths most authentic to us as individuals. These know how to pave ways of evolving us into what we desire to be. Our integral design to self-awareness draws and grounds us from the best developed knowledge systems summarised into four major world philosophies.

Our dreams generate the *I am because we are* resonating with the South; whereas the idealizing *I am because I improve* renews, ascribing to the Asian and Arabic East; the conceptualising and rationalising learning to know, slogans the *I am because I think* popular with the west European North; and finally the practical, operational, educating and implementing *I am because I do and dream* best represented by North America. In effect, this realises our dreams into effective utilisable realisations.

Optimal emancipation and navigation of our perceived scenarios with their need to reveal new knowledge requires us to develop specialised abilities and skills. These can be acquired over time through our implicit, explicit and tacit forms of learning. We may already have what we need within us. How do we bring to the fore what we already have to benefit us materially?

As much as it can be done effectively with what we already have, organically developed and empirically based approaches are needed. Its mandate to specifically reveal new knowledge about ourselves, our families, our societies and everything that impacts our daily lives makes it ideal for one who desires to perform at the pinnacle of things. Putting into practice our individuation journeys results in individuals with the ability to build communities through collective responsibility, development and improvement of services and infrastructure. It equally develops our ability to foster conscious evolution through available spiritual capital and social investment.

The good self is capable of creating new knowledge through self, family, surrounding communities and organisations, collaborating with externally structured endeavors, through social and technological innovation.

The main objective of this experience, but not the sum of all the others described before, is to emerge our personalized integral design that brings about our freedom. It starts with the self and transcends to societally sustainable development through the integration of business praxis, academia, various forms of leaderships to civic and nongovernmental organisations and the public service. These become cognisant and necessarily amount to economic, non-economic and socio political initiatives coupled with specific, measurable, achievable, realistic and time-bound performance.

Introduction

The belief that improperly designed education systems can stifle creativity and innovation is slowly gaining ground within both social and academic arenas. This ist coming at a time when our education curricula are getting more complex and sophisticated. Literacy rates are increasing considerably both in socio-economic and political worlds. Penetration rates into unexplored areas are improving. We applaud all concerned, including but not limited to Non-Governmental Organisations, various religious entities and civic organisations for a job well done in this sector. Formalisation of local knowledge is on the rise but not to desired levels.

Enculturation dominates acculturation in less developed countries whose systems depend on the affluent and materially rich countries notwithstanding that they account for more than two thirds of the world population. How then can we re-visit our curricula to make our learners more self-aware of who they are and relevant to their everyday living? How can we impact their pedagogy to impact their most desired inner imbalances? Corridors of higher learning exclude themselves from societal problems and experiences of learners on daily basis. How can those in tertiary education effect creativity and innovations that contribute significantly to the resolution of existing burning issues on the ground?

Strong beliefs in the superiority of formal education in practice and theory is diminishing, more so when the correlation between education and the impact of graduates in praxis is becoming more obscure. Somewhere in America, funds were availed by a successful entrepreneur to finance enrolled undergraduates with US$100 000. They were required to drop out of university and embark on entrepreneurial creative and innovative ventures. Their mandate was to come up with cutting edge realisable innovations. Would they be able to demonstrate if education per se stifles creativity?

We wonder if at that level, well into the first formative adult years of these youngsters, if more tertiary education isn't required as a tool to enhance realisation paths of their desires? Perhaps the discourse and dialectic tensions emerging between cautious conservative and random impetuous thinking, confined and corridored to unregulated and unmuffled out-of-need creativity, generate semi-coherent voices from within the inner selves. Can these voices be born out of perceived distortions of the teacher to student systems rather than the more interactive and facilitatory approaches where the teacher is a facilitator? Soon after de-briefing cessions popularized as examinations, there is not much left in the student to borrow from in their creative and innovative future endeavors.

Then there is the adage that one does not need a college degree to make it in life. The usual examples of well known financially successful people are proffered in everyday conversations. Local narratives are shifting in that direction reinforced by diverse social, political and economic factors. The historical formal education paradigm that it ejects one from poverty, developed over the century in one form or another, is receding into virtuosity. Arguably, it is not evidenced by tangible results in reality.

The contemporary alternative is the promotion of an entrepreneurial spirit especially within the youths. They are encouraged to move away from the mentality of employment to being employers through start-ups. The vibe is that the world is moving in that direction and examples of China, India, South Korea and the USA are cited as typical examples.

These societal conversations appear overly simplistic and unfortunately filter and enshrine into their narratives, particularly in lower economic classes. In the past century, many countries struggled with cultural evolution to the extent that some of their communities imploded and literally collapsed. Other societies metamophosised into something that adopted other cultures' undesirable traits. Its constant dynamic motion accelerated regardless of where the influence was coming from. Inherent lower level dynamics had strong vertical influence at both quality and quantity of consciousness of individual identities especially in transient environments.

The majority of those that consciously seek self-awareness had great academic potential. They realise their need to act on that perceived potential to be the best of themselves.

We all developed unique ways of attracting attention since we were toddlers. We may not have achieved the success we wished for but certainly got the attention we desired. Unfortunately our education systems were generally not designed to exploit and expose this potential. Instead, it polarized us into uni-disciplinary corridors and socialised us not to care for much else. Those that were in the social sciences, humanities, arts and sports became unconcerned with mathematics, physics or chemistry, and vice-versa. Technical, hands- on classes were deemed as remedial for those considered incompetent in both. Either way, as we move closer to the apex of our academic journeys, we start to realise that we are more similar than different and integrally need the other for holistic success.

Selection and filtration methods that reinforced our mono- disciplinary approaches have impacted our lives in general. They have selectively created favourites and outcasts, with some sectors being viewed as more intellectually superior than others. Instead of encouragement to learn from each other, the less gifted in academics found themselves excelling in the relational side of life. They socialized more, played sport, and developed a common sense that foster camaraderie, learnt to engage and survive from the community and developed the necessary patience to play for the long haul. Inadvertently, they did not confine themselves to specialization to enter and dwell in specific silos. They specialised in the freedom of thought, ability to observe, listening, learning and survival on bare minimums. In short, they learnt to survive in and from their communities and on the hand nature dealt them. They discovered the true selves in the process of their growth.

The other side of the divide's ascendancy up the academic and professional ladders slowly define and confine them to specific fields of expertise, sometimes with total disregard of all else. Their egos and pride appear to correspondingly grow as they get more recognition, respect and accolades in their respective fields, further propelling a strong desire to propagate the mono-disciplinary and silo approach. They realise somewhere along the line that it comes with some level of clumsiness and discomfort with building relationships, not that great at people skills, marketing and selling. They find public speaking and communication challenging. It didn't seem important previously but now is needed to brand and sell one self's abilities to gain and contract with education and health sectors, energy corporations, telecoms, the army, the navy, and with community leaders (etcetera etcetera) for them to buy into their ideas.

Society relegated these areas as less academic and not significant enough to eject one into lifestyles of their dreams. Those that dared grabbed on crumbs left over from natural sciences. They quickly learnt that their survival came out of their ability to talk with clarity of mind, humility, good communication skills and to sell anything, especially their ideas. It is now referred to as emotional intelligence. They mastered these skills previously viewed as too simple and mundane to make a difference.

Unlike obvious University candidates, some scrapped through and barely managed to maintain a 2.75 grade point average. But it afforded them time to be active participants in Students Representative Councils (SRCs). They managed to actively attend University functions, from sports galas to music festivals. They were always well informed about all neighbourhood social occasions and kept their ears to the ground. They knew, talked and hung around with all the beautiful girls and popular boys. Somehow, those considered bright generally sort services outside the main academic arena from those considered less bright and it came at a fee.

The privileged intelligent were quick to rationalise and pamper their egos that they reserved their energies for more important things. After all, what could be better than maintaining a higher than 3.5 grade point average! Society had convinced them that the silos they were in guaranteed an important future and could always beat those outside it hands down.

The academically gifted were considered and treated better. If we fast forward to present day, what proportion of each divide sit at high tables, board rooms and are in networks where important decisions are made? Are the aforesaid areas dominated by those who were obvious candidates, we ask?

Previous graduations were a breeze for the few academically elite. They received several citations and envisaged secure slots in hierarchies of future leadership. They impressed head hunters that were like hound dogs, circling and offering them several career choices. They were in demand and the future looked bright. They were the port of call and appeared to have crystal balls that could decipher the present and foretell the future. One could feel and smell a great career ahead for the chosen few, no doubt.

Being in a privileged position made it difficult to see it coming. How did it happen that *Mussa, the street vendor* surpassed and outperformed all odds to become the COO of the largest energy corporation in the country when them and their peers only achieved department heads status? Something is amiss! They feel cheated because they are not the ones at the helm of successful politicians, entrepreneurs and community leaders.

Mussa is noticeable, visibly becoming wealthier and now lives in a more affluent suburb envisaged to be for yester year high academic achievers. The gossip that Mussa is corrupt, someone's crony, connected, networked and surely must be a tax evader does the rounds. Some are hurt. For the first time, society's torch is on Mussa. He is rubbing shoulders with the elites of society. He now sits at the high table supposed to be their preserve. Egos are bruised! This needs rationalizing. How and where would one even start?

The work environment is proving to be unpredictable. Junior to senior management jobs canbe secured but somehow the top job is illusive. For one reason or another, that elusive position is passed on to the next guy. The *next time* phrase has become too familiar with the blue eyed boys accustomed to first choice picks. They are told they are specialized, unique, highly trained and expensive to replace. They are in special projects and their positions are hard to fill. They are secure in the belief that they are irreplaceable, but on pressing harder sometimes are inadvertently told the higher job requires much stronger people skills they lack.

It takes a while to sink in that they don't have something that landsthe success they most desire. They agonisingly take awhile to figure out that they hardly know who they really are. They are not completely aware of their strengths and weaknesses outside their areas of expertise. Are they sure if they even like the work they do?

Something previously unavailable in the compliment of toys they had in their silos is now required. Who would have envisaged that all that assortment of toys to die for was going to be inadequate for their future needs? The demands of the top job everyone desires require greater skills than they possess. Why are the top jobs seemingly elusive to them as perceived obvious candidates, going to non-traditionals?

Their partners or spouses hinted in the past that they were kind of stiff and dissimilar people found them difficult to understand. Some had courageously pointed out that they needed to emotionally connect better with people. It now makes sense to them. Their ivy league education up to undergraduate degrees and subsequent MBAs totally disregarded emotional intelligence as irrelevant to contemporary demands and dictates. The conventional IQ was particularized. The general approach in technical disciplines sidelined at best, sensitivities to relationships, to contextual communities, culture, spirituality and traditions. And yet we still wonder why that top spot is elusive!

At this juncture, the emerging probability is that we need more thrust to burst through the barrier we now perceive, to improve the odds of the hand we are dealt. We feel great at what we do best but miss something to achieve the niche that obviously looked like ours to take. We feel we should surely be at the top of our game. Title and money are no more as great motivators they were at the beginning. Our demands became more focused since our University days. We now seemingly require less. Something other than the material demands our utmost best. Recognition, fame and peak performance at our archetypical best is now our biggest nag. For some reason, the desire to do something that proves that we are better than our jobs in our acquired disciplines is becoming more impelling.

A greater inhibition stands in our way to do greater good, to excel and prove that we are the best in what we do. After all, what would our peers think if they found out that we now root our future success in first identifying our archetypical Callings, our burning desires, community concerns, spirituality, culture and so forth? Our inner voices propel us on but at times they are not loud enough. It is in part overwhelmed and distorted by interference from all the noises around us. It feels much easier and expedient to go with the flow that has yielded mediocre lifestyles in comparison to that which is lifelike we dream about all the time. How many of those that achieved their success through formal learning-education- training are fully applying the knowledge they acquired or developed in practice? Without further self-conscientising in other areas outside our mainstream, we find that our visibility slowly and surely begins to atrophy into oblivion. How do we counter that negative curve to half- life?

We need to do things differently if we are to reform and ever realise those ideas that formed in our early lives but were sidelined in preference of security found in survival skills. Our original formative years now come forward as external influences probably dominated and overwhelmingly enculturated. Once we begin to deliberately engage our self-awareness initiatives, we find that those pressures start to disseminate and can now be re-addressed with particular focus on inner self interests. Hopefully the egos we developed over the years become secondary and subservient to other voices beckoning us to embark on life changing journeys that authenticate us. We can now resolve that extensive dialectic over-arching our lives to quench that deep yearning.

Our emergence at the end of this long argument as victors draws on our energy resources. It therefore demands us to embark on something that is authentic to us. We need to harness and integrate all energy resources available to us to redress that imbalance resident in us. It may reveal itself through a social challenge we perceive, an inadequacy or a spiritual calling, whatever it is that can transcend our being into balance. Its revelation and resolution synergically peaks when our archetypical callings, our ego needs and a societal imbalance that resonates with us coincide. Their congruence has hardly ever been formally sought before. Close examination of most success cases reveal that this has happened to practitioners to achieve the level of success they realised. The passion displayed by successful entrepreneurs emulates congruence. How do we unfold that trilogy of our archetypical callings, our ego needs and a relevant societal imbalance?

Some extremely successful individuals may wonder what this is all about. They are at the top of their game and are even global leaders in what they do. Their friends, families and communities love and respect them. They may have landed that revered government top post, are First Ladies or Presidents of their countries but still feel the need to take that extra step. Is it the title or the lifelike lifestyles that drives them? Or are they tired of that mister or missus title and now prefer other fancier ones like doctor and president that seem to carry more weight and authority?

It most times gets us the front row, appears classier and has an intelligence ring to it. People tend to listen and give authority to the good doctor more and question their postulations less. We are confident that these titles come with recognition, status, less interrogation of perspectives, respect and visibility. It can immediately elevate one to that class of high achievers with a sense of wholeness we envy.

Our deep kind of inner thirst needs to be genuinely on point for us to get on the road towards the kind of lifelike lifestyles we dream. An insatiable void and curiosity to get to the bottom of things is a good indicator of a living driving force within us. It bothers us that we still feel lacking and empty although we are avid readers, especially in our areas of expertise. There has not been much time for anything else. We considered hobbies as idle time and a waste. We feel we do not see as far as we wish. It usually takes a mindset that itches to take the next step. How do we re-calibrate our mindsets to itch and itch in the right direction?

In some instances, precedence of a family legacy obligates us to show our brilliance to lead the next generation in line. The torch of our family legacy is well established through notoriety and honour in renowned traditional professions that include economists, researchers, scientists, engineers and professors. We may be forced to pass that family leadership position to our younger siblings who are better prepared and are well on their way to obtaining the relevant prestigious qualifications in similar professions. The pressure is on us to carry the Adam Smith dream to the next level. It cannot be anything else but! Do we have the courage to break the legacy, to pass on the torch to our younger sibling in lieu of the demands of our inner yearnings and voices?

At first, motivations pushing us in this direction are unclear. A little voice regularly nags and impels us to take care of undesirable situations we notice and desire to make a difference. These observations constantly bother us that at times we feel helpless. Occasionally we even get cold sweats and experience differing degrees of insomnia from it. Our dreams envision a better life for humanity first and then for ourselves as a derivative of that collective. Envisioned creativity and innovative abilities appear fully capable of moving humanity a step further towards a consciousness fostering greater self determination and more fulfilling lifestyles, as minute as it may be in the eyes of self and others,.

We foresee our intervention alleviating particular deficiencies we perceive and strongly feel. These maybe buoyed in poverty surrounding us or can be a medical condition prevalent in our communities requiring a technological solution or an engineering challenge or a social imbalance.

Whatever the case might be, a self-awareness journey is one endeavor that equips us to better realise the know-how and corresponding innovations to counter imbalances we experience. We must develop the courage, strength and determination first to be able to undertake this kind of a journey. Keenness and clarity of our final contributions out of this undertaking will not sit and gather dust, forgotten in the enclaves of our mind, considered by others as just another egotistical exercise. The change and benefit may not be recognizable or noticeable by the uninitiated, wallowing in the glory of external validation. Our evolution must exude brilliance within our inner selves. Our contributions need and must positively change our sense of being, our families and our immediate communities as an immediate indicator. Our innovations must transform structures and functioning of societies. This is a mouthful, a true challenge indeed, surmountable though!

A trait that has become traditional as a measure of success of our careers is the need to precipitate thoughts into some form of hypothesis, a proposition, an inquiry or a specific statement that translates into material benefit for all to see and experience. But what really is bothersome is that all we mostly have are our dreams and visions peculiar to us but cannot pass the rational and pragmatic tests employed by our peers. There is a formal inquiry into our affairs set by others, unbeknown to us from the onset. Virtual judges sit and adjudicate on our appropriateness in relation to the collective that has had no prior participation and indication of our views. Why is it primary for our inner desire to be contextually relevant and be assimilated for the approval of our peers and those others?

Needs of our communities versus our rebirth in the new impact us only as a juxtaposed secondary consideration to ours. How authentic is this to us, to all those around and beneficiaries we engage on a daily basis during our journey? Are all these factors not part of intimate determinants to the relevance and utility levels of the new us? Is it presumptuous that our involvement and imbeddedness in our self-awareness endeavors we intimately and authentically care about may need to start much earlier? We need to put these through known and established praxis tests? How do we even start? It is an indulging undertaking, firstly through our introspection transcending it to include others around us and finally our societies in general. How involving is it and what resources do we need? It is not as daunting as it sounds because most of what is needed is already within us and only needs to be drawn out. We are the solution to our challenges.

Past academic achievements including our latest MBAs preamble the corner office a few notches up the organogram ladder. Indeed, it advances our awareness and skills at developing business ideas, producing business plans and project proposals. It improves our understanding of conventional business management, accounting and financial principles. Somehow, it does not silence nor abate the little voice that constantly nags us. It awakens the sleeping giant in us.

The giant feeds on continual renewal of our consciousness to participate in our true transformation and that of our contexts and ecosystems. We find ourselves at a nexus of several wisdoms and knowledge systems that can determine lifestyles we will lead for the rest of our natural lives.

We can safely conjuncture that with a well designed integrated self-awareness program we are at the foothills of realising unprecedented success in becoming who we truly are and who we were meant to be. It definitely is not for the faint hearted! This is a 24/7 commitment that does not guarantee any release back into our old selves after we transform into new beings not reconcilable with the old. We develop mindsets tolerant of both our views and those of others that welcome discourse. We acquire skills to integrate all its positive and beneficial aspects into something usable. We become cognisant of the primary need to be inclusive of self, family, friends, community, all interacting organisations and society in general.

We are equally inducted into the bomb disposal unit that assumes responsibility of societal change. The change we see is engaged to transform humanity, hopefully to a better place than we found it. Our re-birth in tandem with our environs emerges a form not even identifiable to anyone but carries the potential to positively impact on all of those it touches. Renewal is inevitable and desirable notwithstanding other ancillary acquisitions assumed throughout the transformative journey.

The majority of us focus on our destination of a defined journey coupled with pre-conceived strategies, pertinent technologies, innovations, people, systems and sustaining initiatives we need to engage. That as it may, the adventure of the journey, self discovery, creation of the new that structurally and functionally changes us and all those around us comes from answering to our authentic demands emanating from deep within. This is addressed by inclusively confronting our core Callings.

Simultaneous engagement with our archetype is considered most synergic, a combination considered to be the stuff those great luminaries are made of and answer to. It is an endless list that is conveniently distributed all over the world for all to see and emulate. It includes amongst many others, Nelson Mandela, Steve Jobs, Strive Masiyiwa, Richard Branson and Mohamed Yunus. We all have in us what they have if we dig deep from within. How then can we traverse similar or bettere self discovery paths, commitment levels and luminance?

Unlike most of us, they delved into their self-awareness journeys early in life and developed inexhaustible motivations rooted in their infinite energies. They engaged their spirituality, community networks, cultures and natural environments, taking from each of these only that which is necessary for their accentuated survival and advancement.

As much as our situations are naturally inclusive of all aspects of life, we may over-emphasise a few to a level where one can dominate at the exclusion of others. This kind of emphasis and minimization is peculiar to communities and confined to parts of the world that developed particular worldviews over millennia. Doesn't it logically follow that they became experts in those areas of over-emphasis and minimally competent in those they did not? It then makes sense that we selectively borrow their ways in areas they are best at over all others. We integrate their knowledge and wisdom in those areas with ours to strengthen and improve our weaker views.

The symbolic South of the world is strong in relational matters that emphasise, are collective and have developed communal approaches rooted in nature ways. The cardinal East metaphorically represents emphasis in renewal aspects through spirituality and cultural issues creating new knowledge in the process; the North in theory development and rational approaches; and the West is great at practice that transcends knowledge into realizable realities that improve economies and politics. Integration of these strengths creates resolute approaches with optimal chances to resolve imbalances we may feel, experience or perceive. The integrated design that results may differ to suit our particular challenges and contexts but the base concept of the Integral Worlds approach developed by Lessem and Schieffer remains applicable.

We learn from them and others that the best approach to any endeavor needs us to borrow inclusively and comprehensively from those that are best at it. We relevantly integrate our borrowings with our own to emerge a new that can holistically heal our imbalances. This in part has existed in natural sciences as they developed various technologies but deliberately marginalised the importance of worldviews of the South and the North. The exclusion of these two worlds is now coming back to haunt us as evidenced by the near absence of relational and renewal considerations that envelop senses of sharing, sensitivity and active respect of nature and our environments, our spirituality and cultures in our daily lifestyles.

If our individual approaches to our enlightenment resumes deliberately develop and engage these integral designs, we will find that we become more relevant to ourselves and others. We precipitate deliverables that answer to both our individual callings and those of our contexts. Where and how do we start a design that promises so much where there is a big outcry on our irrelevance and exclusion? We start with attempting to fully articulate our individual states of being and *who we are* to enable us to influence everyone and everything around us and abound.

Chapter 1

WHO AM I?

Our fore bearers quickly realized the need to experientially learn from prior knowledge and significant others that came before them. Isaac Newton formalised this need in the 17th Century when he summarised it as our need to stand on the shoulders of giants if we want to see further. West Africans proverbial observation was that if you want to travel fast you go alone, but if you want to travel further, get others to join the journey. How do we even begin to think and define what we need to know before we can begin to share? What is itwe require unreservedly as shoulders to stand on?

We must start somewhere and the best place is with self introspection. It assists us to clearly articulate our true states of being. The platform we create is knowledge based and is clear in our historicity, our present and our anticipated desired future. The latter can only be confronted with more enlightenment compared to the present to capacitate us to resolve present and future challenges.

Authenticity is key in the creation of a life history platform. How do we relevantly journey back to the beginning we define at first and how do we ensure presence of the minimum essence? It is only when we can define our incontestable present that we can begin to realistically map out the present and future we desire.

A child born into an environment that thrives on a particular philosophy can be highly any one of, several or all of being spiritual, cultural, collective, pragmatic and individualistic. Conflicting knowledge systems rooted in the local but highly dominated by the exogenous cause further tension. This becomes part of every facet of a child's life, from behavior, emotions, relationships, approach to spirituality and family. Spirituality is a central factor in the personification development of a person. As an example, the idea of witchcraft to an African child is more real than someone flying across the country side on a broom. Its relationship with witchcraft is a lived experience faced directly sometimes. Its reality or lack thereof predisposes the wellness of its being. The inert fear and respect it develops can last a lifetime regardless of what the individual becomes in their later life. This probably predisposes their affinity to highly spiritual religions, possibly a contributing factor to high growth rates of religious practices, religio-preneurship and tourism in Africa.

Institutional African Churches approach communities cognisant of this in-built dogma and capitalise on that tacit belief and their fear of the unknown emphasised through the presence of darkness from childhood. If a parent was to punish a child, the easiest and vivid way was to send it across a dark spot. It was a measure of bravery for one to carry out this errand without exhibiting fear although years later most would confess how truly afraid they were. The fear of witchcraft resembled by darkness manifested in how they relate with others. It impacts on how they view and solve problems. It similarly influences their ability to confront any undesirable situation, definition of the truth and how to tell it. The emergent view of the self is then reserved, introverted and not as outwardly confident. Does it now depend on how much one is willing to sacrifice to confront whatever it takes to get there? Some cultures encourage their subjects to delve into that unknown. How can we extinguish that fear of reprisal from the powers of darkness!

Fears we capture from childhood affect us for a very long time. They can manifest at any level of performance for example solving small village problems, municipality service delivery, administering of offerings of a small church to help the under privileged, parenthood and governance of nations. The failure rate to inclusively come together and sit down, find equitable and collective solutions that comprehensively address problems is enhanced. Obvious solutions become elusive. As one Asian observer commented, except for a few parts of Africa, one really has to push for the truth to come out. It is otherwise gossiped in a round-about way until it comes back to the intended recipient. Unfortunately, more often than not, this happens after the damage is already done.

Local and contextual knowledge systems, including empirically developed ways of conflict resolution are heavily influenced by the worldview particularly emphasised. This is difficult to acknowledge. Even community leaders presiding at prestigious and sophisticated gatherings find it difficult to participate and regard their truth from an enculturated worldview. Those that are enlightened may need to be tactful in the way they verbally communicate, confront and re-define their truth. Lest they may easily be consumed by mystic powers of darkness or some similar inherent fear! As a result, meetings in these environs appear to take longer than necessary to come up with obvious resolutions, some to a point of being ineffective depending on the boldness of the leaders of the deliberations. The power of darkness!

Underlying and silent fear of genuine and visible success that stands out exists in communities that recognise powers of darkness. Those that are free of it at times become prominently successful only to self destruct and stifle their development to levels they feel are acceptable to the powers of darkness. They subconsciously confine themselves to levels they feel do not awaken attention to the self. In their belief, this pacifies perceived forces to keep their distance. Others prefer to call these misfortunes of success, curses, jealousy, destiny and occasionally blame it on a grant scheme by outsiders to keep them down.

Some sections of a society accept these explanations depending on their level of education, exposure, socio-political influence and how difficult it is to access wealth and other resources primary to their livelihoods. Generally, the script ends the same with someone crying foul, blaming it on the invisible forces of darkness that influence one's demise. Those forces from the dark side again! There is always something that caused it and it is hardly ever the self. The self can never self inflict.

After burial, the rituals that follow require an intensive investigation into the cause of one's death. Surviving elders in the clan, both man and women assemble soon after a visit to a traditional doctor, a knowledge person in African Traditional Religions believed to be bestowed with powers to see into the past, present, future and beyond. The deceased could have been over 100 years old or could have positively died of cancer or AIDS, the spiritual cause of death still needs to be established. And yes, the explanations of ultra forces that influenced and caused the deceased's death are rife and generally influence the course of action of the extended family in future. This is something some enlightened individuals do not acknowledge during the light of day but do so under cover of darkness.

Surely the cause of death is clear from the Medical Examiner. This and similar posits are usually met with scornful faces that are clear in their feelings. They wonder on the brevity to question the powers from the dark side. Does one think that they are now above it all because they are educated, wealthy, or well travelled? There usually is one or two elders that are willing to sternly take blended locals aside and elaborately give an explanation on why a seemingly obvious cause of death still needs traditional investigation and due diligence.

Yes, the cause of death was AIDS for all to see but there were underlying causal happenings that push effected the deceased to contract HIV. They explain that the investigation is not there to question the established medical cause of death. It is there to answer why there was no spiritual protection and influence for the deceased to not even think of the sexual act that resulted in one contracting HIV. Why did the spiritual powers slacken in their protection mechanisms to let the deceased think, decide to act, pick on that inflicted partner and worse still contract it when there are stories that some sleep with infected partners and not contract it? Why did the deceased not develop a sixth sense on the fateful event to stop, fall asleep before the act or be called to work or something? Why did the spirit realm not halo the individual from this fatal act? It is that which needs investigation, to establish and correct it for the benefit of the living.

The dark force perceived to weaken spiritual protection needs to be removed and annihilated totally. It protects the remaining members of the clan to walk tall and acquire ultra wisdom to see potential danger, to avoid pitfalls, to be excluded from disastrous events. The living are then guided through the rest of their lives. Even if one leads an illustrious life and lives to be one hundred and twenty, they are not spared of establishment of the spiritual cause of death. Forces from the dark side that could have influenced it all still need to be eradicated!

What has all this to do with wanting to undertake self actualising lifestyles? How does this manifest into self awareness that leads the self and humanity in general into lifelike living? How do we define success against a backdrop of prior inherent cultural and societal beliefs? How hard do we want it? What are the barriers we perceive, conscious and real or otherwise, that get in the way of us realising manifests of our archetypical inner desires? Do we indoctrinate ourselves to be who we are today?

Critical resistance of strong cultural views is usually met with scornful faces intentionally clear of disapproval. Now that we feel fortunate and confident enough to have escaped cultural vices that kept others down, do we feel adequately immune to question powers from the dark side? Are we blaming and absconding it all simply because we are now educated, affluent, well travelled and enlightened of other possibilities,? There are under currents of ostracism and resentment from those that feel obligated to be custodians and preservers of cultural knowledge systems of the small communities some originated from. It is normally from those that remained behind throughout towards those that went away, hunting for their destinies.

But, now that we are all modern, educated, enlightened and religious, how do we relate contemporary selves to dictates of societies we operate in? We are not supposed to be stifled by beliefs we probably believe are archaic and traditional, are we? Is it true in practice that genuine and strong traditional beliefs that exist in our cultures do no ruffle or stifle us, irrespective of where we come from? Can they define and/or enhance us? The American, European, Asian, Arab, Russian, African, Indian, Japanese, Chinese, Korean, Jewish or Mediterranean way. We hear this every day.

We all have our cultural traditions that existed for centuries and remain relevant to this day. What do we do with them in light of enculturation from other global cultures that appear superior and more relevant to our contemporary, future existence and needs? Do we take time to fully understand our own cultural values before we can select the ones to keep or leave behind to replace them with more appropriate ones? Do we relevantly borrow from others only that which makes us stronger? Are other cultures borrowing from us as much as we are from them? If not, is it because we do not have much to offer them or it's because we have not formatted our knowledge in a manner that can enculture others? How do we bring our knowledge to the fore, code and catalogue it to attract its consumption by others?

Again, the dark side rings. Are we so afraid of the unknown to the extent that we prefer it to remain unknown allowing true selves to atrophy? Do we even bother to know what we don't know about ourselves? Why are we more accepting of the exogenous knowledge others re-packaged in an enculturating manner instead of countering it with repackaging and recombining our own knowledge, history and heritage in the best acculturating and enterprising manner?

Various schools of thought impact on our clarity to differentiate the good from the bad within. External influences imposed themselves upon less dominant individuals and societies for a very long time. Knowing what is originally ours is now blurred. Century old systems of passing on historical, traditional and cultural heritage contemporarily appear inadequate and dwarfed to withstand the rigors of artificial intelligence, global information systems, critical thinking and analysis.

Filial piety structures are diminishing. Consultation with elders conflicts and differs at every turn on the origins and foundations of our authentic ways. Do we really want to go back there or should we settle for the contemporary and springboard from there? Who determines that which is genuinely belonging and its relevance to this very complex knowledge based globalized environment? It is almost mission impossible for two adjacent neighbours to agree on minor issues of self determination. How then are we going to develop extension of commons throughout the breadth and length of the vast continent that is as diverse as its population?

Have we reduced ourselves to destitution devoid of free will and without options even in our daily survival? In other parts, they choose to consult those in the know and hold on to their old ways as conservatives!

Discourse on what is truly African, American or European continues unabated at scholarly, traditional, economic and socio-political levels. We blame all else for our limited awareness. Frank and progressive talks are either manipulated for gains outside the big picture of self emancipation. We self emancipate through our own self-definition and determination, through our own understanding of poverty, hunger and development. That fear in us, fear of something out there that can pounce on us anytime and anywhere has muffled, stunted and mutilated our desire for real and true success.

Others vehemently argue for near infinite effective definitions of self identity because we are now a conglomeration of many numerous and different others. Yet we are prepared to accept their definitions of us. They argue that we are too diverse to come up with a consensus. They view its potential benefits as not worth the effort. Globally, each region has had its definition of the dark side, mythical and mystical practices that dwarf others approach to innovations to confront their challenges. Christianity, Buddhism, and Islam to name a few, are the oldest and most popular religions of the world but still experience peculiar challenges of historicity, stories they tell, fundamentalism and dogma. How do we prefer to adopt theirs wholesale over ours if they are worse in certain instances? It appears their dominance in us is very real and prevalent for all to see.

The prevalence of our contextual local systems canbe subtle, invisible and non-existent in other parts of the world. Exception is on a micro level in small enclaves where concentrations of those particular communities domicile. We argue for evolutionary designs well orchestrated by stronger cultures to marginalize, consume and extinct less dominant ones. Some even go as far as positing deliberate machinations to keep the latter on the dark side. As much as we acknowledge these approaches, we proffer the genesis of all else in the world today as having originated from the continent of Darkness. It seems to indicate baseline epistemology for all else to buoy in, to originate from this same cradle that others are thriving to extinct.

The world appears to be re-converging to a common source where it all began to find solutions to its imbalances. The source's highly cultural and relational warm heart rhythmically resonate with the thunderous drums heard at all occasions, be they for thanks giving ceremonies or otherwise. Its high sense in the preservation of nature ways to remain in balance for the survival of its collective humanity can be given to the world for present and future renewal. Its unique relational intelligence is probably part of the solution of what is missing in today's' preferred world solutions. How can we all relate this to a world badly in need of a completely new meta-perspective on how it solves its problems? Major contributors to possible solutions are pioneering and highly self-conscious individuals that thrived throughout their lives, scattered all over the world. They too require correct tools that capacitate them in their considerations to inclusively integrate nature, individuals, communities, cultures, spiritualities and traditions as well as the impetus pragmatic rationalities and possibilities of theorising, be they economic or socio-political.

Some worldviews were excluded and some adopted with greater emphasis and dominance on others from the onset of world order initiatives. Similarly, tertiary self-awareness initiatives in the world are approached with equal biases, lacking in the richness of centuries of empirical knowledge from other worldviews. We start with awareness, emergence and orientation of great minds then transcend to creative beings craving to innovate inclusive contributions that heal humanity.

We all generate an infinite number of visions flooding our minds at any given moment but feel helpless to move them any further. Our simple imaginations die a slow death resulting in our sense of emptiness and helplessness. It is not easy to narrate who and what we are at any given juncture. Developing differentials of who we are at any instance is an absolute necessity. It helps us in substantiating our visions into concise narrations that can reflect on momentous states of being. These visions appear real sometimes and others fail to connect with or reflect on who we think we are or desire to be. All the same, they appear in fragmented shades ranging in reality from what is to what can be in our shadows. They are heavily influenced by myths and stories we encountered in our lives manifest in our long wish lists. Confrontation of these dominant influences requires us to derive the true and authentic us by harnessing all our positive energies.

Derivation of our inner positive energy requires us to answer the question *who is the authentic me?* This question can easily sound like it has neither a beginning nor an end. It can be so formidable and so overwhelming that it lays out a plateau in one's mind. Plateaus of this nature comprise of subroutines of circular causalities, scores of life imbalances feeding into processes that feed into outcomes causing a new set of imbalances. The process can effectively manage to continually feed positive outcomes of these micro ecosystems to the main path of our processes of individuation. The corresponding timeline reveals general commons that may or may not appeal to our families, peers, communities and other stakeholders relevant to our lifelike existence.

There are two nodes that define us all. They objectify anything else outside that domain. These nodes are the day we are physically born and the day we physically die. The two define the context of what is and what is not. It delineates who we are and who we are not including our relevant historicity. Our present being is a constantly moving locus in between the two, interfacing with what we view as our future all the time present in our afterlife. It is a life well lived between these two nodes that fully accounts for our footprint on this earth and pre-disposes our influence into the future.

There can be two other main sub-ecosystems, one skewed more to the left and the other more to the right of each of the two major nodal points. Their extension can be as elaborate as they naturally can be and as much as we wish them to be. It is this futuristic domain to the right of our present we want to influence and control as much as possible. This can be achieved through acquisition of transformative abilities enshrined in a formalized self discovery and development journeys like the self-awareness actualising programs.

Our historicity sub-ecosystems prior to our births impact our meta-physical lives. It then integratively influences our legacies.

We therefore need to unwind back to places we probably never went before to bring out our true sense of being, one that authentically defines us, body, heart, mind, spirit and soul. This sounds easier said than done when it is first suggested.

Journeying back to those depths is not an easy task but can be extremely rewarding in self discovery and projecting our true areas of ability. How can it be done when we know so little about ourselves, let alone about our parents and their past? The little we know is probably not exact and may even contain mistruths interspaced with wide blank gaps. It feels like seating down on a first try to write a will. Several attempts yield blank pages that start to fill as we dig deeper and finer. On the nth try, it comes to us when we realise that we probably need to start with something trivial like our special fountain pen collection. The things that we treasure in life may seem to be of no inheritable value to those that are closest to us entitled to inherit our invaluable junks.

Everyone around Shona had been fussing about his old 1961 Impala

Chevrolet that had unceremoniously decorated his garden for over a decade. He had promised for years to give back life to the old jalopy to as good as it rolled out of Detroit in 1961, maybe close to. This is a project he was slowly beginning to give up on when it occurred to him that his second youngest daughter had always been keenly inquisitive about it. He had spoken to her many times and at great lengths about old cars and his keen interest in their restoration. The rest slowly became easier as he put his thoughts on the old jalopy to paper. His ideas became more alive and elaborate with every visit. He organised two work suits as much as the sum of father and daughter's mechanical abilities amounted to almost zero. What they lacked in skill, they compensated in enthusiasm. The project started and the rest is history. He is happy to say that something that appeared a lost cause is now inheritable!

It becomes progressively easier and more elaborate each time we seat to re-write our wills even if we realise we own very little inheritable material things. We have memorabia that potentially can mean something to someone in the future. There is a tendency to be attached to things we posses. We generally feel every one of them has meaning and is indispensable. What then has significance and qualifies as an inheritable in the mountain of things we have accumulated over decades? What criteria do we apply to precipitate value? Are we able to set aside time to manifest, catalogue and ascribe who gets what of our highly sentimental ornaments whose value maybe truly subjective? Similarly, true awareness of our being and who we are is necessary to ascertain our slots in the hierarchy of things.

Our approach, similar to the old jalopy, is to start with one thing in the present that impacts us the most. What sub-considerables do the slightly bigger ones have to ride on ad-infinitum, ultimately contributing towards the main sub-domain? These reveal themselves as elementary fractals of the main domain, all needing to be considered collectively as key elements of our whole being. As in making a manifest of one's life treasures and subsequently drawing up a Will, similarly, we journey back into who am I.

It was commonly agreed that Shona was a replica of his grandfather, both in behaviour and physical looks. We start with investigating that particular aspect in as much detail as we can. It may start with a single sentence. It develops in scope and depth with each iteration. Once we start, we attract information from quarters we least expect. Ironically, the juicy stuff is usually informally available, from aunts, uncles, family friends and relatives. Slowly, as we get deeper, information we collect progressively begin to provide explanations and make sense in the present. It begins to answer to the persons that we are, our capabilities and failures, strengths and weaknesses, likes and dislikes, areas of life that we are passionate about, our motivations, temperament and our love patterns, and so on. Sure enough, with time, it starts to converge to our objective. How does all this amount to our desires, self-awareness and lifelike lifestyles?

How can we relate this to our present being? We are who we are and always prided in it. Particular aspects of our livelihood came naturally to us throughout our lives? Was it motivated through our unrealized archetype or was it through our socialization and processes of individuation? We can relate findings that come out of our historicities with the empirical objective that is verifiable, from our time of birth to present. How do we do this to find relevance?

Factors that may predetermine, predispose and pre-destine our lives from zygote formation in the wombs of our mothers to present are our genetic make-up, culture, tradition and spirituality. We may not want to overlook the meta-physical differentials that our parents experience! It is therefore important that we start with careful consideration of both our parents and their lineages.

This differs with ethnicities. Some may put importance on their horoscopes whereas some maybe more concerned with their totems, issues of superstition and witchcraft. The *I am because we are, then I am.* The westerners view all the other metaphysical functioning of their state of being as serving their rational and pragmatic minds. The *I am because I do and dream.* In some environments it matters greatly if parentage is from the same clan or not.

Some cultures appear to have liberalised these concerns to a point where they now consider incest as the only outstanding frontier. Depending on who we are, it may be important to find out those elements that directly impact on our personhood today. Heavily enculturated communities now seem to trivialise these attributes at the expense of their true identity and its possible restoration. Such a premise can stifle and haunt our true processes of origination that form the basis of authentic extension to best selves, dreams, creativity and hence our innovations.

Innovations manifest both social and natural paradigms. We are not going to consider other discourses outside those that help us to move towards the differential of our archetypes and callings. These objectify exposure of our best forms of consciousness and hence optimal performance. We can then move to in-depth considerations of our births, childhood, early schooling and our tertiary training.

What kind of person do we visualise ourselves to be and what person does the others around us see? That person we perceive has a life journey that commenced from the day of conception through the union of two people who are genetically different. It differs with different cultures. Some prefer the union of blood relations as genetically enhancing. Others advocate for the exact opposite and everything in between. Whatever is obtaining in our unique situations, mating and mutation on that special day gradually progressed into individualised characteristics that we carry today.

Contrary to the process of personhood or individuation that is perceived to start at birth on a blank template, genetic mutation grounds itself on already existing coded templates. Our parents, especially our mothers' behaviours and characters modeled our foundations in every facet of our lives throughout. Their own prior inheritance is passed on to us during this phase. The initial early formative years of our childhood only builds on this already inscribed *template*. It is definitely not a *tabula rasa*. We start with attempting to decipher the inscription on this template as much as we can and how far it has affected our personhood progression. On it, parenthood, society and the environment begin to continually inscribe their own influences. We note with interest the influence of our ethnicities and our education processes on whom and what we are today. The British, Jews, Indians, Chinese, Egyptians, Ethiopians, Japanese and Nigerians are on the forefront of similar ethnic peculiarities.

Shona's father was mostly a rural boy until his early adulthood. His grandmother was a peasant farmer. His grandfather was employed at the local District Commissioner's office in an area some three hundred kilometres from his own homeland. His father, Naison Ndebele was raised in a strongly patriarchal society. This impacted heavily on how he raised his own children especially the male child. At the age of nine in 1945, Shona's father and his family moved back to his homeland near a well established British missionary education institution. Waddilove Institution comprised of a primary and a high school as well as a teachers training college. This is where he completed his Standard six in 1953 and subsequently trained as a teacher. In 1959, he was recruited by The British Tobacco Company to teach at a local primary school. He then met his wife to be in 1960 through a blind date arranged by a cousin. They married according to his traditional custom, as well as to the more western white wedding custom in 1961. This practice was generally expected of teachers at the time.

Naison's education was sponsored by his elder brother who died in the same year that Naison married. His will, verbal and told to two trustees, requested that Naison takes over the responsibility of his three year old son. This was a normal request at the time that could not be declined traditionally. Tradition also required the widow to be assigned to one of Naison's elder brothers as her new husband. Unfortunately for Naison, he was her choice. He managed to get out of this traditional obligation because of the new western awareness he had developed through his education and training. Further to, there were restrictions from his employment rooted in the Wesley Methodist Church doctrine that did not allow polygamous unions.

As much as he managed to avoid it, it created conflict within the extended family as this was viewed as resentment of one's own culture. His traditional dictates expected him to conform. Shona's mother had to face the wrath of resentment from Naison's family. A new wife was required to stay with her mother-in-law for a minimum period of a month to learn the new marital customs and traditions of her new strongly patriarchal family. The stint expired upon the rituals of the birth of the first child.

As stubborn as he was, a trait that remained with him throughout his life, Naison faithfully stuck to love his new wife. Regardless of the pressure that was brought to bear, he also stuck to his decision not to accept the widow. This immensely affected the dynamics of family members' relationships throughout their lives. Emanating from this, resolution of conflicts, education of his disadvantaged communities and development of support structures of the whole extended family became areas of great interest and devotion for him. He applied his knowledge diligently both to his employment, family and society. He regarded education as a liberator and as a sure way to a noble and better life from material poverty. He was a very fair man to all, strict disciplinarian, open, frank to a fault and a philanthropist. Nick-named "Headmaster", he enthusiastically assisted those that gave their best at school. At times, his generosity to others was at the deprivation and expense of his family. Growing up, Shona had to be a role model of Naison's beliefs. This added pressure on Shona to be exemplary at a very early age.

The local community's expectations for a breadwinner were to provide for the extended family. As his children, Shona preferred preferential treatment. It was not to be. If anything, he got what he considered to be a raw deal.

Later in life, Naison was saddened to see the little he had achieved atrophying into oblivion. Some of the children he sponsored through school ended up loitering unproductively at the small local business centres. At that time, self-employment was despised and anyone engaged in it was considered a failure.

The markers of success and excellence then were renowned and high profile professions acclaimed by Caucasians, especially Europeans and Americans. These included medical doctors, pilots and engineers. Naison's society only recognized and valued employment with an established and well known institutions or organisations administered or owned by foreigners, preferably Caucasians. Whereas one maybe gainfully employed within their communities, the general view regarded that as self-employment and inferior. Employees outside the accepted mainstream were generally excluded and considered as unemployed. This view persists to dominate calculations of employment rates in some parts.

Society regards the development of an individual as bound to the development of the community. It views the creation of a balanced individual to evolve through their interaction with other members of their immediate community. Naison's teaching career and his own calling of wanting to assist extended family members was considered as a stride towards community development. His indulgence to others even before self and own children was to affect and influence Shona for the rest of his life. He later realised that he had become his father through an intense iterative reflection on his early life story and present circumstance.

Naison's young family had a good start. It was blessed with a first born son. This was in compliance with preferred traditional expectations and custom of his community. The first child came within the first nine months of marriage, considered to be highly fortunate for his family. Shona was born with a lot of pomp and fanfare in June 1962. He was bestowed his grandfathers name as a middle name, considered to be a great honour indeed. He even inherited his nickname that has stuck with him to this day.

His grandfather died a year after his birth. Those that knew him say Shona is his replica both in stature and character. Ancestry names bestowed on newly born infants usually carried resemblances to the said ancestor. It could be as simple as gender significance if an only child of that gender in the family. It could be the position of birth in the family, especially first and last borns. It is considered to have a great bearing on one's upbringing, socialisation and privileges. It therefore shapes expectations.

Naming a child after an ancestor is culturally believed to predispose the child to be like the ancestor. Naison's enculturation through western education and his profession impacted parallel clear structures and social expectations. It further compounded how his son Shona was viewed and treated by his immediate community. Being a primary school teacher, Naison had great social standing and respect from surrounding communities up until his passing on.

Shona's early childhood was influenced and developed in the shadow of his inherited "brother", who was three years older than him. He was a very determined and athletic person. A very naughty youngster indeed who was not keen on formal schooling and always got in trouble with authority! He eventually joined the war of independence from colonial occupation as a guerrilla soldier in 1975.

Shona assumed leadership of the family after his father's passing on June 4. His 68 year old mother, now a widow, had to fully depend on all her adult children, especially the first born son to keep the family together. Shona vividly recalls the impact his mother's influence on his life.

****

Contrary to Naison's life story, Shona's mother was born on 23 October 1944 in a family with affluent uncles. One of the Uncles named her Kenya as his ceremonious return from that country coincided with her birth date. This was a very rare fit at the time totravel outside the country, let alone to fly!

Kenya could speak three languages from an early age. She exuded a progressive outlook characteristic of females of the time. She exhibited very strong cultural maternal instincts that included an entrepreneurial approach to life. This faired favourably with her strongly patriarchal society. Her attraction to my father was evident. People of her clan are renowned for being gentle but powerful. They seem to assimilate to the character of their elephant totem.

Most of Kenya's schooling was at Waddilove Central Primary School, the same boarding school with Naison. Kenya transferred to the same school at the age of twelve under completely different circumstances. At the time, Naison was already a young adult. Again, her affluent uncles enabled her by taking care of all her expenses unlike Naison who had to supplement his upkeep with holiday employment at the school Principal's house. She trained in domestic science before she married Naison in August 1961. This made her people very proud.

People from her clan pride themselves in their honesty, hard work, unity of purpose and their resemblance in totem to the biggest animal in the wild. Shona believes that those elements in his character were firmly instilled in him by her and reinforced by his teacher father. There was not much room for anything else. It was a relief when he was shipped off to the same boarding school both parents attended.

His mother was mostly a housewife but took on temporary teaching stints in Domestic Science, cookery, and sewing. She later concentrated on her small tailoring business to the extent that all her children, male

46

and female, can sew and mend clothes competently. They earned extra pocket money by helping in her small sewing shop. She was astute enough to team up as a sub-contractor with a renowned Indian family tailoring business. They specialized in making school uniforms for 20 years until her retirement.

Shona grew up thinking the entrepreneurial tendencies in him came from his father's side. Quite the opposite, as revealed by his life story. His mother was the more enterprising of the two of his parents throughout. It is now clear to him that he took after her in that regard.

Shona branched out on his own to start a new business in Civil Engineering after a mere four years of formal employment, to the displeasure of his parents and immediate community.

Kenya, including all her children considered Naison as a good and responsible husband who never abused his family. He hardly ever wasted his salary on himself as was common at the time. He rarely consumed alcohol, less than five times a year, in line with the Christian teachings of his profession. She administered almost all of her family affairs including all family income. Naison received an allowance like the rest of the children. He supplemented it by hiring out his car in medical emergencies and to ferry odds and ends. She consistently encouraged her children to follow their father's example. Interestingly, Shona's first born daughter tells him all around view him as a Social Entrepreneur. What is the broader perspective of Shona?

A social entrepreneur is a person who has an insatiable passion and dedication towards the upliftment of their communities first before self. This manifests through their philanthropic engagement of broad and critical social issues. They are skilled in innovative approaches and determination executed in a businesslike manner. They, with other members of the community collectively ensure that there is desired social change with all involved benefitting. They are crafty visionaries and are very creative through the engagement of both global and frugal solutions and technologies that already exist. They endeavor to minimise the need for external resources preferring to capitalize on what is at hand to gain maximum coverage and utility. Their initiatives, as much as they are initially designed for local application, at times can attract global attention. They don't consider personal material benefits and profits as a factor but are more satisfied with the social impact their initiatives effect on the ground.

To a great extend, this describes Naison and yet it now equally describes Shona. It may arguably be correct. Shona hastens to add that he equally desires success in all its forms. His preferred form is when it is derived through his facilitation of the success of others around him. We all have different definitions of success and how best we want to achieve it. Personal inner perspectives of success are what need to be quenched per capita, each one consciously fully realising their desire as revealed by their life stories.

Both Shona's parents emphasised the importance of success through a good education above all else. They stressed the need to earn an honest living. Its over-emphasis created deficiencies elsewhere in their children. Kenya did most of the disciplining and regularly meted out corporal punishment. Major problems were dealt with through her husband's intervention. Shona remembers his father belting him only once when he was ten. He got regular spankings though from his mother until he was eleven.

The discipline in earning what was one owns was strongly enforced. This has created a challenge for Shona in business in the short term as ethical boundaries of business are now blurred in most contemporary economic and socio-political contexts. Some societies now perceive, frown and look away at gifts to public officials, corruption, cronyism and marginalised respect for the rule of law including various other societal ills as part of doing business.

We now journey back to Shona's upbringing from childhood to present to actualise his self-awareness of *who am I* utilising his personalised Integral Design. What can he learn from his history to avoid the repetition of prior pitfalls and reinforce past good experience in future?

By the time Shona was born, his father was already at the helm of the education advancement crusade in marginalised communities. The respective communities he engaged obligated Shona, as the advocate's first son to practice what he preached. Cultural pressure impressed upon

Shona to succeed where most failed. Off-springs of community leaders went one of two ways. Either they became exemplarily successful at their academics or they abused alcohol and substances to become notorious misfits. If one was unfortunate enough to find themselves in the latter category, parents were usually the last to know. Other teachers resident at school premises coupled with extra supervision from community leaders marginalised this to an absolute minimum. They had an enshrined collective responsibility to monitor and discipline.

A clear message was strongly impressed upon all of the importance of a good education to counter inevitable poverty evident in most communities. Pressure to succeed was brought to bear especially on those identified to have the potential to succeed. It was abundantly clear that acquisition of a formal education was viewed by the community as a guaranteed way to secure a bright future out of poverty. It was a route to elevating one's family in particular and the community in general into a future of prospects and promise.

Preferred professions evolved over time as communities' exposure and awareness increased. General emphasis was now elevated to obtaining a minimum of a bachelor's degree. In more enlightened families, Masters degrees were now the norm. At the time, Doctoral and PhD degrees were mostly from lands afar and extremely rare to meet a recipient. Shona's father may have been fortunate enough to have occasionally had p r i o r physical contact. The communities' reality of a highly educated person was up to a Masters degree. It is in this environment that Shona was raised.

Shona started school in Sub-Standard A at five-and-a-half years old. That age was then considered very young and could only do so at a primary school where his father superintended. The normal school starting age was seven at the time. The physical test was one's ability to cover their left ear with their right palm, with the right hand going over their head.

Shona was expected to attend church and be a member of the Boys Christian Union popularly referred to as BCU. He was recruited to learn to play the horn trumpet. He discovered he was good at it.

Being a Christian had several advantages to Shona as a young boy. The hermeneutic stories that accompanied its pedagogy greatly expanded a young boy's reality in a society strongly immersed in superstition and spirituality of one form or the other. The community unquestioningly believed in God. Each one necessarily had to believe or have faith in something. Non-believers in any one of the two was viewed as having nothing, soul-less and naked. Without any, who was you? What then did you have?

This was the community's way of explaining the origins of a phenomenon way outside their everyday modes of experience and existence. Enculturation of Christianity suited local communities well. It was a well established institution, stable, structured, had strong narratives of spiritual realities and was enforced through a carrot and stick system by the authorities. It provided opportunities to those that conformed and excelled. It increased one's rare chance of meeting the great man who was the bigger boss to the boss of Shona's father.

Naison was Shona's hero and mentor who knew and had answers to his world. It was that simple and that linear.

Naison maintained two homes like everyone else who was gainfully employed. One was a permanent rural home where he stayed with his family on weekends, when on vacation and on public holidays. He had a secondary urban home where he resided, mostly for purposes of employment. Some of his colleagues preferred their families to stay at their rural homes and only visited after receiving their monthly salaries. Naison was one of those few that insisted on staying with their families in their secondary homes. His family spent a small portion of school holidays at their rural home.

Shona retrospects and realises the importance and influence of his parents' jobs on them, as well as the whole extended family. It smacks of dialectical existence, the other in total contrast to both parents' traditional and cultural indoctrinations. They were caught between the two worlds and struggled with it.

Spending more time at the rural home obligated them to preside over issues that required their participation in cultural norms in conflict with those of their employer. This resulted in their children growing up with a fairly conflicted dichotomy, caught between the two worlds. In some instances, there was direct confrontation between the two. Their exposure to cultural and rural traditional practices suffered from these tensions maiming their true identities in the process. A blend of the exogenous that filtered through formal pedagogy, Christian practices, the world of work dichotomous to local value systems that existed in the tacit oral knowledge systems of our families and communities emerged. The exogenous took precedence and prevailed. This has become a significant consideration in our contemporary creativity and innovation. It is a significant factor of one's sense of that authentic identity.

Shona attended three schools in his infancy because of his parents' migration through various schools in the area. His turning point was when he was shipped to a nearby boarding school after a seemingly mysterious death of his sister. Seemingly mysterious because there was a conflicted explanation to her drowning between the locals, the church and the police diving team that retrieved her body. This was to be Shona's first experience of the dialectic beliefs between the rational and pragmatic exogenous, the relational and traditional local and the spiritual and cultural Christian. Nevertheless, the effect on Shona was the same either way. He was going to be in boarding school from then on. At the time, he did not realise he was going to last seven years in this school as a boarder up to the highest level it offered. It is from here that he gets recollections of most of his early formative and educational years.

An earnest beginning of his education journey in a very formal, mostly exogenous environment that belonged to the Wesley Methodist Church Group of Schools started here. His parents had attended the same school. A significant number of social elites and great luminaries that include political leaders, academics, scholars and professionals in various sectors of society and economy previously attended this great school. It was one of the oldest Methodist Church schools established in 1891 by a Methodist Missionary named John White. Their vision and mandate was to introduce exogenous knowledge systems to educate the locals. It was to pioneer the advancement of local education. Central to the mandate of these institutions, was to instill exogenous church values among the local people. Enrolling into this educational system introduced Shona to that culture, into that other way of life.

Christianity was clearly the dominant value system at the school. Anything associated with the local cultural way of life was strongly shunned and discouraged. At this entry point, one had to almost totally abscond all previous knowledge. They had to die and be reborn, to start on a new slate if they wanted to excel, be considered intelligent and socially correct. This was to be Shona's first conscious death and re-birth.

According to Hallen's treatise of the Congolese Senator and Philosopher, Wamba Dia Wamba, he once observed that the attributes of intelligence, reasonableness and civilisation depended on one's ability to conform to the logic and rationality of neo-colonial structures of governance. Shona must have managed to adapt well because at any given point, he was a class monitor, a school prefect or captain of various school sports disciplines and clubs (rowing, chess and karate). All of these achievements culminated in him being appointed school prefect in his pen ultimate year and eventually a deputy school captain in his final primary school class before advancing to high school.

As a youngster, Shona tinkered and experimented with anything that aroused his curiosity. He was always part of any adventure that happened at school but was never implicated. Those that were in boarding school had to be innovative about the food. They devised trades for better meals prepared at the school farm store in exchange for the school bathing soap issued once every Saturday morning. It was in demand with the local store for re-sale to farm workers. Eventually, their small enterprise was discovered. Culprits were brought to book and punished but Shona was never fingered. Despite all his misdeeds, he was appointed Deputy Head-boy in his last two years of middle school. His friends summed it up in this way: *their survival strategy pushed the system to its limit. They figuratively touched the boundary line but never crossed it.* It appears this characteristic became part of Shona's career: taking risks with innate conservativeness.

At the end of their middle school, they sat for an examination, the Cambridge Ordinary Level Certificate that was administered in England. It was the highest level one could get to at this school. Shona had to transfer to a mixed-race school in an urban environment for his final two years of high school before University.

The experience introduced him to his early adulthood. Morgan High

School was one of the better resourced African-Caucasian, African-Asian and African- Coloured schools. Hereinafter, we will only refer to the four distinct races as African, Caucasian, Asian and Coloured. He managed to enroll here because the education system had just been desegregated.

The majority of pupils in at Morgan were from the Asian and Coloured communities. The latter are people of mixed race, generally between any two or more races. Shona wondered if the mix between Caucasians and any of the Asians was emphasised as coloured in that setting. Or was it limited to a mix between Africans and any of the other races?

All races were required to live in segregated communities before desegregation laws were passed. At the time, each race conveniently preferred and competed to individually side with the Caucasians because of privileged socio-economic benefits and political dispensations it derived. Coloureds, as they were commonly referred to, enjoyed higher citizen status than Africans and the best of both worlds of their parentage.

They were required to go on national military service after high school, just like the Caucasians. Coloureds had notoriety for being highly talented technicians, gifted with their hands but appeared to have little interest in the formal academic curricular. They developed a unique dialect and construction of their English language.

After high school, most Coloured men opted to serve as apprentices in both light and heavy engineering. Motor mechanics was their forte, their cars easily identifiable from the wide wheels and loud noise. Coloured women were versatile and found in every profession.

On the other hand, Asian students were very academic, studious and soft mannered. They lived as communities in large extended families in special and exclusive suburbs. This is the demographic of the school Shona enrolled into coming from a diverse, rural and strong cultural background.

Ironically, Shona was elected Deputy Head Boy for the duration of his two year stint at that School. He was already fairly competent at karate. It came in handy, especially as a deputy head-boy from a minority group in the school.

The school held sports in high regard, particularly basketball. Shona was not good at field sports and atheletics. He hardly participated except in the compulsory events. He quickly realised that one needed to be influential in that area to be effective as a leader. He decided to play a major supportive role in most. He single handedly introduced karate classes with a Japanese master instructor. It benefited him in many respects. He socially became the guy to hang with; a school deputy head-boy as well as a martial arts proponent. He was now in a position to effectively influence school politics. As an Instructor Assistant to Master Chiba, he derived an allowance enough to cover most of his social expenses.

The project was a great success. Shona assisted in disciplining the otherwise rowdy elements in the school.

His lifestyle began to crystallise a discernable pattern from this point. His dreams were demystifying and evolving. The seed of who he was was now in fertile soil. His path of individuation towards defining his being had taken a decipherable shape. Who he was to become was still to germinate, albeit, with proper nourishment and nursing.

How was he to dynamise his present state to transcend it towards his desired future that actualises his Calling? What traits and mindset in him did he need to negate? What impetus awareness did he require? What was his desired lifestyle? What was his desired Godlike life-likeness? How does he now navigate and explore this further in greater depth to adequately tool him to evolve his desired outcome? We now explore this further in greater depth.

It all started with his parentage. We don't choose who they are and we absolutely do not have a say in it. We are predisposed from the day we are conceived. Our genetic makeup: height, physical looks, weight, metabolic efficiencies or lack thereof, the list is endless. As much as we may need to understand this as background knowledge, such predispositions should be disregarded and incinerated. There is no relationship between what that is and our future. We journey back into our historicity in order to understand our present with minimum assumptions, hopefully well informed assumptions.

In general, Shona's community minimally emphasised financial status of a single family. It preferred a collective approach. In minority of situations, scarcity at family level successfully transformed into a need that transcended into a deep thirst. The m ajority o f f amilies w ere s urvivalists. Th ey we re creative and worked hard enough only to make ends meet. Some experienced marginal poverty and were cyclically in and out of it. Amelioration of the inevitable necessarily required related families to pool together. They closely networked aggregating into smaller community fractals. A single person's problem was a problem for everyone in that cell.

The majority of families in the world today has either or continues to experience poverty according to most poverty datum thresholds. It's important to hastily point out that in highly relational and collective societies; there are other forms of poverty that are more apparent and emphasised.

Material resources for a determined and industrious young person could always be raised through the circulation of a plate literally, throughout the immediate community. Obvious fervent advocates of determination like Naison easily attracted the necessary resources to move forward. How could anyone be poor when every individual was the child of the whole community? All aspects, especially of personhood development were the responsibility of that community. It was in education that one specifically needed identifiable individual effort. The rewards were primarily still considered to be for the collective and secondarily particularised to the self.

Formal education was considered to be mostly for one's head and only necessary for future survival. On the other hand, socialisation administered by the community was considered to be for the community first and for one's whole being: body, heart, head, soul and spirit second. It is the soul and spirit that was considered necessary to empower one with survival skills. Collectively, elders in any given community were tasked to manifest their protégés' spirit of hunting in all aspects of life, be it in marriage, conflict in leadership and management of the family. Emotional intelligence was most respected.

Early identification of one's talents was critical for nurturing and encouragement. For Shona, it was specifically his grandmother who was responsible for the early discovery of his special abilities. Her first clue was realising that Shona loved and cared for animals, especially those that needed special attention. Those animals pointedly identified as his seemed to thrive and multiply with ease. This culturally indicated the presence of a strong hunting spirit. Community elders further tested every member's capacity to love, care and respect any form of life. Capacity to extend equal care and empathy towards every member of the clan regardless of their social standing was equally examined. Those identified to possess a dominant hunting spirit became automatic candidates for future leadership. They had to prove that they were inherent providers for all in need without favour, good listeners and natural problem solvers for the extended family.

Discrimination of any form was not tolerated. Vetting was not formal but a continuous, concealed and whispered process. Every elder of the clan was entitled to observe and openly air their observations without any inhibitions, especially on the day of one's initiation into adulthood. Distinguishable family nuclei had one dominant hunter anointed to be its head. Each community member was believed to have a unique archetype that particularised them to serve the whole community in a special way.

The key was in its identification during the individual's infancy. Intended recipients were to actively demonstrate capacity to accept, encourage and nurse the responsibilities that came with such an honourous anointing. The dominant hunting spirit was heavily contested between siblings, cousins and other families of the clan. The individual identified to possess this spirit needed elders' protection by underplaying and concealing the person's identity. Daily treatment of the individual was not to be different from any of the other children. They continued to equitably participate in most aspects of ordinary life, generally shared with the collective in the community.

It was common to see all community members coming together, even those that generally did not get along, to assist each other in times of need. All children considered to be below the initiation age were expected to do everything together. Considered because some were chronologically older but still required to develop to the level of successful initiation. All was shared from herding cattle, bathing at the river, sleeping in the same round hut, sharing the blankets usually on the floor, and eating by hand from the same plate. They were obligated to equally take assignments and instructions from any member of the community without favour. These values were more in line with cultural upbringing tenets rooted in the broader *Ubuntu* philosophy evident in every individual with proper upbringing.

There were notable differences with the individualistic socialisation Shona received in the 40 weeks of the year at school. He began to experience some form of ostracism both at school and at home. While some school mates would consider him too cultural and therefore backward, his cousins at home were beginning to find him not cultural enough.

His "brother" was his invisible hand and protector in the community, although he was secretive about it. He always tipped the scales in Shona's favour whenever he found him at a disadvantage. His other great protector was his grandmother. She used to pull him behind her whenever he was threatened with some spanking from his uncles. Shona held on to her dress with his dear life.

Shona's various other skills helped as they elevated his status amongst his peers. He slowly became more visible as he excelled at most activities he put his mind to. It earned him favours and privileges. Shona was occasionally invited to play the traditional horn trumpet for the Methodist Church, Men's Christian Union (MCU) gatherings when he was still in the Boys Christian Union(BCU).

The Church Bishop of the area doubled as the head of all Methodist schools in his jurisdiction. He would take Shona to these gatherings. They became so close that, at the age of 82, the same Bishop gave a speech on behalf of the family at Shona's wedding.

Shona rarely experienced exerting chores most boys of his age were assigned because of the few minor but special skills he picked up along the way. He occasionally drove his father's car from the age of eight usually in hospital emergencies some 12 kilometres away.

Cars were scarce and rare at the time, especially in rural areas. Shona got easy passage because the Police Member-in- Charge was an "uncle" through a distant aunt. He was allowed to sit in at elders' council meetings, traditional ceremonies, parties and attend funeral gatherings exclusive to much older people. These were great privileges in a culture where children needed to know their place. It enabled Shona to avoid most of the tedious family and community chores regarded as character building and communal responsibility.

Most social aspects in Shona's culture were pro community. Special privileges were scarce, favours were shunned, secrets were categorically not encouraged and solitary individualism was considered anti-social and as pride that led to certain failure in life. The ideal was for communities to function as units totally self- sustaining. Each community quintessentially represented all its members. Family units were fractals of the whole. The collective, the village or community was considered much bigger than the sum of its individual families.

What really was viewed as a successful individual? The divide between normative local cultural community values and those of the exogenous were distinct although in most respects the interface was growing every day. Various tenets were clearly common to both. Parentage and the collective community mentorship played a critical part in laying the foundation of the process of individuation. The need for a good education was emphasised all round. The general development of an individual was apprenticeship style. This was monitored through one's behaviour towards self and towards members of the community especially those of lesser standing. An elevated sensitivity to nature ways was an undeniable passport.

Animals' response towards a person was viewed as reflective of the level of purity of one's inner soul, the part that most did not wear on their sleeve. Local values emphatically focused on the preservation of nature, awareness and consciousness: to acquire from the environment only that one absolutely needs. How has the value system that has surrounded Shona and his whole life story shaped and influenced his overall sense of things in the contemporary and future? Has it advantaged him to excel in some aspects and weakened him in others? Emergence of the true and remarkable self prompts formation of strong mentorship and relationships throughout.

Our world today can do with enhanced pro-community approaches that are relational and sensitive to inherent cultural, spiritual and local collective approaches. It may be necessary to impart direct credit and reward to strong elements, be they individuals or family units, to merit and foster a strong culture of creativity and initiative. This approach embraces a give and take relationship between individuals and societies that is transformational, transcultural, trans- disciplinary and trans-personal.

Contemporarily, there appears to be a gorge between the self and other, a subliminal indifference in individuals in particular and systems in general. How can we learn how best to give more than we take? We seem to be structurally oriented and socialized to become experts at maximizing imbalanced extraction at the expense of sustainability. We are drilled to sweep clean and not leave anything of value at the table.

The contrary requires much more than what we are currently willing to give to achieve that level of outer generosity. Do we even possess the know-how to do it? How can we create the necessary knowledge to confront a future that is sustaining and in balance? Are our education and training systems designed adequately to cope with the transcendent mindset that emerges?

Early in high school, we were made aware of who was and was not University material at the expense of the latter. Information on special areas of competence was included. From then on, identified areas were given maximum attention at the detriment of all others. Some crude form of psycho-analytic evaluation was done by the family and vocational assessment was carried out through the school system. We formulated our possible future careers with this information. Formal career guidance was afforded by more elite schools. Our parents' greatest ambition was to ensure that we qualified for University.

We were weaned of soon after entering university. Some assumed responsibilities after confirmation of acceptance into the local University. The nature of responsibilities was usually to take care of the youngest sibling's needs. The government automatically provided grants to enrolled students at the sole university in the country. It was adequate to accommodate and cover minimal out of University responsibilities. Getting into its engineering school was the beginning of the formation of Shona's dream.

His dream was set on becoming an Aeronautical Engineer. As much as he did not fully comprehend what that was and nobody he knew seemed to know, he liked the ring to the title. His classmates desired careers in medicine, politics, business and education *etcetera*. Shona particularly liked his choice because it was unique and attracted the most attention. It necessitated going out of the country to study, a great feat at the time. As he began to understand more of his chosen career path, he planned to enroll at Nagoya Aeronautical School in Japan. The softer motivating factor for Japan was his exposure to Japanese style karate since he was a sixteen year old.

He got absorbed in his desire to understand the Japanese culture and their way of life. He sort the assistance of the cultural attaché at the Japanese Embassy, a Sensei in Judo who became his personal mentor. Sensei Sasaki organised a Japanese family to host Shona for the duration his studies in Japan. His parents were to be responsible for his academic tuition as part of the deal. They could not afford it. They still had seven other younger kids to care for. Shona's alternative to keep his dream alive was to apply at the only local airline. He was accepted to train as an Aircraft Technician upon successful completion of his high school.

Shona's parents, especially his mother, had drilled into him that his minimum qualification was to be a bachelor's degree in any field. He truly wanted to be an engineer and not start off as an apprenticed technician. Various organisations scouted for high school graduates to train as aircraft pilots and artisans. The local University offered places for those that qualified. Shona's Advanced Level high school results qualified him for an offer at the local University as well as a USAID scholarship to study in America.

The choice was no brainer. It had to be the USAID scholarship. The career change to Civil Engineering did not bother him. He planned on a structural engineering degree at undergraduate level. He intended to specialise in shell design at Masters Degree level. He envisaged that this move would lay a good foundation for entry into aeronautical engineering training.

Shona realised that he had a strong and persevering character sometimes to a fault. This was inspired and instilled by his teacher parents. It was later encouraged by his interactions with a Japanese culture that has a strong filial piety philosophy and respectful of a persevering character. He became fully aware of these traits in his dealing as he matured.

The American scholastic aptitude and placement tests Shona took secured him offers into three American state universities. He was drawn to Colorado State University (CSU) in Fort Collins, deep in rural cowboy country, neighbouring the renowned state of Wyoming in mid-western USA. It was classified semi-arid to an arid region four.

Fort Collins town is very scenic, located at the foothills of the Rocky Mountains range. It receives an average of 48 inches (121.9 centimetres) of snow most winters against a national average of 28 inches (71.1 centimetres).

Aspen, an affluent and world renowned skiing resort was in its vicinity. Fort Collins derived great benefit from its proximity to Aspen. Some of its ski resorts compared very well. It is difficult to get out of Fort Collins without learning how to ski, even for an African from the hottest parts of the Sahara Desert. Shona became an average cross country skier. He found downhill skiing hectic, tedious and dangerous. He did not consider himself exceptionally brave but adventurous. He had the opportunity to experience rock climbing in Mexico, camping overnight in igloos at the Rocky Mountains foothills and ice skating in Larimer County vast water channels. What did these extreme outdoor experiences teach Shona?

Sports and outdoor activities reinforce and instill a character that is no stranger to perseverance, meticulous planning, thoroughness, endurance, honesty especially to self, camaraderie, responsibility for self and others, reliance and a capable team spirit. It empowers one to discover and expose the true self.

The various communities Shona interacted with while at Colorado State showed him power and influence that comes with people that integrally work together as a team, who co-create and how that helps to build systemic cohesiveness.

The state of Colorado has a significant population of rural farming communities. Shona had the opportunity to be hosted by several local families and friends. He found their cultural ways similar to his in many respects and this blended very well with him. It made his four year stay in America enjoyable and rewarding. He was encouraged to become active in the community of his hosts.

Foreign students appeared to cope academically and excelled much better than anticipated. It was not so in other areas. Shona spent a significant amount of time assisting in mathematics and engineering courses, but enjoyed going around high schools the most talking about his home country. A significant number local people knew very little about it and could hardly point it out on the world map.

It was humbling to realise that the things he took for granted and even despised back home were highly valued and respected here. These were mostly issues of preservation of nature, respect for the wild, *Ubuntu* and its collective doctrine, culture and spirituality. He had taken wildlife as an everyday part of his life and not given it a second thought until now. He found himself researching on issues he should have tacitly known to provide competent presentations in the high schools he visited.

His four years at CSU proved to be double layered. Besides the academic main curricula, he was exposed to the dynamics of different races co-existing, a mix of African Americans, American Indians, Hispanics and Caucasians, the deep rooted culturally laden "cowboy" communities and exclusive conservative ranchers. The single digit rated, crime ridden Denver and Boulder cities, the presence of several enclaves of various small communities and other minority ethnicities was enlightening.

On the extreme left was the liberal Fort Collins considered to be a university town. It was made up of the academic world, international communities, researchers especially in water engineering and the general student community who were encouraged to mingle and be open minded. Shona had to learn to get along with diverse communities of Colorado as well as obtain an academic degree from the University.

Social trajectories from experiences of living in Colorado had an impact on Shona in a number of ways. He became aware of the social challenges in individual personhood development, issues of inclusion, conflict resolution and empowerment and how these related to socio-political systems in his societies back home. In context, his impression was that he lacked the required character and qualities to be persistent, patient and perseverance to resolve community challenges. He was socialised to wait for something beyond him to happen and patiently wait indefinitely for external help to come from elsewhere. The differential with the *I think therefore I can* doctrine of the Americans who sincerely believe that solutions to their problems come from within was clear.

Shona was employed as a laboratory assistant in his junior and senior years by his fluid mechanics professor, entrepreneur and researcher in his fluid mechanics laboratory. It helped him immensely to appreciate the American work ethic. His employer had several high profile government research contracts that he exposed Shona to.

This environment connected Shona to the entrepreneurial side of America. It was extremely competitive for the Professor to be awarded those contracts. Ensuring successful results required uncompromising top quality, efficiency and adherence to strict deadlines. Work schedules were extremely tight. Shona had to be prepared to work eighteen hour days. Unlike his relaxed home environment where most people hardly work for more than eight hours per day and have one job, long work hours were common for most people in America. Similar demands were not emphasised at home. Often it was blamed on the collective culture of doing things, contrary to his views.

It was with this American perspective that Shona returned home, anxious and motivated to make a difference. He was armed with a Bachelors Degree in Civil Engineering and a minor degree in mathematics. He was immediately snapped up by a regional Civil engineering consulting firm for three years before resigning to join a state-owned enterprise (SOE).

As the new Chief Development Engineer of a national agricultural development enterprise, he was quick to introduce the skills he had acquired. He started with in-house implementation of most developmental projects that were pending for years. Most of these had been shelved because they were too expensive to contract out. Shona and his team wrestled to bring them back on line.

Shona became competently familiar both from the ground and air with all the thirty odd farming estates administered by his employer scattered throughout the whole country. He had the opportunity to work with all sectors of the community. Success came in small doses. His team learnt to celebrate the little that was generally taken for granted by most. The one development that excites Shona is a narrow bridge they constructed across a very fast flowing river in a highly mountainous region. The bridge saved locals 10 kilometres of walking to reach a service centre a few hundred metres across the river.

Many years later, Shona had an accidental meet with his former Boss at the SOE whose home village is in the area where the infamous bridge was constructed. He excitedly told Shona that "his bridge" was the only one left standing after Tropical Cyclone Eline of 22 February 2000 that devastated the area. That excitement coming from an eighty six year old over a narrow bridge made Shona treasure more the impact and importance of empowering people. It fuelled and rejuvenated his burning desire! It re-kindled the importance of providing basic amenities to empower communities: coffee pulperies for small scale village coffee farmers to process their coffee; irrigation schemes for ten-hectares farms settlers; a 300 hectare irrigation scheme in a region five arid area, boreholes drilling and equipping to provide water points for small sector dairy farmers, domestic and wildlife dotted in several semi-arid to arid parts of the country.

It was Shona's former employer's primary mandate to carry out agricultural and rural development throughout the country. Shona rediscovered that strength, that yearning, that desire in him to succeed as a contextually relevant kind of an entrepreneur that could change communities, societies and the world. His passion to participate in solutions to burning societal problems was rejuvenated. A significant number of Shona's former classmates and contemporaries truly excelled in that regard.

This phase of Shona's life appeared to be fairly static and stable. Mentorships and occupations he formed were strongly influenced by renowned gurus in his areas of interest. Influences from luminaries like Engels, Freud, Gyekye, Hoppers, Hountondji, Jung, Khoza, Lessem, Levinson, Marx, Mandela, Mbigi, Mbiti, Newton, Njoku, Plato, Socrates, Tzu, Venkataraman, Yang and many others were evident. These reinforced his local mentorships programs experienced daily on the ground that included community knowledge leaders, parents, teachers, pastors, karate to taekwondo masters. Now that he was at work and had experienced a bit of it, what challenges was he experiencing in his career? Could he make a difference?

Shona had minimal interest in toys as a child. Most kids used to make toy cars out of wire coat hangers and banjos from empty round floor polish tins, but not him. He was more attracted to playing house (with mock families) and would strive to build the best house structure he could. He played the traditional twelve by six hole local game and board games at an early age.

Much earlier in life, Shona received a couple of chickens and three goats as a present from his grandmother for coming first in his grade 3 class. It was his obligation to build a chicken run and a kraal for them, which he did with great passion and enthusiasm. Animals gifts played a significant cultural role in the spiritual and character identification, development and grooming processes. Their survival and multiplication culturally reflected one's level of inherent capabilities.

Chapter 2

INTELLIGENT OR GENIUS

Models of buildings and cars always caught Shona's attention. His passion for building structures had earned him the Builder nickname in his fourth year of high school. Interestingly, he gravitated to Civil Engineering from his original desire of pursuing Aeronautical Engineering .

It was fortuitous. The aviation industry was not fully developed locally as a career choice. It was dominated by subsidised national airlines. The local one was wholly government owned and operated an old fleet of less than 15 planes with an average age of 21 years. However, participation in general aviation was on the increase. Traditional business entities, start-ups, adventurous entrepreneurs, hobbyists, recreation and tourism were beginning to pay attention. Venture capitalists were on the prowl for highly lucrative projects.

Job availability and security of employment were his extended family's primary considerations. He was now a young adult ready to take the next step. Most importantly, a heavy responsibility rested on his shoulders as the first born son of Naison's family. Two of Shona's younger sisters had now married with baby nephews.

How was his re-entry into the family going to be? How was he going to tackle his initiation into the responsibilities of young adulthood?

It did not take long before Shona married. His marriage was a big elaborate and public affair. He married traditionally in October, the eve of a month traditionally barred from all marriage ceremonies. The ceremony required the future son-in-law to give presents and lobola to his future in laws. It was a process that was used to assess the character and material capacity of the future son-in-law. It preluded Shona's white wedding that came five months later.

Around the same time, Shona had recently branched out from his employment to start a small civil engineering construction company. His bride to be was a graduate in political science. Like his "Brother", she was a liberation war veteran that gave independence to Shona's home country from minority British colonial rule. She was an accomplished public servant and politician.

Shona was a nerd, with very little knowledge of and naïve at mainline politics. He was shy and slowly realised his preference for a private and quiet life. In retrospect, this realisation was a pivotal awakening and an experience that impacted the rest of his life.

Shona's marriage was blessed with two beautiful daughters. His society considered him privileged and advantaged by his marriage to a high profile politician. Subsequent public scrutiny and its perception of his marriage, trials and anxieties of a new business in a new marriage impacted negatively on his new family's development path. Most affected was his marriage, his daughters and the standing of his family in a highly intrusive society.

Evidence around Shona points towards him being a pragmatic person. His exposure has adapted him to become less shy, more accepting of other people and their condition, more tolerant and palatable. A family speaker at his wedding, the former Principal of his high school, wisely pointed out that Shona was a "one plus one equals two person". As a future husband, he advised him to develop skills that consider other possible solutions outside those considered rational. In short, he needed to be more sensitive and empathic to the subjective.

Shona's co-workers and friends pointed out that his weakest link was his limitation at people skills. This, he believes, turned out to be a major contributor towards constrained success of some of his ventures. Over the years, people skills have progressively become primary drivers and a highly valued element of most interactions, be they social, economic, political and otherwise. Shona has consistently endeavored to minimize the effects of his identified weaknesses through out-sourcing expert assistance. From the time he recognized and accepted his incapacities, he has managed to minimise them before they reared their head. A celebrated, fully actualised and self-aware entrepreneur or an afrintuneur needs to maximise his strengths, minimise his weaknesses, identify and capitalize on opportunities.

What is a practical definition of an entrepreneur? Is entrepreneurship something that is embraced or readily accepted as culturally relevant and/or is it fossilized as one matures over the years? Is one born with the special ability? And if so, is it considered a curse to be cast out or a blessing to be nurtured and groomed? These are questions Shona battled with as he ventured through his entrepreneurship journey. It became a major part of his life. He faced most of its challenges including internal and external contradictions, inconsistencies, dilemmas as well as a highly volatile and unpredictable external environment. It has been a challenging, exciting, satisfying and frustrating journey. This is a potent drug.

Some of the many challenging variables encountered were beyond Shona's control. He changed course several times to suit the environment against his instinct or what the so called sixth sense told him. It is this intangible thing called the sixth sense that probably needs to be heard and articulated in developing a desired lifelike entrepreneurial lifestyle worth living. How does a young venturous entrepreneur couple with a young family?

The interface of family expectations, societal beliefs, private and public expectations, that which is indigenous and exogenous can throw incongruences at you. A good number of them can stifle the smooth development of a well thought out, pioneering and enterprising initiative. We therefore need to develop an entrepreneurial self-awareness paradigm that addresses and synchronise all major issues that can negatively impact our desires. A paradigm that brings about broad awareness inclusive of those we interact with frequently and regularly.

It must cause collective consciousness and development of other downstream issues of empowerment. It need-fully and inclusively must embrace most aspects of the contemporary. Its genuine consideration must impact, be fully appreciated and motivate the nascent to tackle this task. It should be the design! How do we enable and engage our present skills-sets to confront this specialised, focused and highly complex challenge? Do we need to reform or be reborn in a new transcendent that can competently confront this dynamic?

Shona constantly questioned the essence of his life. He rigorously interrogated the status-quo, change, new knowledge and even who he was and had become. He could count a few of his youthful ambitions and goals now realised. He settled in his achievements this far and made peace with those that were still in the wind. It was now time for him to face his ghosts and work on those outstanding issues that still haunted him.

It was necessary to establish his niche, a critical mass of likeminded people, initially in his community and spread radially outward. He had begun to acknowledge his specific areas of competence. His life path had a strong bias towards his inner development and eventually that of others. After settling into whom he had become as a young adult, a strong affinity towards the development of infrastructure in civil engineering transcending to residential property development was apparent. How was he to navigate the little resources he controlled into such a capital intensive area? Could he break this into small parts that could eventually lead him to bigger things? How was it related to his inner desire of developing others first and then himself through them?

Asymmetry in beliefs and vision created opportunities for those that are prudent enough to visualise and exploit them. The discourse is in whether this ability is acquired, inherent or both in those that have it. The tensions between the haves and the have nots, the indigenous and exogenous, Western capitalism and Eastern communism, Chinese Confucianism and Christianity, ancient and contemporary ideologies, African traditional religions to Asian-Arabic and Islamic doctrines have inadvertently contributed to the creation of enclaves of dogma and overemphasis of particular views. Exclusive-inclusive dialectics have sometimes empowered or disempowered individual thought processes and liaisons.

Some have been disenfranchised from the mainstream of most political and socio-economic activities, generating inequalities and discrimination at individual, family and societal levels in the process.

What has been Shona's chosen path of individuation?

The decades long journey of defining *who he was* revealed that he had become his father. He was gradually developing an impelling desire to carry those around with him, sometimes at the expense of depriving his family. He extended his meager resources to the larger family to educate and help them through unemployment and their start-ups. This is evidenced by several of them now operating similar businesses in the construction industry. They initially set out as intrapreneurs employed in Shona's enterprise then graduated to start their own. They are in turn developing their own both as people and in business. It is gratifying to observe how teaching someone to fish is much greater than giving them fish. The Siphonaptera order suggests: *Big fleas have little fleas upon their backs to bite 'em. Little fleas have lesser fleas, and so on, ad infinitum* (www. earthlife.net). This manifestation of bigger fleas empowering the little fleas on their back to bite them less is most desirable.

Children envision outliving and achieving excellence beyond the level of their parents to carry on the future family legacy in part. The other parts canbe for their own welfare, to mentor and be role models primarily to their siblings and children; secondarily, to the younger generation, the extended family; to organisations, communities and societies they engage. Shona was drawn to work that motivate others. He envisioned embarking on that journey deeper and further. He wondered if his growing up among school teachers had something to do with it. He worked with young entrepreneurs, small to medium enterprises (SMEs) and generally with empowerment of the disadvantaged and marginalised; impacting information, knowledge and giving motivational speeches at the grass root level.

His business expanded to developing up-market cluster homes for all demographic groups. His enterprise was challenged to produce quality homes at cost plus marginal mark-ups and create nuclei for development in those areas. Shona and his team produced residence complexes of a much higher standard and quality than those obtaining in related areas, at very competitive prices. It encouraged residents and developers in the area to match or better his standard.

Some townhouse complexes they developed were valued at arguably more than three notches above the local standard. They sold them atless than local market price and still made a decent profit. The bigger benefit was on how it raised the value of properties and life in general of the whole suburb. Raising the standard of life of communities as a whole to realise better cohesion and inclusion is partly the spirit of relational entrepreneurship. Downstream effect visibly showed as most residents began to upgrade their properties to match.

Other developers coming to the area benchmarked from the new standard. Shona's organisation intended to groom and reflect archetype intrapreneurs, a model organisation in development that significantly participated in mentoring young and up-coming entrepreneurs. In this way, his organisation directly fed into his community. They envisaged a situation where most of the developed intrapreneurs matured into fully fledged entrepreneurs.

At a point in time, a significant percentage of Bureau-de-Change operators in town were former employees of Shona's family Bureau- de-Change enterprise. It operated at most local airports, border posts, major hotels and holiday resorts. It empowered a sizable number of young intrapreneurs now contributing to the development of their families in particular and the micro-economy in general.

Shona's community, the general workforce, private and public sectors hold diverse views on how to interpret and understand entrepreneurship. What is its relationship with the informal sector and SMEs? How does it directly impact their livelihood?

Participants in self employment, family businesses and SMEs are all generally and mistakenly viewed as entrepreneurs. It appears there is a prevailing negative view of entrepreneurs. The popular view is that they all resist formalization of their enterprises to evade statutory taxes, regulations and legislative compliance. Their contribution to the development of the national economy is viewed as minimal to none and thus trivialized. This is unfortunate given that these sectors are powerful socio- economic drivers in countries like India, China, Japan, the Americas and South Korea to mention a few. Are there relationships between entrepreneurship practitioners and one's quest for self-awareness, self actualization and a deep yearning for lifelike lifestyle?

It is clear from previous bibliographies that a prerequisite for the majority of very successful entrepreneurs is a very high sense of self-awareness. They passionately answer to the *who am I* question. They know who they are in detail: their total history, their parents' history, their support systems, their desires and how that relates to societal burning issues. They know their limitations, weaknesses and strengths, and how to convert those into utilizable resources. Their objective was clear from the beginning and was hardly ever motivated by money. They are highly driven individuals, like they are on steroids!

Their greatest motivation is to provide a pioneering service that solves a burning social imbalance, be it a computer, its software, a cell phone, an airline as a vehicle to finance the development of a space shuttle that can commercially take passengers to the moon, fulfilling one entrepreneurs' lifelong dream. It could also be as simple as an Uber idea, AirBnB and so forth. The list is endless. Regardless, all was motivated by a fully identified inner burning desire fully defined by the individual who has gone or is going through a self awareness evolution. What then are the tenets of this thing globally coined entrepreneurship?

Recognition of the importance of the entrepreneurship sector has been slow in coming to some parts of the world. When it started to happen, there tended to be direct importation of most of the exogenous models, theories and paradigms, generally not ideal for local practitioners. It is important that home grown, contextual, contemporary, and holistic frameworks and theories be developed ideally relevant to its consumers. Critical masses of likeminded people are to be identified to become nuclei of socio-economic development that empower the marginalised and themselves in the process.

It is at this juncture that we need global institutional players at large to intrinsically get involved. They can initially go through their usual institutional channels; government departments, affirmative organisations, contracting local Non-Governmental Organisations (NGOs) and aid programs, the usual. Finally, they can transform into equal partners with local activism that endeavor to affirm entrepreneurship as an empowerment vehicle. As consumers of accruing benefits, local communities are the catchment, liaise and contribute fully with their artistic, soulful, and *Ubuntu* selves. How does an individual relate to this standard and navigate towards it? The boundary of this normative is illusive and requires an elaborate and unique approach particular to the targeted group and environment. How do we broaden our views and opinions?

Further to what we reveal though our journey back into our historicity to tell in detail and authentically our life stories, we interview those close to us. We engage our families, colleagues, former teachers, the local pastors that baptised us, even Mussa the street vendor we saw in our neighbourhoods most of our lives. It is preferable if each iteration documents the whole story. One person that knew Shona intimately since childhood described him as a Builder and defined what that meant as follows:

Mr. Builder is a man driven by vision. I would describe him as a modern traditionalist who gets the best of both worlds and makes it work for him as a strategy to move forward, making him an individual who is in touch with himself. He has a clear idea of what he will want today and twenty years from now. On the other hand he extremely suppresses his emotions except when it comes to his family. Sometimes he is like a skull, hard outside but soft on the inside.

Shona's peers, colleagues and those that have been around him for a longtime concur.

Family is the pinnacle of our lives. Most of the decisions we make are influenced by their welfare. Outcomes of our decisions are designed to best benefit the family and then the individual rather than the latter only. Shona's high school graduating class was highly successful in producing a significant number of today's leading entrepreneurs in diverse professions. Ashruf developed the largest group of private Hospitals with world class trauma centres from a humble start-up. Trevor, his former school Head-Boy started his own church organisation and is now one of the leading Church Bishops heading local religious and civic communities at national level. He is now a revered National adviser on prominent social issues. Mary is a celebrated Neurosurgeon and a Professor at a local University, with a significant number of pioneering innovations. Equally, Michael a senior surgeon in Europe and Mark is an academic advising heads of states on regional issues. There are numerous engineers, accountants, doctors, politicians and community leaders from Shona's school streams and classmates who are making a significant impact on their national and global families. Individuals that are practical, effective, and action oriented with a burning desire to socially and economically empower their collective families - their communities. Who is Shona in all this? What is his contribution to his country and the Diaspora at large? Is he giving more to the world than he is taking from it? Is he making a good return on the investment his national family made on him, materially in the form of taxes that paid for his college tuition grants, hospitals, roads, railway lines, telecoms, water and sanitation that serve him, and so forth?

Shona witnessed most of the political, social and economic changes that his country went through in the past four decades. He is fluent in two of the local languages and in English. His background is half rural and half urban. He grew up in humble surroundings and has personally experienced poverty and discrimination: be it exclusion, racial, social, economic and political. These experiences early in life left a permanent imprint, a burning desire to revolutionise and empower those around him, especially through education, knowledge and skills.

Shona is intimately aware of most of the trepidations, the cyclic failures and successes in local settings of an ambitious entrepreneur. The barriers to entry have frustrated him and wish to make this easier for future entrepreneurs. Generally, individuals and communities in the developing world are socialised to expect unprecedented government or external support for all conceivable challenges in most aspects of their lives. They believe someone must come and be their messiah. Majority of these challenges we perceive can be solved from within, without any outside intervention from other parts of the world.

Outside support is generally intermittent at best and mainly political, demeaning, discontinuous, inconsistent, partisan, ill researched and uncoordinated. Our begging bowl mindsets need reframing to make way for new and confident mindsets. Mindsets that are confident enough to be introspective, independent, self-sustaining and not wait for handouts and interventions from outside ourselves. There has been marked improvement towards this desire despite need for relevant and contextual research that manifests implementable, creative and sustainable contributions to confront obtaining challenges at any level.

The present dependency syndrome we witness today is not in line with the virtues of our hunting spirit that is supposed to be highly adventurous, courageous and proud. In its original form, it is excluded from our contemporary life as it could not rationally guarantee success in a way that our careers offer. Instead, societies tended to shy away from that brave position to almost total dependency. Adaptive redefinition and reinterpretation of the hunting spirit and other aspects of local knowledge systems are necessary to make it meaningful and relevant for a social order desirable to most.

The implicit "traditional mindset" set in the contemporary explicit "exogenous mindset" environment stifled original thinking for most local people. A dependent one reveals itself in some form of a figurative salute, that we can refer to as the *African salute,* can easily be responsible for our willingness and volunteerism to be dispossessed of everything we hold dear including our culture, traditions, spirituality, beliefs, knowledge systems as well as the medium of our communication, our language.

We think in our vernacular but most modern knowledge learning, education, training and interpretation is in foreign languages. The dominant language of any period was dependent on a domineering economic big brother of the time. It can be English today, French and Afrikaans tomorrow to the present day Chinese factor.

The Chinese, Indians, Koreans, Afrikaners and Japanese to name a few made great strides in introducing their first languages to implicit and explicit settings that would otherwise be using exogenous languages. They have thrived to adapt and incorporate most exogenous knowledge into their local knowledge systems.

The Afrikaners in South Africa successfully did the same and strongly resisted the re- introduction of English or any other language as a medium of learning other than their Afrikaans. African pilots, scholars, academics, doctors and scientists traditionally learn second foreign languages as a medium of pedagogy and training. The most common ones are English, French, Russian and Chinese. Surely, they lose some meaning or experience slightly delayed cognition during translation and transmission. Their counterparts understand and cognate instantly the transmitting language as their first language. The micro- seconds delay in relay can definitely make a fatal difference in reaction time to a pilot in a jet moving at Mach 2 for example. It is therefore imperative that bridging innovations are rooted in the local language and knowledge systems, synthesized with relevant exogenous knowledge systems for optimal future use and maximal local consciousness.

Culturally, we believe in and prioritise God, followed by our spirituality, the love and care of our families. We all belong and are raised by a village. We choose peace in most instances but believe that choice must be from an empowered position. Our life stories reveal issues that manifest from family, traditional, cultural and collective influences. These may reveal the source of our strength and weaknesses, our levels of emotional intelligence, control and calmness towards closure of issues, patience, risk-taking, attitude towards productive hard work and the types of leadership we elect. Our derived value systems reveal themselves in ways that are realisable as both tangible and intangible, bringing us peace and happiness.

The peace, happiness and gratitude we feel extends to those we care for. It is evident and reveals itself in ways that make us feel special, blessed and privileged. In return, we enjoy enhanced loyalty, constant care and obedience of those we love when we exude confidence in who we are. It is that support that helps us with our careers in business enterprise, academia, civic, private and public sectors and so forth. It props us to walk tall in our intended paths of excellence. It could be in entrepreneurship, self-development or developing others with minimal re-routing of intended burning desires and issues. We begin to take greater calculated risks because of our confidence and reliance on our levels of consciousness to tackle challenges bigger than us.

The found deeper inner energy we exude makes us appeal as leaders and its natural spirit is brought to the fore. The real world around us appears to magically start to agree with the way we do things and our value systems. We begin to thrive to change our environment for the better for us and all others in our networks. We endeavor to walk the talk through our hobbies, further training, broadening of our horizons, enlightenment and openness to experiences. All of these factors result in us increasing our ability to achieve most of what we set our minds on. We become more competent to a point where we seek to gain visible transformation in whatever we embark on.

Self improvement resumes we engage formally or informally intend to initially deal with our inner transformation. In the process, it enables us to deal with and resolve our internal issues, feelings and thoughts. It simultaneously synthesises the knowledge that we acquired over the years. This phenomenological process helps us to understand ourselves in tandem with our environments coupled with strengths mirrored in our socialisation drawn from our communities. Together, they help us to become forces of renewal, drawing on both philosophical and psychological observations. We equally attempt to build on our unique insights, inner worlds and those of our communities.

Our callings desire to see the death of impoverishment in our communities in various respects. We witness its healing and re-birth through empowerment into healthy communities that are fully conscious, inclusive and engage in participatory co-existence. How does our emergent calling and historicity manifest into functional and structural elements that can benefit our enlightenment and those we interact with regularly?

The search and deep analysis of our authentic selves manages to reveal manifestations over the years of our burning desire. These can be summarised in different ways. For an example, Hilary Clinton's archetypical calling could be summarised into a *game changer*. Barrack Obama's was hope in the form of *yes we can*. Donald Trump trademarked his *make America great again*. Nelson Mandela's was rooted in the *Ubuntu* philosophy of *I am because we are*. Analysis of Shona's life history yielded him as a *builder from within*. It is through our being *game changers, hopefuls from within, derivers of individual success from the collective and self emancipators from authentic inner energies, ntu* that we can achieve levels of enlightenment we desire. Through contagion, we can inspire those around us to equally desire their own definitions of success. They can become equally knowledgeable and be adequately trained with a high sense of consciousness towards the environment to secure their futures. We develop within us a strong ache to carry everyone with us. They may not necessarily be entrepreneurs, but are driven by the vision of collective people development and empowerment. All forms of learning, education and training provide direct opportunities to self development and actualisation.

How can we ensure that there are adequate thresholds of development of relevant local and contextual paradigms and theories for better appreciation? Can we generate more focused assistance to all those that need it? Some of the existing local structures appear untenable. How do we identify appropriate role models, mentors and mentoring programs that are contextual? Asking any young African entrepreneur who their role models are gives you Mark Zucherberg, Steve Jobs, Jack Ma and Michael Jackson. These role models are usually ideally relevant to their environments. Their direct relevance and application to our local communities and societies are sometimes a mismatch.

It is important that we realise integrated transformative frameworks that help to effect innovative endeavors, even from our desktops. These must invariably translate into economic, socio-political and practical contributions that enhance us. Simultaneously, they must needfully invoke serious dialogue on learning and pedagogy of local knowledge systems within our schools curricula to appreciate those local cultural aspects that worked in the past in our communities. Some of them are in fact inherent in their nature ways of doing things.

Marrying the contemporary world view of doing business with cultural aspects that make them distinct in their own cultural setting tremendously benefits us. Indigenous people need to feel proud to share with the outside world their unique way of running their lives and their forms of consciousness that maybe effective for their sustainable growth. How has our process of individuation affected our vision of entrepreneurship as a vehicle of general empowerment of our communities? What legacies do we expect to live behind for our children, families and community?

The final stage of the first of our infinitely iterative and spirally cyclical journey integrally incorporates all prior stages to bring our essence of elevated self-awareness. We expect visible change and tangible evidence of our transformative evolution. Our personhood, in accordance with the dictates and orientation of our respective cultures are also improved as we begin to find ourselves. In retrospect, we can visualise how all along we actively indulged in helping others around us increase their personhood by recognising their internal struggles and strengths and hence their full potential. It's an enabling realisation that consciously reinforces our capacity to navigate through our collective callings.

Focused and committed answering to our inner demands provides us with a much better chance of living a worthwhile and lasting legacy. Synthesising our known capacities and capabilities as ontological platforms are good places to start to identify fortified programs of self-development and empowerment in that respect. From that self-actualised position, we reach out more boldly to the outside world. The outcomes of our initiatives are rewarding and may culminate in something that has high utility levels to effect and achieve the goals we may desire. Are we, at this juncture, prepared and willing to draw from our own knowledge systems those aspects that are relevant to the contemporary and be proud to share them with the rest of the world?

Some of the knowledge that is available emanates from ancestry wisdoms that went through rigorous experiential development from fundamentals. Who are we to doubt it now without fair adjudication of its relevance and efficacy to our contemporary livelihoods? Abdication of what is truly ours preferring the new, foreign and seemingly dynamic has been easy, done at the stroke of a pen. Driven by imbalances we now feel, it has become critical for us to find common cause between our imbalances with those of the other worlds. These necessarily motivate us together with the global community to best serve our broad constituencies. We all must play our part in striving to empower others through increased self-consciousness. Appropriately identifying, directing, exploiting and channeling of latent creative energy abound within all of us; empowerment from within at individual and collective levels can go a long way in helping us to achieve this. Its broad inclusiveness eventually results in societal transformative shared benefits broadly significant to all.

Through our life history, we showed how we can subjectively consider our callings and transcend them integrally with our societal challenges to precipitate a unique area of imbalance that needs healing. Our personal issues that arise out of our callings must relate with the broader societal callings. How do we integrate all these seemingly divergent aspects of us without losing value? The desired integration needs capacity to converge our dualities to a synthetic both or to various perspectives without standing out from all others. But we should still be able to differentiate them.

Aspects of our lives considered here in part are viewed from multi-perspectives in a holistic and sustainable manner that takes our contexts into cognisance. We notice they align with our individual journeys, with those of our communities, organisations and societies we desire to serve. From these considerations, we raise higher order complexities that exist in us all. Carl Jung posits the concept of the *shadow* that houses the unconscious in his *Red Book* as a possible approach to resolve them.

We need to bring the unconscious into the conscious by letting ourselves step into the unknown and be explorers and discoverers so to speak. This process at a personal level is *Individuation* and it also embraces an individual's self-awareness path. The same process works in our dualistic thinking of opposites, of either-or into that of both or more. How do we learn to view both competently, without fear and skewed over-emphasis? Why not the continuous conscious and unconscious back and forth? How does this develop our self-awareness trajectory? The last section manages to bring our life story and history to successfully define ways of bringing forward our states of being, our soulful, spiritual, mindful and physical selves to the fore. It essentially maps out in detail the ontology of our state of being and the episteme of our immediate contexts, as they are.

Assumptions made in extracting both situations must reflect what we perceive as the truth on the ground and be able to withstand acceptable levels of reasonableness. We become aware of what truly defines us. It reveals our true strengths, weaknesses, our callings, desires, dispositions, brevity, capacities, motivations and imbalances. The desired awareness fully empowers our archetypical talents into related areas.

We followed an example of a life trajectory that has led us to whom we are today. Most probably, it has also led us to who we will be in the future if we do not change course to reroute it towards our desired zones.

It took us this long to realise our need to thrive a little more and blossom that which we deeply hungered for all along. We proved to ourselves and those around us that we can make things happen, mobilise families, communities and organisations into activism that brings people together. We showed that we can renew ourselves from a worm into a beautiful butterfly and vice-versa as need be each time we fall. We can catalyse ourselves and those around us for similar rebirths and renewals. We possess the ability to educate, learn and train ourselves, but questions still linger on our adequacy to confront what we most desire. We question the normative.

We are now cognisant of our ignorance against a vast ocean of unknown and untapped knowledge that can address all our world problems. Our impending legacies are far from complete and in jeopardy without us. How can we bring all this forward into our consciousness? Are we even capacitated to research it into reality given our present skills?

A venture of this magnitude demands pragmatic approaches and prerequisites special evolutionary forms of renewal in knowledge. It requires design methodologies that can be interpreted, can develop and result in more acceptable us. They need to be intelligent, coherent and practical enough to be recognised and admired by our peers in all four corners of the world. If we are capacitated to do this in our present states, add-ons we engage relevantly enhance our positions in the hierarchy. If we don't, we might as well take a very deep breath and psyche ourselves to take a marathon of our lives blindfolded. Our wiggly legs may even support expedient transgression to our demise.

Our perceptions change as we project into our transcendent journeys. We gauge our levels of happiness and contribution this far towards the status of things, regularly comparing it to when we started. We may occasionally feel despondent, helpless and excluded to the point of opting to not see nor hear evil. We dissociate and become numb, and eventually indifferent to it. How do we arouse, stimulate and heighten our curiosity to further sensitise ourselves? Heightening of our thirst is known to manifest from elevated dreaming that originate most creations and innovations. We require deliberate and focused decisions on what our lives should accomplish. It must be extraordinary with imageries vivid enough to feel like lived reality cherry picked from high up in the sky.

It is the identification of that desired present we wish our lives to be re-born in, supported by a deep quest for the truth and base knowledge that drives us to propel constant transformation and evolution. Our re-birth possesses that special ability to recognise a deeper painful wound, a nagging challenge that is difficult to see to an unsophisticated eye. We most definitely would not want heroes out of our subliminal, where our best vision is from the one eyed. We all, as part of collective humanity, owe and thrive to play our parts towards remedying any discomforts that may befall us.

We harbour an insatiable desire to live lifestyles of our choice to their fullest extent; lives that are so original, free, without fear and as unique as we individually imagine them. We hold the bull by its horns; eat the elephant in terms of self-development if we need a fighting chance to ever taste our desires. Anything less may not bring out the necessary inner latent energy we require for an exceptionally capable self.

We prepared throughout our lives, often involuntarily to be who we are today and tomorrow. Those that progress further than others develop the potential to consciously engage necessary preparations required for the paths of their destiny. As our journeys engage our chosen paths, we develop skills along the way that can demolish our self connectedness. We move forward easier once we become devoid of most of our self inflicted inhibitions.

Our ability to conquer the self becomes the first biggest huddle towards our intended journey. Over time, we self-inflicted with limitations that include desperation, unworthiness, all forms of complexes, fear, anxiety, perplexity and despair omnipotent to unleashing our full potential. These are mental conditions that can be overcome. With a little help and cognitive introspection, we can gradually pick on them, slowly minimising them to final eradication.

In more situations than preferred, the inner self overwhelms us, annihilating our dreams and desires to shreds in the process. We become our beliefs, our words, our behaviours, our conscience and eventually that character we tell. It canbe tainted further by the negative of what we don't desire to be but continuously cognize and over-emphasise in our minds. The stronger we hold on to who we are can exaggerate the mountain we want to climb. It can feel insurmountable, a true Mount Kilimanjaro to hike but can equally be reduced into a mole hill. How can we regenerate, develop skills to create and re-create ourselves in a continuous renewal mode that brings forth a dynamic self-awakening lifestyle we long for?

It is possible that transformative processes we engage can turn what we viewed as inhibitants into drivers of inspiration and motivations. It requires us to holistically draw on our being: the physical, heart, mental, soul and spiritual to fully get onto our healing journey. Outside our total indulgence, we relevantly borrow from the collective. These initiatives engage all of the self, drawing on higher cognitive, psychological, leaps of faith and commitment for their total disposition. The level of engagement carves the realisation of our paths naturally enshrined in our archetypes. This, as we will emphasise throughout exists in all of us but we need to take individual initiative to bring it forward. Achieving the peace, comfort and joy we all seek in our lives requires that we transcend from mechanical responses to organic knowledge based ones that can be reinforced by meditative cognitive contemplation. With the right kind of focus, it can result in realisable outcomes that we desire. It is the praxis of the final awareness outcomes that brings about collective healing and the peace we seek from within and without.

Lower levels of the educational and career ladder emphasises transformation of an individual into a person that fits the cultural and institutional mould. Depending on the collective culture, tolerance to deviance from the norm varies widely from extremely liberal to extremely conservative. The range and distribution is not unique to any part of the world as each society has its peculiar and particular traits.

An individual's creativity has generally been influenced to the extent directed by the immediate society, albeit the strengths of collective creativity within those confines. Total cultural genocide that at times has resulted from heavy enculturations in some parts of the world from whatever influences gradually destroys the basic fabric of creativity. The result maybe a deficiency in locally generated, contextual and innovative entrepreneurial endeavors. How does our furthering up the ladder through learning, education, and training counter inherent mutations from our cultural and social processes of personification?

The ability of self-developmental and actualisation programs to liberate one's way of dreaming, creativity, ideation processes and innovative realisations has threatened some communities. The perceived threat is reinforced by unfavourable but successful products of these engagements occupying leadership positions becoming moral compasses to societal challenges in its daily existence. Even the state tends to end up exploiting those that float to the top in the promulgation and support of its policies and laws for elevated legitimacy. In the process, those that achieve visible levels of awareness become highly regulated, structured and monitored. This mentality greatly influences enlightenment and transformative initiatives in those societies along the confines of what is institutionally acceptable.

Inherent limitations witnessed communities around the world importing **S**trategic **T**echnologies, **I**nnovations, **P**eople and **S**ystems that are **S**ustainable, acronym *STIPSS*, along with their respective cultures.

It is the importation and enculturation of external cultures that are concerning. The advent of the internet, availability and penetration of mobile phones has created untold challenges in this regard for societies intolerant of unique and divergent views towards creativity.

We should make a note of issues we generally need to answer in our lifetime for elevated self-awareness journeys. How do we focus on the things that authentically motivate us to continuous forward propulsion, sometimes seemingly against all odds? Universally, humans are keenly and insatiably interested in everything within and without them, intra and inter-relational from an early age. We are prepared to satisfy this interest in diverse situations. The only difference is some develop the courage to try at some point in their lives and some continuously procrastinate until their demise.

As we grow older, our senses of curiosity appear to slowly diminish in areas we consider superficial and irrelevant. We begin to focus on specific domains that interest us, just like we were as children. We start to intentionally thrive to reorganise ourselves to bring forward our sources of particular energies. We deliberately harness, capitalise and expend on those selected domains. Our affinities gravitate towards our root realm that radiates peak motivations to reveal our Calling. It demands an undeniable desire to want to know, to acquire knowledge on how things work and to act on them to the best of our abilities.

The spirally and iterative effort that emerges is re-energised or refueled with advent results we realise from our unique engagements with our Callings. They interface with those of the collective and society, be they physical, material, spiritual or emotional. These include, amongst others, reactions from recipients, visible activism in societal consciousness; mobilisation and collective networking; general improvement in approaches with integrity to social challenges; tolerance, open mindedness with a positive view towards boundless possibilities; resilience and a sense of sustainability rather than pessimism. These transformative initiatives desire to answer to the why of everything that affects us as individuals, families, communities and societies. It responds and transcends through the chronological issues of *how it* happened, what happened, when it happened and where it happened.

Evidence is accumulating around us on what happens when an integrated design is not formulated just-in-time to arrest the side effects of prevailing unintended current positions. The world is witnessing adverse effects from a cumulative chain of incremental negatives that are now a Mount Everest to climb. A butterfly flapping its wings in Gaborone can initiate a *tsunami*, the magnitude of an Omicron! Unprecedented heat waves, landslides and Elninos result throughout the world unlike ever before, leaving devastating trails in their wake.

The marginal per-capita output of sophisticated and highly conscious people coming out of the developed economies of the world is atrophying to an extent that its aggregate population is diminishing in real terms. The impact is felt more in developing countries reeling from incapacity challenges to build critical masses that can realise significant and measurable positive returns in their national development programs. How can they best confront this challenge?

Considering academic doctoral programs as an epitomic initiative at the height of self-awareness in a particular field, there has been considerable success in introducing their untraditional forms. These have had positive impact on throughput of these terminal degrees. Unfortunately, some older accrediting and traditional institutions are resistive and reluctant to fully engage these technology driven seemingly liberal methodologies.

These include, amongst others, distance education, online interaction, seminars and facilitation through the internet. Reluctance and resistance to change, holding onto the old they consider as the conventional has continued to limit capacity. Capacity to innovate, develop strategies responsive to the contemporary and introduce widely accepted curricula more applicable to areas with similar contexts. To mould the desired present that leads to the desired future. The obtaining is limited to continuously create conducive ecosystems responsive to the dictates of current dynamic and complex-chaotic environments.

A few countries in the world have achieved the requisite densities of doctorates necessary to make positive impact on the ground. That demography has shifted from career academics that go for it from start to finish. It includes significant populations of mature part timers that are in full employment or are already professionals in their own right. This mature demography embraces distance learning facilitated by the advent of the internet as a major supporting structure. The use of video conferencing, Skype and emails has created virtual universities that offer virtual courses delivered and quality controlled by a virtual supervisor.

As much as this created other challenges in guaranteeing quality control, that the work is in reality being done by the student, meeting desired objectives and thresholds, accountability issues and competent assessment methods in an environment where student needs became highly dynamic and transient. Their success has been most effective in areas with satellite access and fibre optic networks. They provide desirable high speed data resumes for the necessary impetus resolutions. It seems outstanding challenges can be overcome through innovative and optimal blending of conservative traditional approaches with the more liberal modern initiatives.

The onus is on us to promulgate initiatives that capacitate us to realise set objectives we want to achieve at defined points in time. We examine our consciences and reconcile capacities in self consciousness targets that we set for ourselves and those desired by our contexts. Certain thresholds in levels of competencies both in knowledge and skills can be prerequisites to enable us to present, articulate and defend our discourse with acceptable minimum levels of rationality. They are generally very demanding of high discipline and diligence. Our tolerance of others with different perspectives and our relevance to most aspects of collective lives of these academic and scholarly institutions elevate and adapt almost instantaneously at first. We then must maintain minimum standards of performance and pace as we progress throughout our journey.

Our achievements that confront more complex scenarios ascend explicitly with permanence, not to backslide to our old selves. Importantly, we simultaneously develop learning profiles during and after the doctoral journey that become permanent and continuous tacit processes for the rest of our lives. These are accompanied by an insatiable thirst for knowledge, brevity to confront unprecedented change that has become a way of life and to constantly welcome diversity. How does the doctoral experience equip us to successfully resolve most of these challenges in the most enlightened manner?

At various pre-doctoral programs orientations carried out by accrediting institutions or their representatives, we are told that one of its major objectives is for us to end up as enlightened rational thinkers and thought leaders. We must be able to derive objective approaches to diverse views of the world and its realities eighty percent of the time. We view and resolve global societal problems as our own with heightened consciousness and with a high degree of success especially in those fields that we have expertise.

The process of self conscientisation is a painful one and is accompanied by infinite deaths of the self with corresponding immediate re-births in the next level. We desire to transcend the new us through our decisions from habits of naturalness to more competent decision making processes that are more successful. It requires that we endeavor to fully understand ourselves psychologically and behaviourally, developing greater levels of intuition on how these influence our lifestyles. How can we develop capacity to the best of our abilities to identify, develop and fully apply ourselves enhancing our exposure to optimal praxis?

The integrative learning-education-training journey at terminal level puts a cap on our tertiary education and lifelong learning through self discovery and exploration. It authenticates our conscious endeavors in the creation of knowledge through its accompanying implementation methodologies. We want to come out of our shy, conservative, private and personal selves to be party to societal socio-political and economic challenges. We need to develop paradigms most of our peers throughout the Diasporas agree with especially those that practice in our regions. This objectifies us to be sensitive to local knowledge systems in our processes of creating new knowledge for its consumption by anyone in the world who desires to acquire it. It is prudent and insightful then for us to consider and be relevantly inclusive of those worldviews supporting locally developed knowledge through areas of expertise and best practice, allowing us to derive global acceptance and recognition to our inventions. What do we broadly expect the doctoral journey to achieve for us individually transcending to the collective?

We will be empowered with cultural, spiritual, philosophical and contextually rational approaches to practice as we move along our self-awareness journeys. Its evolutionary tenets allow us transcendence to expertise in chosen critical areas. We can, at this point develop integral designs competent to confront the full spectrum of challenges we perceive.

All developmental stages need to be consolidated and internalised. These transformative processes have to start with the self by developing skills positively self critical and abilities to filter intelligible creativity relevant to the context of existence. It is through these processes that capacity as shrewd, analytical, meticulous and fundamental individuals are born. High levels of performance to think intelligently in excess of 80% of the times instead of the 20 to 26% generally obtaining in highly demanding higher order complex; even chaotic situations usually accompany this birth. We can learn from following the lives of those that successfully went through similar processes before us.

In our life experiences, we are exposed to many successful people viewed as college drop-outs. On familiarization with their autobiographies, we realize that the same guys went through educational processes equivalent or even better than some doctoral programs. They achieved it through informally apprenticing themselves to the best mentors willing to share their wealth of experience as well as through contagion with and exposing themselves to institutions of higher learning.

Their implicit learning styles developed in them that special eye, mental frame and mindset that can fish out a developmental frontier existing in minute cracks of liminal societal space. It is in this space that a gap exists for one to rise from mere obscurity to a globally recognizable individual of substance. Many liminal and marginal persons chatted and carved their life paths from minimal existence to world class social and technological scientists, philanthropists, humanitarians, business persons, Nobel Price nominees and winners.

Beings described here are created and capacitated to operate outside the norms of society. They constantly search for crevices that when sealed result in positive benefits to society. To locate the crevice existing in the liminal space in any society, we need the tenacity to ask the right questions. It is the nature of these questions that draw out the desired outcomes. They lead to the ability to extract the right assumptions about the past, the present and the future, the chronosophy of a given context. Inappropriate assumptions in approaching complex situations have been found to provide out of context solutions.

Knowledge and hence assumptions of the past need to mainly serve as a grounding platform for the design of desired future outcomes. Emphasizing them can influence the tendency to repeat the same outcomes similar to the ones obtained in the past. We then need to concentrate on the desired present and future basing it on our strong sense of imagination to give birth to a new that is not contaminated with failures of the past. How then do we minimize the influence and flaws of our individual subjective realities emerging out of our processes of individuation? What is our reality?

Reality becomes not so obvious when it begins to depend on our subjective perspective, view or opinion. The reality of personal views and knowledge of something are considered as person specific and unique to the individual. Above all, through these infinite realities, we strive to bring out the truth and beauty around us motivated by our particular levels of enthusiasm peaking to levels that we set for ourselves.

The first challenge that hit us when we stumble on a true liminal frontier and precipitate a unique challenge is to realise what its objective is worth. We do this through interfacing singular with collective perspectives, starting with the immediate society transcending to global realization. Each society has a strong sense to over-emphasize a mono-cultural perspective rather than inclusively consider other relevant multicultural aspects that enrich our particular challenges.

Considerations here will exclude specifics on methods and methodologies on how we engage our self-awareness journeys; on how we approach intermittent process resumes. They will consider motivations that lead us to successfully achieve our objectives. It will not consider in specificity structures of the journey but will touch on its integral preparation and how to successfully achieve the objective.

Can we answer to why we need to continually develop our self-awareness? Most manage to realise their full potential enough to actualise their dreams to a level. The remainder needs to put more effort towards digging out their deeper and inner selves to bring forward the impetus self-awareness necessary for their best to manifest. In-built within us is the capacity to achieve our wildest dreams but the responsibility to draw it out of latency lies with us. Without it, we miss one of the critical aspects to a full life well lived, filled with aspirations we truly desire.

What role do the individual forms of intelligences we assign to ourselves and at times assigned to us by society play in all this? It appears, of the various forms of intelligences in existence, as much as they all have a role in our lives, still require further development. Most are complimentary to each other although we are occasionally made to believe otherwise.

The discussion of our intelligences as they influence our aspirations in life emerges from the differentials of how our minds function. They seem to be a direct function of societal influence and our egos. The challenge is that our minds appear to pull in directions of the most demanding domains of influence at any given time. It impacts on our perceptions and how we deal with our inner emotions and motivations, including those of others we interact with.

The view of traditional intelligence directly relates itself to the prediction of one's level of future success in life. This probably explains why we are surprised with how some of the most brilliant persons during our formal education and training days ended up uncorrespondingly unsuccessful.

How can we competently differentiate those that are academically successful to equally succeed in the real world? Today, brilliance is credited with only a fifth of successes in life. The rest that demands an inalienable right to full life, liberty and pursuit of happiness on our terms is excluded and accounted for elsewhere. How does our perception on the impact of our intelligences in our lives explain it?

The subject of intelligence and/or genius has been on the forefront of discourses that attempt to pre-empt one's success path. The two are loosely used interchangeably assigning them an infinite number of definitions. For more than one hundred years of debate and research, there is no single universal definition and it appears we may not get one soon. Quintessential proponent researchers in the field like Howard Gardner, Robert Sternberg and John Horn posited definitions of various forms of intelligence that gained considerable prominence, recognition and application. However, the collective broad definition from classic proponents averaged at our ability to learn through interfacing of formal and informal education, experience and training. One is equally required to continuously develop abilities in posing and precipitating problems out of a given context as well as finding viable solutions to them.

Finally, intelligent people need the ability to solve complex problems through clearly defined transformative action. Sometimes these actions result in the development of creative and innovative social and technological products. These three tenets appear common to most traditional forms of intelligence including multiple, practical, experiential, componential and other successful intelligences among many others. On the other hand the usual twin, genius, is intelligence that results in unique creative and innovative performance. We can venture to say here that genius is steps further than intelligence.

Development of what is intelligent and genius has arisen with dialectic differentials and in various forms of discourses of our societal demographics. Its intensity has not abated with globalisation. In effect, it has become more complex as interaction levels increase and intensify between communities, societies, races, social classes, schools attended, subjects undertaken, religiosity, spirituality, careers, material success, inter and intra the haves and the have-nots down to the choice of a spouse. All these and more are in the arena, significantly making contributions to the discourse of intelligence and genius of an individual or a collective. Its pertinence increases almost exponentially as one transcends the academic or career ladder.

Informal and unsaid peer approval is required in this regard. Otherwise may spell untold suffering and hard times revealed through tendencies of exclusion, subtle ostracism and lack of support and co-operation from already established peers. Many were stifled and others were stopped in their tracks to realise their academic dreams. Interestingly, retrospective consideration of the same provides completely different outcomes. What has retrospection on intelligence and genius revealed to us as the world fast globalizes?

The advent of the knowledge era has revealed wide influences overtime on the world's view of great men and women that came before us. Some situations witnessed subsequent revolutions, posthumously or otherwise that followed their dreams, ideation processes, creativity and subsequent disruptive innovations. The paradigms that manifested and the related shifts in human behaviour did not affect and influence only those communities of domicile of the creators but spread to all parts of the world. Communities far and wide were encultured to unprecedented levels. It transformed them to an extent beyond recognition of original cultural acculturation processes. It was to the detriment of their internal contextual creativity and learning abilities.

Of note, prominence on world enculturation has built on the works of Plato, Socrates, Descartes, Galileo and Newton amongst many other western European luminaries. Their scientific views enculturated the world to think and see the world in sectors considered rational, governed by reason and linear simplicity, with all other sectors summing up to the remainder. In our little spheres we strived to meet their bench mark at the expense of our other natural insightfulness.

Desires to dream of contextual creativity outside the western view were negatively considered and compromised. They were viewed as not rational and reasonable to pass the test into global integrity, hence unacceptable. This kind of mutilation has reduced beneficiaries to machine like behaviour that is mechanistic in approach.

If we were to inclusively consider other diverse insightful worldviews, we would see that the spread of influences of eminent persons dominate at the exclusion of local knowledge systems. These may or may not have viewed intelligence and genius differently. The cultural, spiritual, religious and collective views of the context took centre stage contributing to the contemporary world order. Other capacities more cognisant, sensitive and knowledgeable in relational and renewal knowledge systems reinforced the view of empiricism, measurement, rationalism and reasonableness. Unfortunately, relationalism and renewalism did not measure up therefore did not get a seat on the table to discourse in the intelligence and genius measurement tenets. How then do we relationally, renewably, rationally and realisationally consider the intelligence and genius capacity of anyone or anything? Is there an empirical template that we can refer to?

The view here is that we can categorise intelligence in an infinite number of ways. We proffer to sum it up into four main general categories. These will be referred to as relational, renewal, rational and reasoning intelligences and finally the realisation intelligence. Each individual form is inherently enshrined in the archetype of a particular worldview. In that particular domain, it is optimally and extremely potent especially if integrated with at least one of the others defined in its particular worldview. The definition of any of the intelligences needs to be context sensitive. As an example, an Indian national intrinsically defines it with its originality and peculiarity to Indian cultural tenets.

We can see that those that are relationally intelligent are successful at working with people. Related communities and societies can be considered as realisationally intelligent. Some of the luminaries that are identifiable globally for their unique forms of intelligence are Nelson Mandela for his rainbow nation, Julius Nyerere for his UJAMAA, and Nkwame Nkurumah for his African form of democracy and Steve Jobs for his realisable android.

Renewal intelligence has its roots in hermeneutic spiritual processes that provide emphasis and capacity in psychology, philosophy, spirituality and religious related work. We can site many spiritual innovations that renewed the world albeit the mutilation they received and hence had lesser impact on it. Many spiritually charged initiatives had the guise of Christianity, Judaism, Islam, Buddhism and Confucianism as guiding philosophies. The Dailar Rama, Mother Theresa, Mahatma Ghandi and San Tzu gave renewal intelligence prominence. Rational and reasoning intelligence is great at new knowledge, concept and theory development. Similarly, it can formalise and transform all that is considered empirical or measurable.

Those with realisation intelligence have abilities to translate, implement and put into practice any of the rationalised, conceptualised or theorized knowledge. Steve Jobs, Bill Gates and Richard Branson are typical examples that quickly come to mind. They advanced and displayed specific forms of intelligence and genius giving birth to innovations that went a long way in healing the world. What and how then is intelligence and genius defined in a way that is broadly inclusive of all the others?

We posit here that intelligence and genius are individual, community, culture and context sensitive with each having primal claim on specifics unique to it enshrined in their archetype. It is through the revelation of our authentic Calling and archetype that maximally tap on our genius resulting in novelty creativity and innovation in areas of our best performance. Communities that took the initiative to define intelligence and genius for the world confined it to their environs basing it on their specific prototypes that excelled exceptionally in areas of their Calling and archetype. Carl Jung in Brooke (1991) suggests that the archetype exists in one's potential with a strand unique to the individual. If the archetype is correctly identified, it makes one a unique achiever. When archetype confluences with one's ego demands, a deepest sense of uniqueness and individuality that submits to the greater whole is exposed.

Sometimes our desperate need to perform to the requirements of the conventional definition of intelligence and genius results in dreaming-creativity-ideation-realisation paralysis. We usually put ourselves under tremendous pressure to be the first at something or at times to be the only ones who ever did it. The odds of this happening are slim, but possible. It appears that at best we are able to borrow from our mental archives that bank all life experiences we encountered. We draw out, filter and converge those that are relevant to a perceived challenge into combinations unique enough to give birth to something new. The new is so pioneering it solves the challenge that has persisted to exist until this initiative. Michael Williams posits that *there is no such thing as "first" in any creativity associated with any human creativity.*

Application of what is conventionally considered as intellect is partly motivated by competitive survival. It is driven by our desperate need to be the centre of being and universe regardless of our marginal abilities to make real difference. The less challenging route is for us to assimilate, to blend and be like our environments both psychologically, physiologically and behaviourally.

The advent of information and communication technology (ICT) has made the processes of simulation much more sophisticated that we can disguise ourselves to fit our intelligence and genius on our terms. These occasionally result in perceived innovations and technological advancements when in reality, it is all unintentional plagiarism or otherwise. How do we rise above the simulation tendencies that are well orchestrated by highly developed enculturation and acculturation subtle processes confronting us constantly? How do we de-centre, unmutilate, become unmechanical and liberate ourselves into the societal liminal frontiers eighty percent of the time?

It appears there exists a form of intelligence and genius that can best suite a particular worldview as well as incorporate other worldviews notwithstanding their context. Inclusivity and integration of the best from the other worldviews appear to be one logical way to do that. Contemporary definition of intelligence and genius has correspondingly shifted from exclusively embracing rational and realisational intelligences at the marginalisation and complete exclusion of the other two intelligences. This integrated and inclusive realisation comprehensively incorporated in its definition some of the other missing sensitivities to recognise emotional intelligence as a true measure of an applicable form of intelligence. What is it and how does it differ with the positivistic approach to intelligence?

In its approach, emotional intelligence embraced and integrated all the four forms of intelligences that we discussed here into something that is contemporarily relevant and desirable. In the past, mostly the rational and realisable forms of intelligence were emphasised at the marginalisation and even at the exclusion of relational and renewal intelligences. Over a century of intense discourse, cracks emerged resulting from their deficiencies, especially in our contemporary environment. The perceived gap required another social innovation that could attempt to close the gap, hence the birth of Emotional Intelligence.

There has been a strong attempt at defining emotional intelligence both from the social and empirical sciences. Common to most of its interpretations are three major areas that primarily define its domain that the journalist, Daniel Goleman posits in his book, *Emotional Intelligence*. Traditional intelligences have been criticised for their deficiency in relating their definition to our daily experiences and existence. It remained in silos that have not been easy to translate in performance terms.

On the other hand, emotional intelligence has incorporated operational capabilities experientially enabled and hence its measurement. It drew its energies from the positive aspects and prior knowledge of its predecessors, complementing itself through surpassing pre-established sets of benchmarks, adding cohesive value in the process. Its value is evidenced by how traditional intelligence empowers us to be accepted as competent in mental skills envisaged to translate into usable practical genius. As a result, the merit to secure a career is enshrined in it. In practice there are significant shortfalls and unexpected turns of events.

High traditional intelligences did not necessarily manifest in obvious practical performance success life stories. Formal educational and informal experiential development mostly remained exclusive of each other to a point where they even contradicted. The dynamic environment that is constantly changing faster than we can is fully considered in emotional intelligence. We need to stay ahead of change! It has capacities to deal with determinants of the success of life exemplified by strong market forces and human emotional imbalances. Our hierarchical slots in society became highly transient because of accelerated advancements in globalisation that need an emotionally intelligent approach.

Emotional intelligence was found to improve with age, education, training and experience, be it implicit, explicit or tacit. These are impacted on by the practical experience we get from our daily lives.

Its approach is open, flexible and adaptive. We can postulate on its emotion sensitive inclusive approach that integratively envelopes relational, renewal, rational and realisational intelligences positive energies in all of us albeit in varying unique combinations. It therefore relates well to the work environment that it has been credited with excellence and hence advancement in a work place or entrepreneurial environment. Maybe we already took positions on what we perceive to be intelligence, but what is our informed view on emotion as individuals, as cultures and as societies that form the global society?

Invariably, our wish on emotion is to approach it from the way it impacts us and how we react to it in our quest towards our self initiated self awareness processes. Overall, how does this contribute towards our desired lifelike living that manifests and culminates in our individualised sense of good living?

The basic question of what emotion is has been a subject of intense and raging debate for over five centuries. Its formal discourse was introduced then by Socrates but failed to bring consensus on its definition up to the present. The Merium–Webster dictionary defines it as being *a conscious and cognitive, subjective experience, a strong disturbance, excitement and feeling directed towards something specific usually accompanied with psychological, physiological and behavioural changes in the body*. The most recent posit relates it to a more formidable definition, to what can be considered as a more globally acceptable definition of intelligence by Meyer and Salovey in their emotional intelligence differential from previously existing ones.

The psychological and physiological concepts proffered this f r remained provisional for short periods of time before they were overtaken by counter and sometimes contradictory discoveries. Socrates, his student Pluto, David Hume, Descartes, Hegel, Adam Smith, Immanuel Kent, Friedrick Nietzche, Aristotle, Seneca, Baruch Spanoza, Sigmund Freud, Edmund Husserl, Max Scheler, Martin Heidegger, Paul Ricoeur to Jean- Paul Sarte and now through the pair of John Meyer and Robert Salovey. In the beginning, emotion was considered as subservient to reason. On the other hand, it has been considered specific to individuals, respective cultures, spiritualities and specific settings with dichotomy tensions between the psychological and physiological.

Our ability to reason was advanced as the first and foremost impacting differentials to and of our emotions. It is the way we view, cognate and judge our worlds through our life experiences and our slots in its hierarchy. This provides us with explanations to our sense, our nature, our humanity and the environment we live in. In the process, it addresses our epistemological as well as ontological concerns that bring about an inner and deeper understanding of our sense of being – and self awareness.

When we empower ourselves through self development and enhanced awareness campaigns, we objectify our strong desire to strengthen our position in that hierarchy. As much as reason has been considered to impact on emotion the most throughout its formal evolution, it is considered to exceptionally disturb our passions. The latter found itself in the ethics definition of cultures as well. However, most appear to be driven by passion. How does emotion fit in the global realm of things that influence our well being, happiness, love, desire, lust, hatred, jealousy, threat, fear, moods, joy, sadness and human compassion?

The elements listed above create part of an infinite ecosystem of elements in us that influence our emotions. It manifests emotion on emotions, ideas feeding on previous ideas and impressions on impressions each feeding on prior conditions of infinite and continuous deaths and rebirths of a seemingly chaotic but hierarchical and orderly progression. Adam Smith goes further to relate emotion, sympathy and ethics as bedrock to capitalism in his treatise *The Wealth of Nations* of 1776, impacting directly on the core of human existence, social survival and morality values.

A child is not afraid of a fire unless it has been burnt before and is not scared of heights unless it has experienced falling. The in-built data banks that capture information from zygote formation to our present, consciously or sub-consciously informs us of our emotions based on a minimum compliment of a minimal stimuli enough to trigger either bad or good emotions and everything in-between. This means that every emotion we get is rooted in something or a relationship that has happened or is happening in our lives whether we are aware of it or not.

It is perceivable that our emotions can function as our barometer or the proverbial sixth sense we generally credit ourselves with when we experience moments outside of what we perceive as normal. In the process it determines the quality of lives we lead relationally or rationally, subjectively or objectively. It is clear therefore that we need to be highly self aware of who we are through exhaustively journeying back as often as necessary digging deeper and deeper into our life stories. Without it, the good life we desire becomes elusive.

How does this contribute towards the way we think and our abilities to make our situations exceptionally successful? How do we bring out maximum benefit out of all our encounters including inter-relationships with others as well as their diversity?

How do we logically, conceptually and positively define the domain of our emotions? How do we determine them more elaborately as we grow, finally cognitively and cohesively enabling them to function in our favour in the majority of cases?

Overall, this implies that there is no empirically developed prototype of intelligence or genius template for self development and advancement in life. We can develop ourselves into exceptionally unique intelligent and genius units that can archetypically excel unabated, uninhibited, unrobotic and unmutilated to realise that life like existence we most desire. Top shelf training tools capacitate us to actualise these epitomes. How do we pre-mentor in preparation for the related life changing and significantly transformative self development journeys? What do we opt for, intelligent or genius or both? How much of it is enough for our full enlightenment?

We all puzzle on when exactly we triggered onto the life trajectory that has led us to who we are today. All those events, some unfortunate, make us wonder how in the world they could have been helpful.

Ironically, even the fortunate, wealthy and comfortable had the expected good as well as the unprecedented bad. We are who we are because of every crummy occurrence that has happened in our lives.

What role has our fore-parents, parents, families and communities played in the unfolding of our life historicities? Could we have maneuvered ourselves somehow to the same destinies as those we look up to, admire and try to emulate? We may or may not have obtained any living examples, just their hazy mythical images. There was no-one to hold our hands towards creating any form of a horizon let alone a desired one. Chances were limited to enable us to create horizons of substance in our minds. All that darkness!

Some had the fortune of having long histories of related prior knowledge in our areas of natural ability. They had choices from birth and could pro-actively be referred to as doctor, astronaut, rabbi, engineer or nurse from the time they were in pre-school. Their orientation towards the particular started then. Notwithstanding, their processes of re-discovery could have revealed something different later in life. At least the beautiful horizons to alter to suit had been created.

Career days at sixteen revealed for the first time what possible careers or professions we can embark on. Through it, a significant number has settled on those they perceive as most lucrative or secure regardless of very loud screams to the contrary coming from deep within. We later feel and regret not having listened to those voices. But did we really have the luxury of choice?

We are made to believe that the truly intelligent and genius did not have to go to college. How could they when they tacitly realised its equivalent in their first year of high school? They were apprenticed early, exposed to informal learning through problem based learning (PBL) and they embarked on numerous self-motivated and self- discovery journeys before most of us could recite the twelve times table or the alphabet. They were totally aware of who they are at that early and tender age. They knew their hobbies and even pursued them. They were clear about the sports they liked, the type of foods they preferred to eat and they chose their friends carefully.

In most cases they became loners because they could not find compatible friends. They even creatively crafted revenue channels to finance their ambitions and desires. Occasionally, they had the support of their immediate societies but equally, they were alienated by the same as a sign of disapproval of deviance from the societal norm. All in all, they inadvertently exposed their callings and archetypes and engaged areas of their passion unapologetically. They were motivated by the disapproval around them and dared their peers, families and communities. Those that truly dared won.

Who of us successfully broke the barrier, from genuinely generating dreams authentic to self, conceptualising them through emancipation of the static self to total enlightenment? Its movement has allowed long, arduous and critical idealisation processes that are collective and inclusive. Implementation to realise applicable and relevant contributions has been the greatest challenge of all. Those that fail had limited capacity in creating a feedback loop back into more enlightened dreaming. What are the special circumstances that enable those that successfully walked the tight rope?

All humans have a peculiar archetype whose disposition dominates all others if authentically identified and intentionally emphasised from an early age or as early as possible. This is a diamond in the rough that needs polishing soon after its discovery and extraction from the ground. Its mining is followed by proper preservation and meticulous polishing. High sensitivity to its prominent features is critical in revealing its most hidden secrets. Skilled polishers can identify these features to enhance its essence and unique sparkle. The desired inherent glow can best be revealed by that special someone, never to be recognised nor enjoyed by those that desperately seek it to satisfy their dreams.

Similarly, we all need those particular others and our societies to help us shine. Shapes unique to us mustbe revealed to shine in the form of that special archetype equally existing in nature. We believe it can optimally enhance our creative genius visualised through that unique polisher who can bring it to sparkle.

It is the polishers, the mentors, the role-models, professionals, academics, educators, trainers, spiritual leaders, our parents and families who had the pleasure of grooming us to realise our shine. They played the role of the most pleasant repudiators, greatest informers that awaken our conscience moving the unknown-unknown in us to the known-unknown and to known-known in our minds as their protégés. Has this been done to the best of our interest as individuals or has it been to the best of others interests, especially society?

We can choose to point a finger at those that took that responsibility. Did they know any better to do it in a manner that brings out the best of us? They probably emphasised what they had learnt and known over time, the Italians with their tailoring, the Jews with ruthless trading and bargaining, the Indians with information and computer technology, the British with their need to see reason and rationality in everything, the Japanese with *kaizen* approach of small incremental improvements, the Chinese with respect for filial piety and family networks and the Africans with their *Ubuntu* approach to life.

We can see how such over-emphasis has resulted in something contemporary is mistakenly considered as inherent. Their levels of self-awareness directly impacted on the development of ours at the time.

We can only transcend to something new and greater once we know and accept who and what we are. It is from that platform that we can evolve to the next level. The autobiographies of luminaries of our respective societies are clear on how desperately they listened to their inner voices. They unrelentingly introverted on who they are. It was critical for them to know what their capacities were, what they could and couldn't do.

Steve Jobs adopted a vegan diet singling out apples as his preference. Richard Branson moved out of his parent's main-house into their garage as a youngster to concentrate on developing his creative freedom of self discovery. Similarly, as much as his parents insisted on him following the family tradition of becoming lawyers, Bill Gates could not be dissuaded from his passion in computers.

We notice that in many life spheres, be it religious, spiritual, cultural, sociological, humanitarian, philanthropic, physiological, psychological, philosophical or scientific, most of the respective luminaries started early in life to work on strengthening their convictions and in knowing who they are and what they represent. Available resources at their disposal were not a factor. The critical resource they needed and was wholly at their disposal was their inner energy buoyed in the strength of their self awareness. They had big dreams, quintessential dreamers from early childhood.

Richard Branson had a clear dream of venturing into space long before he turned sixteen. His vision was so clear that he went ahead and reserved the name Virgin Galactic, a name he uses today for his venture into space. At Virgin Galactic, their ethos is that the *future of sustaining life is in space.* Expanding earth life into space provides us a clear view of fragile earth *with a new perspective inward and outward.* It's a dream come true for its founder and promoter, archetypal entrepreneur, Richard Branson. He had his maiden trip into space on the 11th July 2021.

The success of these dreamers from tender ages came with resilience, first degree bruising, passion, commitment, one ten thousandth success rate, agony, frustration, solitude and focused constant searching. They continuously researched for and dug deeper into that inner self that propelled them on even in the face of seemingly insurmountable adversity.

How could they stop when their vision of who they are and who they desire to be in the present and future overwhelmingly consumed them dominantly and crystal clear? They knew exactly what and where they want to be in the global hierarchy. Their number one goal was to effectively transform the world into what they desired. It was imperative to be archetypally best at what they do. They craved for the number one jersey, but were not in competition with others but themselves. Only they could do it their way.

Commitment to constantly compare and contrast provided them with snapshots of current creativity platforms to operate and spiral from. They slept, dreamt, ate, agonised, toiled, pilgrimaged and literally crucified themselves over it.

We all change the world albeit at varying degrees and in different directions. By denying ourselves our dreams, we invariably deny the world something it could have gotten from us to better itself into balance. The unique us existing in who we can be has to be extricated, exposed and celebrated through empowering ourselves to exercise it in optimally effective amounts, effort, timing and purpose.

Through repetitive extra effort, failures, dusting ourselves and trying again, we increase our chances of realising the desired outcome through deeper enlightenment manifest from each failure. It benefits the generality of the world in the process pushing ourselves up to our rightful destinies.

Socrates, the father of reason even posited that we need to know ourselves intimately first because an ... *unexamined life is not worth living*.

A large proportion of emerging communities' demographic strata, the youth that constitute more than fifty percent of current populations in most developing countries yearn for the success and stability they perceive in other societies. They fancy the same for themselves. They fervently follow the lives of their celebrities with active imagination and interest, unfortunately sponging everything portrayed by their chosen role models as living gospel. Their communities seem to lack in eminent role models and mentors with desirable narratives to match future desires of the unintended protégés.

Similar role models and mentors with familiar stories that meet societal predispositions are glaringly lacking. They are a primary need in developing communities to mentor, role-model and motivate the youth to become conscious of greater possibilities early in life. We all individually have unique callings coupled with peculiar archetypes whose combination can synergise to serve specific causes that contribute towards healing humanity. In the process, it simultaneously emerges and engages our unique contextual entrepreneurial skills globally integral. It evokes best possible journeys to realise dreams of our Callings.

Our collective focus is to develop a continuous process of births, deaths and rebirths of an infinite series of renewals. that the latter constantly engage deliberate integrated designs that draw out and build on our authentic states of self awareness. Our holistic sense of being is drawn out; the *I am* through the progressive frames that life deals us on a daily basis. It is the true and genuine identity of our states of being to ourselves by ourselves at any given moment and time. It provides us the best potential to manifest lifelike existence we choose and desire on our own terms. The state we seek is fluid, transient and so shifty that our yesterday's reality of the self can be our today's illusion.

This is a journey of self discovery. We really don't know what we don't know until we embark on the journey. We can only do our best to develop the necessary shock absorbers for all eventualities that come our way.

Such preparation includes our preparedness to work alone. It consumes us full time even in those moments we are not aware of it happening.

How does this impact on those around us, our partners, parents, family, siblings, holidays, and physical exercise, walking our dogs, hobbies, peers, celebrations and funerals? Most importantly, we need to exhaustively answer committaly on how we are going to provide for our responsibilities and obligations when we are not available. Prior consideration of all perceivable outcomes is absolutely necessary.

How does this impact on our career plans as the highly transformative journey may revolutionarise this?

Our integrated design requires us to competently confront and deal with all our lifelong aspects that feed into and manifest from our journeys. It must awaken and motivate the dormant action oriented spirit, the archetype, the genuine being in each one of us. That awakening provides us with inner power to propel forward regardless of how insurmountable any challenge lying in our paths may look. It must constantly and wholesomely renew us, exciting us to maximally excel in the face of adversity and individual quests. It is therefore imperative that we shift our capacities from the implicit through to tacit processes that allow us continuous change reactive to our states of reason and emotion, keeping the two in tensional balance. From here on this can be mentored and exemplified by going through pinnacle processes or journeys whose philosophies are rooted in continual revelation of our individual whole, pumping our creative and innovative juices to our unique maxims.

Over time, the space that was allocated to our hierarchical domains in the world system of things has been exponentially decaying especially in areas of mastery and expertise. Doctorates in traditional areas such as research and tenure at universities reduced significantly for every one thousand people served. On the contrary, their domain of relevance has greatly expanded in other non-traditional sectors. They include business development, entrepreneurship, non-governmental organisations, civic society, philanthropy, humanitarianism, the private and public sectors.

All aspects of our lives evolved over time. The contemporary now demands us to create dynamic spaces visible and plausible to those that see not only with their eyes, but with the authenticity of their inner selves.

Other none traditional opportunities exist to those that are confidently aware of their limits in liminal abilities and inabilities. Their levels of self awareness capacitate them to define liminal challenges for society as they perceive them. As these are clearly frontal and hence unknown to the infected society, it remains their responsibility to sell and justify their relevance and need for immediate attention by society to balance the perceived latent illness.

Why are some of the challenges we see more critical than others the society experience on a daily basis? How do we then find relevance to society's fractal organisations that keep our daily lives in balance and we desperately seek to serve? It attentions us to the need to relate our desires and the direction we intend to take with a particular political or socio-economic sector of the macro economy at the beginning of our intended journeys.

The impetus is directly upon our heads to ensure that whatever we see and visualise, our families, communities, organisations and societies also see and visualise. The traditional approach is pitched so far away from humanity's direct needs and daily application of our communities. It has been so Newtonian that the only people that could understand it are those that specialise in related areas of expertise. Those that are passionate about what they do were labeled as nerds. Most cannot explain issues, simple or complex, in layman terms in a way that John the plumber can fully comprehend. How can we immediately convince those that cannot see what we see? How can they visualise without doubt that an imbalance actually exists that warrants resolution? Without it, all may just belong in an ivory tower.

High conceptual and arbitrary initiatives are desirable for pioneering and cutting edge discoveries but they may need to relate to everyday realities and practicalities. Those that cannot be reduced to simple language need to be exceptions rather than the norm. We require an approach that carries perceived societal challenges and realities, with enough densities of practitioners. Noticeable concentrations of them per every one thousand of our general populations have measurable impact on our collective awareness and developmental initiatives.

The current advocacy emphasises that national governments must lead and finance initiatives to massify the production of doctorate holders in developing nations. The reality on the ground is contrary to this belief. Individual and creative combinations of individuals' initiatives are more effective. These seem to emerge and nucleus around a senior Professor who develops a strong sense of being and gets frustrated by the sluggishness of institutionalised frameworks, too cumbersome and awkward to respond to timously.

These, on self cognisance, act as catalytic activists making life simpler for the would- be doctoral candidates, especially the mature and working ones with families. Their efforts are producing impressive results yielding higher numbers of graduating doctorates within four years of enrollment. Their quality is comparable to or even surpass traditional channels, generally referred to as conventional. The per capita cost of production is much cheaper.

In short, we implore all doctorates to ensure that they directly influence the production of at least two other doctorates within the first five years of their graduation. It could greatly massify numbers to optimal critical thresholds fostering noticeable transformation in reality. This effectively happens if the origination of our self awareness is truly authentic to the self and throughout the continuum to bring out the desired relevance and structural change in our functionality.

Personified integral designs to self awareness are typified by a doctoral journey as an area whose demands actualise us towards lifelike living. It necessarily must successfully effect transformation and innovation. We notice that truly successful people living amongst us are fully engaged and passionate about their learning processes up to pinnacle levels. They push for the best out of their strong curious minds by immersing themselves in spheres related to their Calling. They are extremely adaptive, health conscious, religious and love their families, communities and organisations. They live passionately and lifelike to the maximum possible.

This comes with uninhibited, unmutilated and unmuffled interaction with their environments. An open two-way sponge like relationship exists with each keenly absorbing and learning from the other as much as possible. The sponges eventually start to drip back to the giver extras it cannot hold. The two way flow is interdependent with one ready to give and the other ready to accept. In the example of the PhD or doctoral journey, desires are heightened to that maximum.

We will explore ways to engage our preferred philosophies that bring out authentic callings. These will provide self discovery processes that enhance our personal life rooted in *STIPSS* as we get to know ourselves better. How can we enhance our journeys to include our families and all around us?

Our approach will attempt to stay away from any one particular and established methodology. It is best for each individual to identify and choose known knowledge systems they find relevant and compatible to reinforce their integral designs. We believe the oscillatory and iterative processes suggested here are capable of enhancing any of the existing formats in use today.

Forecasting anticipated outcomes enable us to prepare to handle the success of our self-discovery. As we transform, we may not realise our progress if we do not continuously re-enter our environments as we progress. How do we encourage our environments to enthusiastically keep up with us? This journey may appear to be ours as individuals and not theirs as a collective? How do we minimise strong resistance at nodes of interception? Can we increase the number of nodes to make interactions frequent enough to relate to continuous presence?

Lifelike existence can be a heavy responsibility in an environment going through diverse experiences. The environment may choose to stifle our efforts and achievements. What intelligences do we require to manage external pressures contrarian to our objective?

CHAPTER 3

INTERFACE OF VISIONS

We are now going to engage a phase of formal education or training available to us as one of the key routes towards our self actualisation. Post high school, we find ourselves in one place or the other. In some situations, we do not get to choose. We take what we consider to be the best option of that which is on the table. There exist numerous formal structures that offer us opportunities of advancement towards what we perceive as the best avenue towards our most desired future. Some will be better prepared for this occasion than most. We all pray and hope that our choices at this juncture represent our aspirations. The experience soon to be provided is adequate and firm enough to be a rung in the ladder that lifts us a step closer to our desired lifelike lifestyles.

Success of this part of our journey, similar to our former self-awareness engagement, builds on a solid process of origination that exposes one's strengths and weaknesses from its onset. It directs impending participants closer to their burning desires. It relates them to societal challenges that fall within areas of their archetypical calling. It is a highly transformative stage that demands total attention and cognizance of the self. Research has shown the *STIPSS* process to be very effective in that regard. It's an acronym that stands for implementable **S**trategic thinking that is **T**echnologically sound, **I**nnovatively viable, has **P**eople at heart and carries them along, evolving simplified **S**ystems that encompass all related networks to result in **S**ustainable outcomes *(STIPSS)*.

At every stage of consideration, we ideate and attempt to clarify our Strategy, identify the Technology we will engage, Innovate relevant tools, inclusiveness of People that we collaborate with through well crafted Systems to realise Sustainable practices in continual self-awareness initiatives for desirable lifestyles. This means we engage actualising Strategies, Technologies, Innovations, People, Systems and Sustainable practices and outcomes necessary for continual growth in our quest.

What processes are we going to use to approach our journey?

Our envisaged integral design that we slowly began to organically bring to life in the last two chapters is rooted in a philosophy that hierarchically and integrally builds on prior processes, inputs and outcomes. It comprehensively objectifies dynamic actualisation of our states of being at any given point. The integral part indicates that it is wholly inclusive of transformational, transcultural, transdisciplinary and transpersonal initiatives borrowed from world views that are best at it. These have empirically evolved and mutated over hundreds of years. They have learnt to adopt general omissions in the past and buttress weaknesses of the methods that exist this far. Over emphasis of one aspect at the marginalisation of other pertinent considerations has been the order of the past. These are action oriented processes we now need to immerse ourselves in.

Once the stage of passive consideration of embarking on our self-awareness journey evolves into action, it clearly starts to emerge our need to broadly define dedicated sub-ecosystems around *STIPSS* that we can work with. These become pillars we can reliably lean on to achieve our objective; functionality, co-operation, positive effectiveness and commitment. Once started, this process slowly and increasingly becomes more critical and demanding as we delve deeper with each cycle. It also progressively becomes clearer that not all those we engage are necessary. We may also discover some necessary others that were omitted. However, our full commitment reflects strongly on the process and to realise that the journey has started in earnest. At this point we make visions of our desired outcomes clearer to feel like lived reality. Notwithstanding, they may turn out to be completely different.

They are nodes throughout as we progress. We are awarded tokens of achievement that encourage us to soldier on. These tokens are epitomes of achievement and success at the battles we encounter and fight to win. They push us forward towards our goal. Our success in desired areas of excellence inevitably moves our minds forward that we can literally feel and smell our intended outcomes. This imagined reality must grow to the extent of overwhelming us, and be a constant nag at the back of our minds.

We are going to be working with something intangible and invisible to sight. In reality, our creation is something that will totally renew us to a level that may even shock us. We want the outcomes to most importantly be alive enough to positively impact us, our families, our peers and our communities in a way that carries them with us. It cannot be a zero sum game. Thereafter, we are perceived differently, in way that may feel strange. Outsiders may feel as if we are mucking up the steady state our families and communities worked on so hard for generations to achieve. How do we derive loyalty from people we engage and ecosystems we create?

Our focus is on lifelike lifestyles we envisage after we become fully operational at our optimum with full awareness and consciousness of a complete sense of our total being. Similarly, just like freshmen apprentices may fully visualise their graduation day and elevated contributions that impact their communities at large will. Besides self development, our impact on a society to operate at an elevated level of awareness is phenomenal. We can imagine the elation and the out of self zombie like feeling that zaps the spine like an electric shock. The ululating, whistling, clapping of hands. The odd crying like a mother coming out of those ladies that were part of the team, so proud that the journey raised their senses of values, awareness and self consciousness. How then do we continually design a formidable and fully immersed and energised meta-ecosystem with impetus dynamism characterized with intermittent births and rebirths throughout its life?

Before starting any of our developmental journeys, we normally engage what we consider to be a rational approach. We search the internet, read a myriad of books, widely consult and listen to a number of prominent practitioners in the field. It helps in building a platform to start from. Much of it weakens instead of strengthen our resolve. Each experience is unique and different. What it mostly leaves out is how these journeys are peculiarly tailored and most enjoyable experiences if we design them properly to fully engage our creative and innovative selves. Once done, it gradually strips layers of discovery that get better with each cycle, like an onion, getting softer and increasingly palatable as we delve into it deeper. We will experience crying and eye watering moments as we slowly peel our way through to the core. Albert Einstein summed it up well when he posited *"I never made one of my discoveries through the process of rational thinking"*. This hardly ever comes out of our pre-rationalisations and formal researches we engage.

A significant amount of discourse exists, whether or not these processes truly empower beyond the usual that may have happened anyway in one's normal course of life. Are we able to bring out, realise and formalize our creative and innovative abilities towards self- awareness through our normal daily lives? Some schools of thought believe time and energy is better spent if directed towards other formal and rationalised advancements. This thinking advocates that it should really not make much difference if we were already so inclined.

Various individuals, families and communities, especially in developing countries do not wholesomely ascribe to the notion of apportioning some of their scarce resources towards counseling, psycho-analysis and self-developmental programs. They need realizable and tangible outcomes that benefit them in the moment. Benefits from conscious self- awareness engagements do not seem to hit us on the forehead as lower level initiatives do. Thus, it obligates us as individuals or small enclaves of like-minded individuals to be resourceful regardless of our needs, be they material, cultural, spiritual, emotional or intellectual. We find that the spiritual, cultural and emotional are not emphasised.

We can hazard to say traditional forms of intelligence are inadequate to fully embrace the demands of the contemporary. We are gradually realising the importance of engaging consciousness enhancement initiatives from all worldviews to adequately confront our world order today.

Self-awareness processes do not require special skills, special capacities or structured mainline forms of intelligences. It is independent of prior knowledge. It mostly requires our full commitment and energy to apply ourselves. It is intrinsically a personal journey that necessarily demands resilience energy from the inner self. Proper preparation, creation of external structurally functional and sustaining support structures, holistic and realistic enough to serve the ultimate integral design is equally important. Such an integrated design at the beginning of the journey provides the best possible fortitude for success.

There will be a significant amount of impromptu pop-ups to deal with. We are enabled to deal with them as our levels of preparedness increase with each cycle, capacitating us to cope with dynamic challenges that arise. We gradually jell with our meta-ecosystems in the sub-conscience to a point, converging as our levels of consciousness and our realistic needs simultaneously begin to increase.

We came a long way to where we are today. The long walk is slow, tedious and unique. All lifestyle maintaining aspects function in harmony albeit at differing levels to achieve this fit. Some of our dreams may never be realised in our lifetime, unfortunately to be realised posthumously. If we casually browse at the lives of those around us that appear to be making it, are we proud of the roles we play in their lives? Or do we pass a cursory look to those others that we view as responsible for our demise? Regardless of our beliefs, we are totally responsible for most aspects of our lives. We play a major role in the qualities of lives we lead and are the total embodiment of our being.

We cannot begin to imagine the billions of things happening within an hour that can completely change the courses of our lives. It may not be immediately imaginable or realisable the roles we played in wading them off to get here. Just in the past hour, Shona could not finish his torso plank exercises because he developed an unprecedented sharp pain in his lower back. His girlfriend made a personal decision to terminate their relationship. She believes he was exhibiting a minimalist lifestyle and cannot cope. There was power outage in the hotel he is staying at. The backup generators could not be started in a town notorious for its very high temperatures and humidity. His spiritual father could not recognise his regular mobile number so he did not answer his call for their scheduled morning talks. He called back at a time when Shona was experiencing an excruciating back pain. In the same hour, major television channels are carrying saddening and depressing news; the BBC, CNN, SKY and Aljazeera. Shona smiled at his 24 year old daughter's text message that her longtime boyfriend had proposed to marry. Shona considered him a total loser. He knew he didn't have much say in it but how come it still messes up his day!

All this in an hour of a life total of 455 520 hours! How are we expected to decipher the essence from all this? What and how many parts do we need to break into to reveal our strengths and weaknesses? What is our unit of measure to determine how far out we are from the realities of self discovery? Time always inevitably reveal our realities, our truth!

We are individually aware of how our lives come to a screeching halt when the best pump ever made residing in us decides to pack up. It always appears too soon regardless of how old we get. We get adequate warning if we pay enough attention. We forever need more time and are never ready. Is it because sometimes we start late to live the lives we truly desire? Do we spend too much time on regret? What is regret and when do we realise it hasn't been that bad, that we have realistically been happy? When something worse than ever before happens and awakens us a little bit more, we reckon and acknowledge our prior worst as better. Is it at this point we come to realise all our prior experience was probably what happiness is?

In some societies, the collective consumes us that people may procrastinate to start living their lives to as late as fifty. Even that may also depend on marital, social and economic status. The level of success of our children can be thrown into the fray. God forbid, it is a different ball game altogether if we harbour tones of regret for whatever reason!

If we assume a healthy minimum heart rate of sixty cycles per minute, our hearts pump upwards of 3600cycles every hour. Every one of those is an opportunity; the prior one determines the next. Sadly, our lives are determined by the quality of those little tick-tocks. Failure of our hearts to pump continuously for over four minutes can spell our demise. We can only guarantee the quality of future heart beats by ensuring that prior and present ones are of the best quality. Otherwise their quality and strength slowly diminish, putting us on the road towards the undesirable inevitable. How can we extend that nexus with our lives?

We all desire healthy, painless, stress free, comfortable, inclusive, productive and connected lives. Lives full of love, joy, peace and leisure in a manner of our individual free choice. How do we make each heart beat count? At the prime age of twenty-five, the quality of seven hundred and eighty-eight million and four hundred thousand expended chances guaranteed that plus one we will desperately need when the time comes. To put this into perspective, at the age of thirty-two years, we will have lost a minimum of a billion chances. Invariably, some of them are squandered by external influences obtaining in our surrounding ecosystems. This only stops when we take full charge of whom and what we are after realising what that is first. We stoically realise how our lives were just but a flash of light, the uselessness of it all. At some stage, we may realise our imperative contribution to the universe, solely unique to each one of us. Unfortunately, most of us can go through life without ever realising that self-best.

It begins with us realising that desiring to know ourselves better is a need not a want. That enables us to dispense the best of us, most importantly to ourselves and then to others. Without it, what we view as our best might just not be it. It maybe a few over-emphasised aspects that we excelled at enough to tower over all others. In most cases, we measure ourselves with posterior success factors. These in most are reflected and dominated by material gain glamorous enough and in compliance with the dictates of the meta-embodiment. Our families, peers, communities and societies stand in wait to police, approve, admire and emulate.

How can we break into parts of who we are through our visible successes and failures to reveal our strengths and weaknesses? How does its unraveling expose imbalances in us and in our ecosystems, refining them to bare essentials with each scrutiny? How do the stories we reveal fit into our long range visions of satisfaction, realism, sense of originality, expectations, unjealousy, sense of comfort, sentimentality, calm, peace, empathy, faith and most importantly – LOVE?

Knowing who we are and our capacities in detail is a pre-curser to our success. It is necessary in tackling daily life challenges we face. It enables us to proactively and adequately prepare for most realities and eventualities, avoiding inherent pitfalls in most areas of our weaknesses and strengths.

Our life stories we unravel determine our Callings and imbalances, including those of our contexts. The process refines them deeper with every cycle of journeying back into our historicity. It is the revelation of prior terrible happenings we considered insurmountable, now dwarfed by recent ones that help us define and realise how happy we have been. It requires imaginative and cyclic re-storying. Simultaneously and dynamically, other undesirable demands and complexities are espoused.

This moves us to an even higher dimension of complexity as it incorporates our emerging stories with those of our families, our communities and societies. There is great need for us to re-generate and re-author the emerging stories to encompass everyone and everything in them. We necessarily must engage ourselves at experiential, imaginative, conceptual and practical levels. The perspective that validates our revelations is that evolving reality is neither wholly subjective nor objective.

All outcomes we reveal are generally built on some state of already existing knowledge basis and the nature of how, why and where that knowledge basis developed. What are the belief systems and assumptions we make in re-storying our life stories? How do we synthesize interplay between all the necessary elements we engage to wholly absorb and integrate them to a level that cannot be differentiated in the end?

Our ability to combine the inner subjective and outer objective of our emerging stories enable us to continually renew ourselves as we go through the processes of continual self discovery. It is that ability that actualises and revolves our life integral designs. The two develop hand in glove, each energising the other. How do we use our discoveries to strive for individual empowerment, increased self-consciousness through identifying, directing and exploiting latent creative energy which abounds at every level within our inner selves?

We can facilitate this by utilising our inner core and inherent archetypical omniscient capacity unique and imperative to every one of us. As all these aspects of our life stories co-creatively and evolutionarily unfold, they significantly differ in functionality and structure with the immediate precedent. They inevitably incorporate the integrity of our contexts, our every day processes and contents of existence.

In essence, all our efforts need to resolve the quenching of a deep thirst within us bringing forth a deep gladness not realised in the past. It must be self reflective on personal, collective and professional levels as they holistically develop us. Fully appreciating our individual Callings provide us with a whole new dimension of inner wholeness that is individual and particular. Total reflection through meditative contemplation that is relationally intra and introspective originates our Calling energy that comes forth with vitality, excitement and re-journeying of our lived

116

experiences. Buechner, Hansen and Hall and Chandler concur with this observation.

We emphasise the need to remain in our best sense of objectivity on a very subjective matter. We can find ways of unbiased engagement but remain true to ourselves as individuals first and fore-mostly. Our rationality improves with every iteration of re-storing and increased self-awareness. We may need to limit our emotions, opinions and our tendency to rationalise through the eyes of experiences. How do we achieve this, avoiding the pitfalls and pollution from all the communal decay that embodies us, manifest through exclusion, conflict, fundamentalism, terrorism, bureaucracy, dogma, corruption, closed and failing systems to open & transparent knowledge creation, materialism and abject poverty as Lessem and Schieffer put it. How can we achieve our best self-consciousness that sustains equitable, sustainable and lifelike livelihoods?

We are saying here that our journeys build on our dreams from an informed position of knowing exactly who we are. We don't mind whether these dreams are based on the conscious or the unconscious mind as long as they transcend us into the next realm of awakened enlightenment. We want our visions at this stage to simulate dreams of a blind person. Individuals that are blind from birth never knew the sense of sight but compensate from heightened senses of touch, smell, taste and feel. This means that they perceive colour from how it is narrated to them, something that is not easy to visualise. We are implying here that their dreams can either be rooted solely on the heightened four senses minus colour or it is imagined from the unconscious mind. All the same their dreams are like everyone else's.

Let us impregnate the blind person's dream with our experienced reality. We are woken in the middle of a dark night to be told this dream, whose imagery is better than our sighted lived experience. We are reminded shape is a felt, sensed and heard experience. How is the shape of a ship or a space shuttle brought into reality? A blind person's mind is intuitive enough and highly creative to figure out all this and come up with colour and shape preferences to become great artists and musicians. Their dreams' visions have better odds than the sighted. It allows them to interface with creativity and ideation to emerge their reality.

We are gifted with all the tools we need to dream as we wish when we are awake or asleep. We can relate and interface our dreams with scenarios we experienced without anything holding us back. We need our dreams to be as good as or greater than those of a blind person figuratively for us to engage our creativity, ideation and realisation processes at their peak. How can a girl child raised by an abusive father who divorced her mum when she was two, shake the inert feeling of internalised insecurity especially in self care in adolescence and further?

Both her parents immediately re-married and abandoned her. She lost all sense of belonging when she had to move from one abusive home to the next regularly due to undeserved wrath of step-parents and step-siblings. Male relatives of the step-father would try to sexually abuse her at every opportunity. Her favourite uncle once came to stay temporarily, something that she welcomed in the beginning. Little did she know that the uncle was an abusive pervert and an unrepentant womaniser who smuggled different women into her room at night, thrice a week and forced her to watch!

She was raped by a car sales man in an elevator at the age of sixteen and had an abortion from that encounter. How can this young woman counter the negative image of men she has in her mind and replace it with her overwhelming desire for a strong, gentle, caring and loving man?

The nearest thing she got to a partner was a brief fling she had with a guy who abandoned her as soon as he discovered she was three months pregnant. The male infant died within forty-eight hours of a caesarian birth. She moaned for it for close to eighteen months. She now dates much older married men, most of them more than twice her age. She claims being the other woman in a relationship absolves her responsibility of attachment. Her most recent relationship was with a married man that lived across the street with his family. It didn't end well.

Through the turmoil, she managed to scrap a Bachelors and then a Masters Degree in Sociology. She is gainfully employed as a junior high school English teacher. She has since significantly reduced the partying, alcohol abuse and engagement of multiple sexual partners. She has managed to interface her visions. Who cares?

CHAPTER 4

SELF DE-CENTRING (DECENTRATION)

It is comforting for us to feel that we know ourselves enough to function optimally in any given situation without having to introspect further than we deem necessary for immediate survival. We would rather not go around digging things up that we prefer to forget anyway. Let sleeping dogs lie. If it's not broken let's not fix it sort of attitude especially if we were managing without it so far. Some are on a genuinely successful growth path making great strides in almost all aspects of their lives. Regardless of where we are, our current lifestyles success levels are directly dependent on how much we really know ourselves. The differential between the actual and authentic primarily accounts for the lifestyle we lead today.

Our mental, spiritual, emotional, soulful, psychological and physiological capacities aredirectly influenced by our self awareness levels.

Who we are is related to and correlated by our true life stories we tell both to self and others. They have a clear distinction with our life histories. Ivor Goodson's view is that a life story is *what we tell ourselves and others about our life* but a life history is a *life story located within the historical context.* How does either of these two impact on the process of comprehensively authenticating our states of being and knowing who we are, how we function, react, think, create, innovate, love, hurt and desire? How do we continually story and re- story our life stories and life histories to represent our true selves to manifest the best of us?

Depending on approach, it can be an isolating journey but does not have to be. There are various ways to go around that challenge. It includes both singular and collective effort through formation of a winning team that may co-research and co-create whole stories resonating with us in all related areas. Some may engage with various established social protocols and take advantage of online resources. It is not easy to find those that specifically talk to us. We are exposed to infinite alternatives that may inhibit or hinder our open mindedness to fully engage and expose ourselves. Belonging to some ecosystem may provide the essential minimal companionship necessary for us to survive this highly personalised and *solitary journey.*

We begin with drawing on all available resources to energise us. How do we awaken enough introspective juices to thrust us forward on a trajectory that safely lands us on the island of lifelike existence? How do we draw on that infinite inner energy that is insatiable and inexhaustible? How do we awaken our *ntu* – our infinite inner energy? How do we develop the ability to extricate our individual and collective inherent energies that naturally reside in us? Once we do, we objectify them with what goes on around us in our particular communities and societies as a starting point. We necessarily ground, immerse and anchor ourselves deeply into those energies.

We move onto those areas we are aware are authentically great at and interest us to our core. We transcend these into a format that relates to the immediate environment and integrity at hand. Relatively, different areas of the world are strongly connected to varying aspects of our lives. For some, it might be their land. It roots them to particular places and spaces grounding them in nature and culture. Others have limited sentiments to this, but more-so to their spirituality. Whereas for some, their senses are more in-tune and relate better to economics, business and politics. Sentiments strongly impact on the emphasis of an individual's sense of self-awareness and dreams of their lifestyles.

Synthesis of our individual paths to self-awareness with those of the collective aids us in elevating our identified imbalance to higher dimensions. Objectifying this, coupled with experienced real life challenges and the dogma in us influences our progression. It forms strong foundations that energize us in our inner core and throughout our future journey. In the process, we realise a much deeper understanding of how we function in relation to our realities. It is critical for us to pave pathways that originate and ground, found and emerge, navigate and emancipate and finally implement and transform those challenges residing in us that hold us back. This comprehensive approach borrows from strengths and capacities, simultaneously learning from subsequent imbalances. It is inclusive and emphasises some aspects that are omitted in most self-awareness design methodologies.

In some communities, a prevalent sense of nihilism exists, a hopelessness that manifests in loyalties to external enculturation. This form of uprooting disorients one's faith and belief in our senses of origination. Henceforth, it disorients our motivation to original thinking that brings out our genius. We then require infusion of abilities. These re-enable us, through metaphysical transformation of doctrines, philosophies, paradigm shifts, the stories and myths we tell to break perceived confinement. Our narratives need to correspondingly evolve to stimulate, disturb and change our minds to higher sophistication, directing us towards our lifelike lifestyle desires in the process. It allows sourcing of the necessary consciousness to ignite competent energy, unbound drive and desire from within that can confront what needs to be done.

We give re-birth and re-energise our stifled senses of dreaming and imagination. This connects us to the root of our ultimate view of our reality. It is imperative that this rooting is developed further, continually re-storming fantastic mathematical, scientific, societal, psychological, philosophical, motivational, humanistic and heroic stories grounded in our contexts. Without these, we are stunted, mutilated and perpetually self imprisoned to stew from within.

In different ways and forms, we continuously strive to better ourselves. We backslide and fall many times, enough to question our way. The falling gives rebirth and revitalizes the zeal to propel forward. Comparatively, we relate our way to organic bio-systems that are constantly evolving adapting to the constant challenges obtaining in their environments. It is not static but dynamic. Similarly, humans constantly synergise towards the creation of the best possible being in every dimension. A human that actualises into a faithful, empathic, affectionate, original, unirritable, unjealousy, calm, collected, realistic and satisfiable being. Most importantly, we desire a being that has LOVE and full of FAITH in something that totally respects all forms of life.

The Chinese in their forms of martial arts, especially *Tai Chi Chuan* exhibit similar elements in their vital force (chi), we refer to here as our *ntu*, metaphorically as a tree that spreads its roots in all directions. It strongly grounds and anchors in its context and culture drawing its energy from it but giving life and vitality to all living things. Branches and leaves extend upward into the atmosphere to draw energy from the sun and heavens above. This resembles existing infinite knowledge systems associated with other energies residing elsewhere in the universe, constantly enriching our way of life. But rooting signifies fixation, statically locked in one position, lack of flexibility and active dynamism.

Unlike a rooted tree, the wind that blows is transient, flexible, malleable and takes any form or shape. It can be condensed from a gas into a liquid or a solid showing its abilities to adapt to change given certain specific surrounding conditions. A combination of the characteristics of the wind and roots of a tree would be preferable. Tree roots and the wind create and develop our energy source, a vital force, *ntu*. It provides continuous processes of transformation and actualisations that fully engage the collective environment and its nature ways.

Similarly, the development of the self is a lifelong and a dynamic process with constantly changing levels of consciousness. We develop the ability to fully connect with our *ntu* consistently. Our continuous mental awareness of it, the Descartes *Cogito ergo sum (I think therefore I am)* provides continuous snapshots of our new realities at any given time. They are infinite and relevant to our sense of consciousness and hence creative self.

The *ntu* energy found in *Ubuntu* philosophy has a vast network of roots grounded in the sense of collectivism and nature's ways. It embraces its various bio-ecosystems relevantly into its societal ecosystems. It simulates the wind that allows imbeddedness, mobility, flexibility to take any shape, form and multi-dimensional approach embracing   a multiplicity of other energies from other cultures, spiritualities, disciplines and personas. Our personal approaches are limited to minimal dimensionality fixed in our dominant individualised ways if we simulate the tree exclusively. Those that are like the wind lack the necessary strong groundedness that spreads adequately throughout the engaged knowledge systems. We must approach our integral designs as the tree and as the wind.

Prior exposures have impacted on tenets of our individuation processes and this may recur in our formalised self-awareness experiences.

Through contagion with, family, peers and the collective that includes academia, scholarly work, business and civic induction, we are exposed to methodologies formally elaborated elsewhere.

When we start considering the energy and mind frame we require, we find all that surrounds us. Our desire is focused vitality that transforms us throughout our mortal lives. It plunges us into and emphasises on knowing what we don't know. It endeavors to increase that domain coupled with impetuous curiosity to want to know the unknown. Complexity becomes familiar through sophisticated integral designing that allows and provides capacities to deal with higher order challenges in a manner wholly comprehensive and inclusive of all possible discourses.

We need to ensure that we stay balanced. Our inert or active aspirations are superseded by who we are, enshrined deep in each one of us, sometimes lagging slightly behind in our shadows. The *I am* in the present has to be extricated, exposed and celebrated. Once we manage that, it authentically brings forward our inner stories to transcend us to our destinies. The journey to realising our destiny engages others for a collective approach. It is inclusive of all possible paths available to us, an enabler we need desperately in this modern world to quench our material thirst. Denial of the inner self stifles our origination processes to expose the true self. It does not only short change the self but all others that benefit from our stories to heal them. Basically the whole world loses the imperative singularly intended for each one of us as our unique contribution to the Cosmos. Self, life and enlightenment!

There are five major pillars in our lives we pay attention to define our being. In random order, these are our hearts that essentially give us life. This is an organ we all strive to preserve the most, notwithstanding that all the other organs in our bodies are its fractal. They can cause unparalled difficulties that equally result in very undesirable outcomes. It is therefore incumbent upon us to maximise, to the best of our ability, the quality of feed that we provide it, from our spiritual, soulful, mental and physical being. Like a colony of ants whose main purpose is the preservation of their queen for continued procreation! The rest of our bodies serve to preserve the heart in the final analysis.

On the other hand the heart has the significance of being the generator, the storer, the giver and the arbiter of arguably the greatest need of all humanity, love. The heart then has the dual responsibility of preserving our lives and also providing us with our collective need for love. Contemporarily, it appears love is still most elusive to humans. We managed to make significant strides in most areas of our lives with devastating results in some.

Minds, not the same as our brains, navigate and steer the course of our lives, providing us with our cognition abilities and perception to anything we sense. It includes all our evaluation processes, data into information and activates all systems utilising the brain, our central processing unit (CPU). The mind can be simulated to the software of a computer that processes sensory information throughout our bodies. It regenerates, renews, enhances and develops in the same way our bodies, hearts, spirituality and souls do. We free the mind more when we untangle it from influences of our ego, enabling us more consciousness to the demands of answering to *who am I*.

We can simulate the brain to computer hardware as a container, a storage device and a centre that cognates all mind activities. The two are not the same. The brain's power, like a computer, is to generate stored information from its in-built capacity, to provide information with speed and its dexterity to maneuver comes from its highly competent software - a great mind.

Bodies enable us to perform and respond to physical demands of our lives. It represents the outer person and has primal responses to the *id* stimuli. What it perceives and likes, it wants. The success of the outer person is controlled on the most part by the inner person. The latter either allows or denies us impetuousness that has negative effects on the well being of the body and person. What is reflected by the outer person is an integral part of the inner person therefore is indicative of our spirituality, soulfulness, strength of mind and physical prowess.

Spirituality provides us with a conscience indicator, influences our feelings and willingness levels, triggering the little voice existing in all of us on what is wrong and right hence our renewal. It is considered to occupy the highest order of all the five pillars. It interfaces with all of them but our soul is the direct younger sibling. A combination of the two interfaces with the body and with the mind that acts as the neuron information transmitter throughout the entire functioning of our being. It does this through its concerted attempts to understand the mind which in turn is significantly influenced by our egos and society. It is considered profound to be responsive at the spiritual level. When we do, we develop the impetus faith levels necessary for the mind and body to draw on inexhaustible mind potential and insatiable energy to prosper most of our desires.

Our soul, as much as it is the first cousin to our spirituality and lower in hierarchy to it, is responsible for our sensory well being. It is dynamic, situational and transient. The Merriam-Webster dictionary defines the soul as *that which gives life, moral and emotional value.* It gives us capacity to feel kindness, sympathy and appreciation of other things including other beings, life, art, beauty, music, dance and so forth. Religious circles consider this aspect of us as immortal, that which continues to carry on after our mortal lives and our legacies. A combination of the higher order spirituality and our souls is considered to form the inner person.

We can argue that one takes precedence over the other, but striving to develop all five simultaneously in balance to the highest levels possible is preferred. At those levels, we can experience and realise panacea lifelike existence originally intended. It happens differently in real life as we have preferences and emphasise on one or a few depending on various influences impacting us. We need to come up with some form of a plan, consciously or sub-consciously, to steer ourselves towards individual objectives. This plan of action is normally informal on the most part. We will discuss how we can manifest their development in harmony in each of us. Regardless of our preferences, over-emphasis of one affects the development of the other four.

Superficially, a super-model, a race car driver, and a high performing athlete all appear to be primarily concerned with their physical being. It quickly becomes evident that beyond a certain point of performance, other aspects are engaged and may even take centre stage. In this example, it could be the capacity of the mind and spirituality that excels either of them to go beyond the limits of the physical. Similarly, a College

Professor maybe overly concerned with bumping his head in an accident and the pianist with breaking their fingers during a social basket ball game when in reality their abilities at that level are determined by the trans-pillar development of all five without marginalising the other. The saying *mind over matter* is fairly common; we relevantly draw on each of these to synergically access the capacity of the other.

Religion emphasises the development of our spirituality for it to salvage all the others. A strong mind is an added advantage as a vehicle to superintend over the soul and the body to contain the marauding *id*. How can we get to be wired this way?

We are significantly influenced by where we originate from, what we did in our short lives, how it was done when it was done and the causalities related to the whole of it. Four stages of formative development are possible in life. Broadly, these are the youthful phase, the strong age, the consolidation period and finally the legacy stage. They are very similar to David Levinson's life stages discussed earlier but with a slight twist.

The Youthful Phase, as the primary stage, influences the rest of the stages through chronology of experiences and learning processes. In the early stages of this phase, they directly imprint on blank templates making impressions that last us our lives. These impressions gradually transform into characters through further reinforcement to finally become our reality. It is an adventurous and exploratory period strongly influenced by the environment, with parents, family, peers, culture and community playing a critical role. We are not capable of questioning and rationalising whatever we are fed at this stage. We are impressionable and vulnerable to manipulations. Our formed reality starts to form a personality in our early teens that is fairly rudderless and seeks exterior approvals. The self is secondary and experimentation tainted with rebelliousness takes centre stage.

The Youthful Phase transitionally blends into the Strong Age where individual characters start to emerge albeit with a strong desire for peer approval. The primary driver here is sex. We are totally absorbed by it that almost everything we do has sexual overtones and appeal. Some level of vanity starts to creep in. The outer person significantly takes precedence over the inner one. The inner voice is muffled. Our behaviour, emotional intelligence, the friends we pick, the sports we take, our performance in college or at work and our relationships in general all converge to sexual rewards. We become territorial with all aspects that impact on this need. It even influences our career paths. Those that are more vulnerable to the Strong Age dictates tend to gravitate more towards highly luminous careers like the electronic media, politics, pastor hood, teaching, visual arts, music, drama and so on. The less driven probably end up in less frontline and less glamorous careers like research, bass guitarists, consultancy in technical fields, medicine and the military.

The latter category is not so much into the hunt but the wait and trap game. Their job domains are their hunting ground, preying on those within their professions as it is less demanding and less awkward. Researchers will most likely target research assistants, doctors for nurses, engineers for technicians and so forth.

The Consolidation Phase is when we realise that we are running out of time. We become less adventurous and target the sure thing. We gradually stop to take rejection personally and our risk averseness increases to the extent that it influences our sex attractiveness. We begin to be unconcerned with our physical being as much. Our capacity to resist those aspects in our lives that feed our imaginary greatness anchored in the material increases.

Genesis of our spiritual birth that most of us may never realise in our lifetimes makes us regret the time we wasted in our earlier lives monkeying around the unimportant and mundane. We could have concentrated more towards our true inner desires including answering to our callings. Becoming renowned experts in areas of our archetypes would have given us the satisfaction, recognition and respect that societaly reflect as success in human beings. Our material security concerns would have been limited to primary and basic essentials that do not feed unwarranted consumerism. Early pragmatism could have provided us with impetus capacities to help those that are not as privileged and secured the futures of our families better.

Stock take of that which we have achieved so far reveals lost opportunitie that may never reoccur. We wonder on our short lives and how much of it is left. There could be very little time left! This revelation causes us panic or excitement depending on where we find ourselves. Reactions from within and those around impact us strongly. If their effects are not handled carefully, they may result in grumpiness, pessimism or general despondence. On the other end, if they are positive, they may bring happiness, non-convergence and risk taking at an age where prudence may be necessary. Depending on our disposition, its impact on the next final life stage can be significant.

The four stages are usually successful at creating a certain kind of being who has a unique disposition, an opinion, a particular mind frame and varied philosophies to what they believe is life. We can get ourselves out of these structured boxes we find ourselves in that pre-dispose our functionality in a particular fashion, mutilating our rational vision to other possibilities. How do we uncentre ourselves from what has made us who we are this far? What pillars of enlightenment do we engage to re-align and re-calibrate?

The physical being of members of a community have lifestyle tale-tells peculiar to it. Eyes, body postures, their gait and even the type of foods they consume on the streets are further indicators. Major towns of different economic regions are representative at societal level. A third world city like Harare, a second world one like Gaborone, a combo of the two like Johannesburg and a first world city like New York. The reflective mix of urban demographics impresses the soul of survival and spiritual motivation to be a participant in life in the present or in future. Distinctive patterns that emerge are indicative of each respective sample's desire to be included in the mainstream of society and contribute towards their sense of self determination. Its presence or absence impacts the actualisation trajectory of their self-awareness relevant to that particular demography.

A sense of suffering, helplessness, exclusion and submission to the status quo as determined by the special others stifles that flicker necessary for a community to creatively implode. Whereas the presence of the opposite provides a positive and conducive environment that breeds beneficial experimentation to the self, family, community, the work place and society in general. Can there be prevalence of such creative abdication in one and seemingly abundance of it in another? Are we able to bring ourselves to rise above and eject from situations we find ourselves in? How do we transition from behavioural psychologies to function either within the box as defined by our personification processes, or move back and forth between the inside and the outside of the box? These two are acceptable modes desired of us but either way; we still remain attached or confined to the dictates of the box.

The final scenario is provided by journeys that actualise our self awareness to the fullest, to the best of our advantage. It allows the individual, preferably collectively with a few others to develop the ability to function comfortably within and in relation to the box, but only as a spring board to eject into a zone that functions independently and without reference to any box. Thus, with the self playing the role of an initiator, activator and catalyst to a given nuclei, they all develop the capacity to dream, create and ideate at peak within, outside and without the box. We will have de-centred!

****

Continual self development programs have the capacity to de- centre the world of an individual. The Psychology dictionary defines de-centring as movement from *ventured thinking to open minded thinking*. It is alternatively referred to as decentration. Jean Piaget's theory of cognitive development that originated the concept of decentring includes and exposes other worldviews. It comparatively considers and critiques their similarities and differences. How do we walk away from that which we believe to be true to us, that which is our identity but best articulated elsewhere? Do we have the capacity to learn cognitive processes that are outside ourselves?

We are referred to as centred when our norms and value systems congruent with expectations of our societies and other overarching embodiments. It encourages us to conform, in the process heightening our sensitivity to the point of being judgemental of deviant behaviour from societal expectations. Centring then can be stress inducing and can confine our senses of creativity within societal expectations. It is critical for us to develop the ability to be mindful of those discourses but still maintain authority over our uninhibited cognition. Individual insights toward elevated dreaming and imagination that embraces alien experiences and knowledge systems develops. We necessarily must manage to hold on to ours existing in the desired new.

In that vein, we are comfortable to accept and believe those views that provide us with illusions of immortality into perpetuity, with dreams of Godlike lives after death. We are more prepared to compromise our mortal lives in lieu of promised desirable lifestyles of the afterlife. Societies developed supportive philosophies around such reality. It refuses to accept that we possibly can be nothing after this mortal life, and that sense of nothingness, just like a dysfunctional computer, instead of something in whatever form is what escapes our imagination.

It is imperative that we awaken, contribute, prepare, engage and exist for the lifestyles that we envision in our dreams. How do we become originals of our dreams? Are we able to capacitate ourselves to face the demands of free living that allows us to transcend and hover above all that which ties us to conformity? It seems that this kind of liberalism and freedom is not encouraged by societal philosophy. Society sets its boundaries and norms of behavioural modes beyond which it becomes abrasive.

We can choose to counter these societal machinations of conformity by de-centring ourselves and developing critical thinking. It enhances our ability to generate our own thought and behavioural processes unique to the self. This can be a basis to critique that which is not within our perceived reality.

Herbert Mercuse differentiates our critique discourses into uni and multi-dimensional ones. It is from this differentiation that we view the meta-systemic platform as allowing us to be components or fractal parts of the whole culture. According to Bruce Tyler, in *Philosophical Legacy of Behaviourism*, it allows us to *compare, contrast, transform and synthesize individual's perspectives*. Tyler further questions how our independently constructed realities and those of our environments can be co-constructed through dialogue collaboration.

In decentring, one may need to view themselves as a spoke in a wheel, as a distinct entity but still an indispensable part of the whole, strongly influenced by nature's ways. Both need to work reciprocally and in unison, collective, inclusive but still individually identifiable. Learning, advancement and development of the self becomes that of family, community and society.

Our prior processes of individuation gradually pre-empower us to handle structured linear and simple situations. Parental guidance, community involvement, education and learning curricular all worked towards one's enablement to deal with steady-state domains, those that are contained within the norms of society. Success has been measured against one's ability to succeed and excel within the defined cultural boundaries. Subsequently, the voice of the individual and independent initiative has been muffled to different levels depending on the varied global cultures. Do we still have the capacity to build our unique sense of being and co-exist co-creatively in this den of cultural centredness? How do we break away from this trodden path but still be able to interface and carry with us selected objectives of that cultural path to our desired destination?

At this stage of personal hunger and thirst, it becomes clear that the conversations, the dreams and ideation processes we are exposed to do not necessarily conform to the everyday discourse around us. We realise we want more, but feel mutilated and imprisoned to liberally explore those voices making noises from within.

The linear, the simple and the uni- dimensional becomes inadequate. It does not quench our hunger and thirst anymore. Our reality now requires us to action and reciprocate, to cyclically move from the simple to complex and back, from the complex to chaotic and back, linear to non-linear and back, and finally from uni to multi-dimensional and back. As we action and reflect through these processes we are empowered to decipher complexities in our lives to the easily comprehensible simple, linear and uni-dimensional that is practical, usable and implementable. This cannot be achieved without moving ourselves in tandem with our various eco- systems through de-centring or decentration temporarily disrupting, unraveling or destabilising societal perceived steady-state.

The steady-state is responsible for a particular sense of knowledge we base ourselves and exist in. It provides us with our state of being that is mostly static when our need is its combination with varying degrees of dynamism and movement. The ontology existing within us is born in and out of an ecosystem that defined its truths, limits, ways, methodologies and methods of doing things over long periods of time. This nature of knowledge that we exist in cannot be ignored in our desire to find our space towards our perception of lifelike living. We become more alive as we sophisticate our state of being, our awareness, consciousness and platform of knowledge.

As we climb higher up the ladder of knowing and consciousness, we progressively realise the little we know, an insignificant minute fraction of an ocean of knowledge. We cannot even begin to imagine the magnanimity of how massive the domain of the unknown is! Analogously, in the realm of sound, we cannot hear pitches lower than 20 hertz and those higher than 20 000 hertz, loudness outside the range of 0 to 85 decibels. As far as we are concerned, there is nothing that is happening outside our realm of sight and hearing.

These ranges vary slightly. A few of us are born with the ability to detect intelligible noises on the extremes. If one of our friends had the hearing capacity of a moth, we would probably freak out and think of them as weird and abnormal. There exists plenty of activity in the lower ranges that elephants and whales can comfortably process. Dogs, bats and dolphins are capable of much higher ranges. The moth has a whooping hearing capacity of 3 megahertz that is in excess of 149 times higher than that of humans.

Unlike in sound, the beauty of knowledge and enlightenment is that we can increase our awareness of that which we do not know. This is with a view to bringing that unknown knowledge into the known realm, existence, understandable and utilisable domain.

The process of self development must be lifelong and continuous. Its benefits can be so subtle. It may initially appear as if those that are not engaging with knowledge pursuit, creation and development endeavors are living more fruitful lives. Deeper enlightenment subtly sneak through as we grow, develop, experience, learn, research, discover, create, ideate and hopefully get wiser. The challenge is that sometimes we reduce these processes to thresholds much lower than those required to achieve empowering marginal positive growths.

Real and realisable empowerment that accelerates the pace of contemporary enlightenment transformation is desirable. Such a pace needs to outstrip that of natural knowledge decay at individual level. Half life of acquired knowledge is very short, contemporarily put at less than eight months. We must keep developing at a much faster pace throughout. How do we handle all this knowledge and wisdom we acquire? Is it proper for it to be shared by the whole world, passing it on to even one person at a time? Can we continuously desire to change and grow our individual ontology by engaging any means necessary; to teach, teach and teach, share, share and share at every opportunity?

The short finite lives we exist impel us to live lifestyles we desire from the earliest possible moment, but we waste so much time wishing to be something else outside our reach. We have very limited time to debrief and share all that we have in our heads to avoid making the graveyard a knowledge bank. How do we acquire this ability to share generously with anyone that cares to listen to what we have to say and do? Our knowledge only benefits humanity if it is shared, usable and implementable for the benefit of its consumers.

Previously, opportunities to share our experiences mostly existed through formal teaching, learning and training. This is not the obvious case anymore. Other more exciting avenues since opened, especially in the digital world. The internet revolutionarised some of our knowledge needs and accesses. But, these are only helpful when we seek them for a defined purpose either at individual, family, community, organisational or societal levels. It allows and capacitates all of us to be teachers or learners and deciphers of knowledge in the informal sense, to teach and orate all the time, to put it all out there like a virus.

We can employ any method available to us to spread passionately our enlightenment, creations, and discoveries. We can preach and even become missionary about our praxis at every opportunity. Or we risk atrophying. Equally important is that we formally develop, format, catalogue, code and, I emphasise, share unreservedly with all communities our discoveries in a truthful, meaningful, intelligent and relevant manner.

******

When we start to find meaning to what we hold as the truth, we discover that such endeavors furthers away its accessibility. The related epistemological platform enhances its truth and meaning. What is causal between the senses of truth and meaning as derived from the world around us and our given belief? It appears like a chicken and egg thing where the latter predisposes the former and vice versa. Tensions of dialectics in the truth being causal become the other, simultaneously finding itself in the meaning it sets out to be the basis of in the first place. We ask whether our beliefs and sensitivities cohere with what we considered as our epistemological grounding philosophy to the truth and meaning as they relate to cultures and societies as their basis.

In the process of regeneration and rebirths of the same, how do we empirically spiral through the cycles of subjectivity, objectivity and rationality to arrive at knowledge we desperately need to revitalise us and our societies towards desirable enlightenment? What are the fixed conventions of our perceptions of the truth and meaning? How do we push these boundaries or frontiers from self, to the next person and to society bringing it all into our everyday discourses? Can we do this without rocking the overall societal boat that thrives for a steady-state? Society is known to ignore, ostracise or discard anything or anyone that threatens this desire. Usually, over long periods of time, *qualitas occulta* (hidden quality) in the truth and meaning is exposed contrary to the wishes of society.

Our success in exposing the truth and meaning of a life worth living depends on who we manage to carry with us from the onset. Who will be with us on this journey with capacity to be supportive and add value to our objective at the same time? Do they appear capacitated to sustain it for a long period or even, for the rest of their lives? Strong loyalties are paramount, especially if they can come from people we interact with regularly. Strong *Ubuntu*-like way of life that is not only humane and compassionate it is inclusive of balanced and ideal thought processes that are totally humane. How do they assist us in defining our senses of meaning?

Derivation of a sense of meaning is a long gradual process that comes through infinite encounters with various cultures we deliberately expose ourselves to. These broaden our senses of meaning domain. There are formal and informal guiding parameters existing at every level providing us with snapshots of our perception of meaning. It is influenced by prevailing views of spirituality that correspond to our metaphysical frame at any of those times. It forms the basis of our mindsets that cumulatively relate to dictates and influences of the dominant society, sometimes inadvertently. It directly impacts on our sense of things in relation to those we came into contact with. It is imperative that we rise above this confined way that limits us to mundane daily existence.

Limitless engagement is key for us to realise the life we desire to live without diminishing our abilities to imagine, to dream and hence to be creative. How does our present lifestyles ascribe to the realities of our desired forms of life?

Sometimes we are impelled to live in this desired future, estranging ourselves from the present, depriving us further of the quality of life we live. We then fail to develop a clear structural vision of our lives reinforcing our need to resign ourselves to the establishment. Higher order learning empowers us to disengage from developing modular mindsets inherent to societal and institutional structured approaches. We combine discourses in our personal lives and re-orient them with the dictates of our environments. It provides our present the voice of the future, the impetus imagination that rises above repetitious existence. Our self-consciousness journey will have started in earnest.

The self consciousness journey demands almost all we can give; body, heart, mind, spirit and soul. Total commitment, especially on our time is paramount. It gets so demanding that we are tested more than ever before, to our limits, at times wondering why we are doing this   to ourselves. The endings and beginnings; deaths, births and re-births; destruction, construction and re-construction of a continuous new at every stage can be frustrating and overwhelming that we may even wonder if we are not going crazy. It is only when we constantly review our development path, do a cost-benefit analysis and justification at every turn that we will obviously favour continuance. It is imperative that we fully consider our status and the load of non-synergic commitments as we continuously reframe and develop a mindset able to concentrate, implement and produce a very high standard of lifelike lifestyles we most desire. Sometimes, we may need to use an evangelic approach.

Approaches may differ. Some of us may want to consider it as a job that needs to be done. Others may want to consistently and gradually chip at it in a parrot like nonchalant manner but with commitment and at a pace that accommodates other vicissitudes of contemporary dynamic living. We alternatively choose it to be our lifestyle. This is a journey that anyone of us can start on and does not require any special skills or abilities.

It needs full commitment to transition from the dreaming and imaginary to the metaphysical, illusionment to disillusionment and finally to the realizable physical. The process can be in a random order starting with the physical, then illussionment and finally disillusionment. It is important to still be able to decipher and filter reality or go scherzo. The ability to do this successfully elevates our cycle into a higher order conservative one. It enables us to zero in on more complex detail and issues relating to the creative process. Again, it all originates with more focused dreaming and imagination stages whose imageries get clearer with each cycle. Our dreaming need not shut everything out but keep a very attentive eye on all the other little dreams and their related happenings that may pass us by.

Dreaming and subsequent creativity derives mono-directionally from natural phenomena. It does not have the reciprocal ability to positively enhance nature ways but only to imitate its near perfect order of things. It is God given so to speak for the benefit of humanity. It follows then that dreams, creativity and our philosophies of existentialism are all rooted in nature and our knowledge of it. Martin Heidegger concurs when he posited that our creations reflect our view of nature with a desire for it to expose its secrets more as a potential resource towards healing of humanity's injuries. He further observes that the advancement of our creations with time as we begin to understand nature deeper improved our quality of lives and our longevity. We don't seem to easily connect our life experiences as mostly derivatives of earlier knowledge clusters we encountered. At the same time, dialectic tensions emerge of bad and good, right and wrong. The jury is still adjudicating which is better for humanity. The process affirms our needs and our humanity.

What then is the importance of knowledge in all this? How does it contribute to the relationship between dreaming, creativity, ideation, conceptualisation and realisation! Contrary to nature, we were socialized to compartmentalise and imprison our dreaming and creativity into cells of disciplines or professions. These were over emphasised to us in domains or clusters at the exclusion of others. Unlike in nature, all functions in harmony and in-tune complimenting each other integratively. Over millennia, they developed a uni-language universally understood by all phenomena in part or in whole. We now need to change our storyline to an organic and a life-enhancing one rooted in our humanness. Why are we imprisoning and maiming our will power and freedom of the same creativity? How do we ensure that most of what we endeavor is born and are extensions of the same nature we totally depend on? Can our approaches to creativity not be fully aligned with our challenges, meaning, purpose and the very nature ways?

Clarity in cultural images form part of the core of highly creative minds coupled with ideological orientations from our philosophies, institutional frameworks represented by models and systems. These need to be inclusively and collectively put together. In-depth understanding of our creativity in our Eco-systems shape, map and influence the direction of our creativity within that Eco-system.

The subsequent storylines both for self and those of our respective societies as they relate to our areas of imbalance bring creative origination exposing the initial possibilities and potentials that feed into that creativity. Engaging the creativity of our cultures helps. It affects us through organic creativity rooted in the soils of those cultures and transformatively combining indigenous and exogenous knowledge systems. It enables co-creation, evolution and sustainability of our societies. It then purposely engages trans-disciplinarily the development of our creativity. In the process, it creates a dialect between our sense of creativity and that of our context. This is influenced by the culture of the origins of that creativity represented by the subsequent innovation.

It is creativity with innovation that results in wealth creation, refines and extends knowledge, creates new knowledge, generates new theories and paradigms that are sorely needed for us to live desirable godlike lifestyles.

CHAPTER 5

DELIMITATION –
ENLARGEMENT OF HORIZONS

There are infinite phases to a total self awareness journey. The one that directly concern us in terms of mentoring is the period starting from the time we become conscious of our need to embark on this journey to the period we settle in rewarding engagement that precipitate our gains. The meta-phase can further be segmented into three, starting with the period of pre-engagement, then when we become conscious of our need to embark on the journey and actually do, to full time engagement. Everything we do cumulatively adds to our journey. The first phase of pre-engagement narrates our self conscientising processes that bring us up to speed with our as we are. The second phase is the duration from *as we are* we accredit to self enlightenment to the time we start realising the fruits of our effort as small as they maybe. The third and final phase is when our enlightenment tacitly become part of our lives like second nature.

Each case requires a unique design specific and cognizant of gender, traditions, culture, social status, survival engagements, marital status, ethnicity, race and a given context. The integral design approach collectively and inclusively views the meta-ecosystem components as co-collaborators. These are accommodated and embraced as functionaries of unique mentorships that emerge at all levels of enlightenment. Approaches we engage holistically confront our needs that cannot be fully addressed from any one level as has been generally offered by the conventional mentoring programs. Limitations of some latter approaches contribute to contemporary imbalances attractive to most of us. They literally endorse corruption, amassing of wealth, consumerism and over-emphasis on mono-views, dogma and widespread poverty within communities.

A strong presence of mentorships encourages strong and intimate collaborations holistically inclusive and equitable in deciphering of meaning. Subsequent enlightenment is born out of progressive outcomes of the journey. Self discovery skills are enhanced with elevated acceptance by the immediate family, peers and community. It increases self awareness and consciousness to individual development on the social, emotional, scholarly, economic and professional trajectory.

The mentoring process is more effective when it is broadened to more than a couple of individuals who are usually luminaries of a family   or community. They canbe spread throughout the whole social meta-ecosystem and networks spectrum, creating a neutral domain that truly flows openly and multi-directionally. Our families, peers and social environments are now too complex for just a few seasoned knowledge persons or luminaries to mentor protégés. Contemporary demands are infinitely multidimensional and spirally non-linear.

Levels of mentoring complexities spiral from one rung to the next as the protégé develops from a potential, to an enthusiast and finally to a lifestyle that has relevance. Once our way of life starts to spontaneously traverse the paths of consciousness, enlightenment or self awareness frontiers, discourse becomes our daily bread. We find ourselves thrusting hard into these arenas, but shy away when we feel we lack the requisite knowledge or facts for that level of interaction. We progressively become skilled at recognising environments that seem not to add value to our knowledge base.

This far, we subliminally and constantly, formally and informally had a *laissezz affair* pace towards self awareness. It mostly manifested through our families, friends, communities, learning systems and work environments. We embarked on hobbies passionately without even thinking why we prefer one over the other, developing strong beliefs and taking positions that currently impact us. As long as it earned us recognition and popularity.

Our association with people has been limited to a point preferring partial engagement. We hold back much of what we competently know. We realise our importance to the big picture of things, but choose to use this to derive influence and significance. We care strongly, hence the drive to empower ourselves with various self improvement engagements that we undertake continuously and intermittently. We tool ourselves to be more significant in the quality of our contributions and the difference we make.

We then radiate slowly and cautiously to our immediate environment expanding further outwards.

Cutting edge things are life changing and impact on our daily lives and the way we do things. They shift paradigms and challenge communities' traditional way. At times this infringes on the status quo of societal existence and conservative livelihoods. The impetus change it brings maybe undesirable to some who may have a totally different view or approach. The frontier of change is infested with change landmines. Everywhere we step in this zone is exhilaratingly transformative and has a potential blast that can give us a high never experienced before. It can equally be extremely frustrating. We must be prepared to accept more failure than success only to get up every time with more zeal and energy to get it on and get it right.

Processes and outcomes in this zone are vulnerable to continuous critiquing by others but we must take it all in constructively with a positive attitude. We in turn provide constructive and conciliatory responses that are inclusive. We develop armor to accept criticism wholesomely in any form. We display the patience to capture from it its essence that enhances our specific areas of concern.

Zones of change can be identified constantly through earnest indulgence and broad engagement of our contexts. We carry particular views as we start but enlarge them to synthesised energies much stronger than the sum of their individual energies.

The liminal change frontier, either on an individual or collective basis requires us to thrive on an insatiable thirst to know *what it is we don't know*. We will struggle with the ability to differentiate that which is knowable from that which is not knowable.

We can testify our need to authentically rationalise an initially subjective us, born out of an uninformed hunch or an intuition. It can be extremely tedious if unattainable. Occasionally our peers, in their quest to achieve their goal, end up resorting to undesirable and unethical behaviours. They manifest in deception, cheating, faking, plagiarising, posing, fabricating and role playing to conceal their inadequacies towards realising the desired outcomes. How then do we perform at the highest levels of what we consider and believe to be the gospel truth?

Self development at higher levels has a tendency to recognise and revolutionarise loose ends that we chose to sideline in the past. Our questions and our lives transcend from the seemingly linear upward career projection that we are accustomed to, to a multi-faceted trajectory with several deaths and rebirths. The level of engagement suits the challenge in lateral, vertical and cyclic projections. Self evolution that accompanies this process can be overwhelming. This canbe harder for others looking in to understand the changes that will be happening. It is not unusual to occasionally find ourselves at odds with what our community envisioned for itself as we progress. The community is usually particularly sensitive to its endeavors towards steady-state in all communal aspects of life, including forms and direction of leadership.

Cognisance of our collective episteme helps us to transcend our journey of self discovery. An inclusive approach broadens our sense of obscurity as we become more conscious of the self and all that surrounds us. Parts of most things that influence our life integratively become part of our whole. We become strongly aware of the need for all inclusiveness, for these parts to be fully representative of us and the dynamics of dismembering one part in relation to our total epic functionality.

As we progress along, we increasingly sense how this elevates our senses of discovery, our desires and curiosity to know. Our levels of ignorance of that which we know in part in contrast to the vast infinite world of that we don't know are phenomenal. How humbling this is! All of a sudden, the more we discover and learn, the more we become self aware of our ignorance. We become conscious of that awareness of our inner and outer need to be broadly inclusive and integrative in this highly transient, complex and chaotic global village we now exist in. The unfolding journey transforms our lives wholesomely and continuously rather than at specific points in space and time. We rather are not identified only by our jobs, titles or material status. These can follow behind our paths of consciousness.

Ascribed titles and labels can confine us to a pre- determined course with set rules, structures, codes of conduct and measurement criteria. Our chances of making history are curtailed before we even try. We can be popular and be assimilated to success at certain points in history without adding anything significant to what is already known and exists. It is possible that we make better strides if we borrow from Schumpeterian thinking of creative destruction. At every point, no matter how infitisimal, we supersede the existing status quo, that level of honesty, love, care, co-existence at all societal levels, scholarliness, academia, spirituality, creativity, innovation and technology that enhances but annihilates precedence. In the process we enhance our worthiness of existence.

Our main objective in this maze is to find meaning and purpose unique to our individual lives but collectively relevant. Mike Martin postulated three intentions we need to confluence to realise this objective. Firstly, he postulates that our careers must quench our thirst enshrined in our archetypes and callings. It is best if our careers are directly and strongly related to our archetype and calling for maximum derivation of meaning and purpose. If this happens, our careers become our hobbies to the extent that we realise elation of feeling unlike our work and employment can ever achieve. We begin to immensely enjoy what we do and to derive remuneration from areas that are metaphysical and material.

Secondly, he identifies the need for rewards that satisfy our total sense of being; the body, mind, heart, soul and spirit as demanded by our Calling's inner deep need. This transcends easily beyond the material into spiritual, religious and cultural needs and expectations.

Thirdly, it is the collective benefit we get from work we do daily. How does it benefit us including our families, networks, communities and societies in relation to our expectations? Three postulates cited here can be linear, cyclic, simple, complex and spiral assuming all forms of combinations and permutations. It responds to our needs and wants at any given point and time. Once we manage to define and express these for ourselves, we develop dynamic instantaneous combinations responsive to any given scenario. We experience total engagement with our individual senses of meaning, worthiness, happiness and fulfillment.

Over-emphasis of the rational position of natural sciences decidedly promoted, advertently or inadvertently, the mechanistic view that took dominance over insightfulness. Formational, cultural, discipline and personal views depending on the importance and power of the promoter, be it economic, social, spiritual, religious or political, monolithically prevailed as the accepted view of integrity. Philosophy desired to root itself in logic and languages, politics in ideals of controlled and engineered societies that generated structures like socialism, communism, capitalism, Confucianism and fascism. How have these prominent features faired in the contemporary era?

Most of these have since diminished in stature or completely atrophied into oblivion. The coming together, synthesis and amalgamation of some of these, especially in the 21st Century has followed a trajectory that is unpredictable, open and evolving with emergent properties indifferentiable from their original free standing selves. It is now very difficult to predict order in most of our situations today.

How do we incorporate either of social or natural sciences appropriately to our self-awareness journeys one enriching the other? It is important for us to borrow relevantly from existing knowledge fields both in catalogued, coded and oral literature.

There are clear lines of dialogical and dialectical tensions that unfold to balance re-orientation of our mindsets. Its manifestastion releases collective energies caught up in those tensions.

Clearly, the development of our personhood and individuation is anchored in our societally existing imagery, especially those directly linked to our experiences. It is considerate of our past and the present, and how it impacts on our expectations of the desired future, more specifically the future lifestyles we envisage. How then can we clearly reveal our pasts for potential utility in the present and future?

The dynamic contemporary increasingly and continuously becomes chaotic and very complex. Deciphering and separating it can only be momentous like a moving target. We can only take stroboscopic shots. Our ability to clearly articulate these elements including related assumptions is important. How do they directly impact on our envisaged outcomes and their relevance to our journeys?

Definition of what it is we desire to achieve in the present and future depends on how close we get to the reality of these two aspects. We cannot change the past but only extract from it what is relevant to the present.

Retrieve what is usable towards our advancement socially, technologically, politically and economically! We should not lose focus of the impact of all this on the world around us. Some aspects seem to need renewal and some need total rebirth to create the necessary present that trajects us towards the elusive desired present and future.

Differentiation and integration cycles of possible scenarios mapping become the order of our mindsets. They now constantly dream and idealise. Imageries in our heads relate to the reality at hand. We become truly pre-occupied and entertained by what we envision. Some observant family members may notice the change. To some, we may appear a bit aloof and self absorbed at first. The switch will have turned on and the release of infinite inner energy, *ntu*, begins to flow into our life systems. How do we manage to let go those inhibitions, the impulsive demands of our egos and the machinations of our id?

The ability to ground and immerse ourselves completely in our enlightenment journeys lets go some of what our peers, colleagues and society considers as normal praxis. This may mean letting go of long standing relationships. We will realise that some of these' severance was overdue. We may have been unable to, had the new not begun to be born in us. This new can be so strange sometimes. We become aware that something alien to us is gradually taking us over. It gets increasingly difficult to cope with the change. We become extra-ordinarily inquisitive and enthusiastically engage in discourse that enhances us.

These informal discourses from all walks of life are very insightful in assessing our mindset's gradual emergence in the new. Articulation of our desire with clarity to those around us reflects our depth of understanding of the objective. Some may strongly argue against the changes that they view as negative both to self and community.

We superficially appear as if we are becoming more complex, confrontational and argumentative to those we encounter. The opposite is closer to the truth. The more complex we seem, the greater we need simpler explanations. It brings out marvels, constant transitions and spiral loops that perpetually require us to actively delve into. The origination and foundation it gave us, those we constantly interact with and our contexts, is phenomenal. Its critiquing and exposal of our origins is critical to our success and cannot be over- emphasised. How then do we manage to build on the very grounds of our originality and foundation without being consumed by it? How do we extricate ourselves from dogmatically following a path that has been well trodden?

Like a new baby that only has paternity history and the present, lie in a cradle completely oblivious of that history but is totally connected to the present. It is incognisant of the future but whatever it experiences in the present will forever impact on how it views and behaves in it. Its awareness trajectory is exponential as it absorbs new things like a sponge. It probably dreams a lot but in practice is highly experimental and exceptionally creative. Subsequently, it learns to apply acquired knowledge to innovate the lifestyle it desires. It tries strongly to make itself comfortable, in-tune with its natural organic development and in congruence with all possible influencing aspects of its eco-system.

Similarly, it is important that we bring our eco-systems to the fore to enable us to systematically create knowledge fields recognizable throughout our utility spectrum. This sits well with our modest and continual self-development processes we evolved throughout our various stages of individuation. Our initial view of our eco-system appears fragmented and our approach to it may be a challenge.

Enculturation of our mindsets from various sources took residence in us, overwhelming local application. It is necessary that we continually reframe them as necessary for common approach and understanding. This greatly boosts our competence and conversance with subjective perspectives already coming out of our eco-systems.

It is through reinforcing our resolve from within that lasting effective creativity and innovation is exposed. Sustainable sufficiency hierarchically manifests through inclusion of inherent nature ways, collective knowledge systems, be they historical or contemporary. The co-creative approach benefits and broadens our appreciation of what it is that needs to be included from all possible stakeholders. Our horizons are immensely enlarged and our energies synergise.

Contemporary global villages are impacted by an infinite number of perspectives constantly. Over-emphasis of the Western worldview on the rest of the world at the expense of all the others is now biting. Its world historic legacy to present day relevance and futures of other worlds is fast diminishing.

On the contrary, meta-perspectives of the other two worlds, the South and East are fast increasing. It now appears it is up to these two to fundamentally hybridize all four major world views. Individuals, communities, scholars, academia, Afrintuneurs, civic organisations, business praxis, private and public sectors cannot then continue to view their success or failure through the eyes of Western philosophy. We need new pathways rooted in empirical experiential models that are socially equitable and ecologically sustainable.

In the early 1980s, Japan's economic development mostly originated in its organisational rather than technological breakthroughs. Informal networking and subordinate revitalisation of small businesses was instrumental to vertical integration of existing large corporations. It was able to tailor make a very successful interactive relationship between its small business developers, labour, government, larger corporations, academia and scholars. All was based on the *kaizen* principle of continuous small increments in equally minute time lapses. This was applied across the board from standards of living of nuclei small families, small family businesses, individual development, production levels, labour relations, organisational affluence, training programs to the general work ethic of all stakeholders of the society. Application of the *kaizen* innovatively brought about higher order dimensions to Japan.

It is imperative that we transcend to our perceived higher order dimensions. Our personal development usually comes in infitisimal increments from the very beginning. It is perceivable that at the time of birth, we are similar to a functional computer hardware system devoid of any software. At that juncture, an infant maybe totally oblivious of its stimuli. It cannot relate or cross-reference it with its empty database or prior experiential processes. Its recognition processes are triggered with a birth cry and opening of the eyes.

Animals, like birds imprint in their memory the Chinese breeder they see first at birth as their mother. They follow the perceived mothers wherever they go. Similarly, a human infant is not aware of its environment only to initiate learning processes at birth. Sensory to sight, feel, emotion, sound, discomfort, real time experiences etcetera initiate instantly. All forms of its intelligence systems start to accumulate data by simulation.

One's inherent archetype is also triggered albeit unrecognisable to the infant and those surrounding it. Further development through this simulation or mutilation processes thereof commence immediately. Who we are today is a product of that entire process of individuation from that moment on. How then do we continue to influence the course of our paths of personification from the moment we realise our role in it?

Building of various knowledge systems in the human intellect starts from a position of arbitrariness, irrelevance and aimlessness compared to those existing in nature. The relevance of human intellect seem to be only self serving as we, on the most part, define the basis of what we consider to be the truth of our knowledge. Its importance is provided for in its origins by its initiators and those that advocated for it to serve specific purposes. Its significance only relates to not much beyond that initial domain of influence but then gradually radiates outwards as it engulfs those it acculturates. At times it spreads all inclusively without consideration of those it colonises.

The basis of that truth is out of us and on the most part excludes the possibility of other forms of truth as perceived by other forms of life. These early stages in a baby's life create nucleus of the universal truth of those particular knowledge initiatives in varying degrees of discourses. Who has the responsibility of creating the initial discourse to the established basis of the truth? What tools do we need and are necessary for this ability?

It has been implied here that the basis and perception of truth is knowledge realised through a spiraling cycle. It is initiated in total subjective sensory intuition that results in thousands of dreams. These funnel, consciously or sub-consciously into creative imageries. Depending on their frequency and intensity, they can be intelligent to the dreamer.

Those with that merit are further developed at this stage through ideation processes, individually or collectively. It merits less than one in a hundred to the next discourse stage of what is true.

The next stage of conceptualisation emancipates those few that emerge from the first couple of rounds of rationalisation through cycles of ideation, applying existing knowledge fields. Most do not pass this stage and are either discarded or put into a recyclable bin for further development if necessary. From here on, the death curve of these initiatives exponentiate to levels of survival of less than one in a thousand. Implementable praxis of those with potential becomes the driving consideration. They may promise but remain unsound both in theory and practice.

It is the high failure rates of our initiatives our minds need to wrap around and fully embrace if we truly desire to push the frontier of the truth of things. Most truth carries varying degrees of a sense of faith that may not fully actualise into realisable facts. It brings us full circle back to the relativity between its subjectivity and objectivity.

The relativity basis stands on the shoulders of that originally perceived objectivity premised in the first truth basis.

In our searching for the truth, we find levels at which we seek inherent truth in our knowledge systems and environments. It includes dynamics that constantly influence vibrancy of that knowledge. That epistemic standing at any given time provides a platform on which any developer of knowledge spring boards. At this standing, related relevant chonosophies we make regarding these truths on our knowledge, questions we ask and strive to answer and enlightenment we experience empowers and skill us to continually engage with the battle. In the process, it increases detail and complexity levels for greater objectivity and praxis.

One of the primary objectives of our consciousness processes is to foster our objectivity growth with propositions, hypotheses and postulates in knowledge that we bring forward. This can be achieved through authentic self discovery processes that yield realisations good enough to pass the review of our peers with varying degrees of subjectivity biases. How can we diminish its inclusion at every iteration but ensuring that the relevant initial subjective social motivators are rationalised? We remain cognisant that the subjective and objective are two domains that are mutually exclusive even though their lines of demarcation appear to be blurred. It is impossible and contradictory to find causality, correctness and expression in the objective that is in the subjective, in the egg that is in the chicken!

Only an aesthetic relationship exists between the subjective and the objective that increases our sense of its realisable application in praxis. We can accept as evidence the tangible in technology and social innovations. They all should be regarded as equitably competent, without one taking precedence over the other, but as co-existing twins and synergic allies depending on each other. Discussions are limited to that which has chosen to emerge from secrecy and reveal itself into the known, only to as far as us realising that it exists. We remain in the dark on anything deeper as it hides pending discovery. We can now claim to be conscious of its existence but the rest remains a mystery. An insatiable quest for the truth of things propels us forward.

Life with no societal loyal tests, no restrictive traditions, no retribution, cohesion, provides us with openness. It allows for mutuality between self, family, community, institutional and societal flows. Included in this equation are active and collective participants that resonantly foster individual voices and authentic inner initiatives from the integrated inner person. How do we all responsibly move towards these levels of consciousness that openly and frankly allow us to share ourselves with others, our unknowns as well as our knowns, our fears as well as our brevity, our indigenous as well as our exogenous knowledge systems without fear or favour to rebuff or embrace?

The initial phases of our self development initiatives, especially as we go higher up the ladder of consciousness, are deeply and intrusively inquisitive of the inner self. It questions all pillars of your being, especially the state of your spirituality, soul, mind, heart and body. In the past up to present, we had inner self inquiries in all these areas but never pushed them to this depth and intensity.

We are required to find new depths where we thought there were none, discover unknowns to things that we believed had nothing more to be known. Our previous journeys into inner selves were instantaneous visits that did not last very long. Sometimes they scared us so much that we lacked the desire to go back there. They were incomprehensive attempts to liberate all five pillars of our being. Missing depths that existed were revealed. Those that remained still exist and are unclosed creating fissures with structural and functional weaknesses. They continue to deny us as individuals to perform at our utmost best.

The first pillar to consider is the preparedness of our bodies for the impending rigorous self development and awareness journey. Its demands are as real as a nine second one hundred metre dash. It is a great investment especially in commitment and time. Occasions will arise when we need to commit long sessions, consuming a couple of hours at a time. It is critical to discover early in the journey best times to have these sessions and environments for maximal concentration.

They include locations of working stations since we do not necessarily need to go to any particular venue, types of relaxing foods and drinks we prefer including time and place of consumption. We must consciously generate our exercise and sex resumes as the latter can be a major issue for those in relationships. Healthy supplements are a necessity for those over forty. Normal food intake may either be too heavy or may provide inadequate nutritional value. These are issues we probably considered independently but had not paid enough attention to.

Health issues are most critical as they impact on the quality of final outcomes of our journeys. It determines the level of manifestation of our commitment, concentration, creativity and innovation. Ill-health compromises all our senses including our perception of things, the collective and that of our humanity as a whole?

Perception of the context starts with us crystallising perception of self. How do we view ourselves? We need to know our strengths, weaknesses, things that threaten or invigorate us, our fears and desires, our capacity to love and hate, our abilities to learn and unlearn, to stress and relax, our physical, mental and spiritual capacities and soon. We ascertain what we know of everything against how much of it we know we don't know. How much of the unknown are we capacitated to know?

We objectify the subjective in us that compromises us. How do we objectify our subjective elements through our societal imbalances? These could be sociological or technological. They boost the objective elements in us like manifestation of our Callings, our Archetypes and the state of our mindsets. Rationalisations and contextual applications raised elsewhere other than from our particular ecosystems can be a major misapplication. We visualise two negatives in our lives at this stage, the compromised subjective definition of our collective consciousness and misappropriated rationalisation of our context.

Origination and foundation of our discovery journeys already stand on quick-sand. We require deep piles to support our positions. These piles are born out of negatives we engage like posing, fabrication, deception and so forth. We are aware of the levels manipulation was engaged to get our discourses on course! It at times shows in seemingly genuinely intended initiatives that may never see the light of day. They end up as illusions of what could have been. Unfortunately, we can end up totally immersing ourselves and believing in our illusions at our peril. At this juncture, our senses of morality, ethics, belongingness, authenticity, rational, praxis and relevance to any context are lost.

The illusions we feel encourage us to sincerely believe, to the best of our knowledge that we know enough and at times more than we need. As children, our learning processes where almost exclusively experiential. We possessed an insatiable curiosity of discovery and inquisitive minds of anything that we came into contact with. Either our little oral laboratories tasted it or we touched for confirmation. This necessitated constant supervision. Slowly, as we grew older, our watchers gradually reduced constant watching and began to perceive us as becoming independent and not a danger to ourselves. The journey of complacency, diminished inquisitiveness, less experimentation and conformity to the dictates of our contexts ensued.

We hardly were ever left to our own vices since birth. Our parents were the first frontier, generals of society engaged to ensure that we orientate in the right manner as expected and desired by our respective communities. We were required to tacitly know the right things. As parents, they were convinced that their primary function in our lives was to ensure that we grew up into well behaved kids to their standard that complied with those of society. Only a handful of parents taught their children the venturous spirit, to find out things for themselves or burn. They did their best to stick to the syllabus of society that set the standard of good and bad as defined by it.

Our upbringing became a communal responsibility from the time we turned four, or old enough, starting with the extended family, peers and the relevant community that included the schooling resume and the broader society. Our journeys of individuation became a duality between controlled self-awareness and total mutilation ever since. It took a village to raise a child. We were allowed to know only that which was known as good for our individual and collective good.

We learnt unquestioningly. A minority escaped the net early in life but could not escape the societal rod. Those considered deviant were viewed and treated as different and undesirable. Parents and communities encouraged their children not to hang around with those sorts. The nerdish were made fun of, teased and bullied. Communities generally ignored them because it believed those who were that way deserved what they got coming. They were considered to have brought it upon themselves. It was paramount for communities to bring them back into line like prodigals.

Ostracism was punishment for those considered outcasts. They in turn neither had the chance nor will to lose the inadvertently new found space. Some found the exclusion tough so they curved in and conformed to a seemingly obvious chance at success especially in same environments. Every generation and group had a couple of individuals labeled as deviant and had notoriety in the collective community. Some of the fibs that were told about them still exist to this day. The "culprits" currently occupy varied positions in society.

We occasionally find comfort in thinking that those that appear to be unsuccessful by our standards deserved it. Why is it that way though? Would more tolerant and broader approaches have yielded different outcomes? Or, did it make us feel better about ourselves? Scrutiny of the autobiographies of those that became the greatest innovators of our time, or any period for that matter may change our minds!

Feelings we harbour are a reflection of what we know. Known- knowns strongly influence our view of what is and is not our truth. The greater part of those knowns are passed on to us through generations as granted reality. In some progressive and dynamic communities the known truth is tested. It become something entirely different but has stagnated in conservative and traditional ones. Our sense of dreaming and future desires and hence our creativity operates within the domain of those societal senses of reality, known–knowns and senses of truth. This leads the creativity and evolution of our communities towards uninspiring and unexciting known outcomes. It is only when we push the liminal frontiers of our societal knowledge domains that we create a fighting chance of breaking through. Pushing these frontiers a little further make a difference at individual, community, local and global levels albeit still mutilated and muffled by that containment.

The foundation of deviance we craft for ourselves early in life equip us with abilities to probe deeper within our inner selves. We reinforce our resolve around our strengths and weaknesses much more than the sheltered. We focus on our emerging self-awareness from a half full position and strive with all our might to fill a bath-tub with spill from it. It becomes survival and strives to know first and further than anyone what is known in the areas of our desires. We are challenged with knowing the unknown and become desperate to find answers, developing special skills to identify and map out such areas.

Knowing the unknown stimulates and arouses our curiosity to broaden our realm of knowledge with practical capacity unparalleled in any formal setting. We become obsessive about dreaming things, engaging our creative juices, constant idealisation, conscientising our being to a height unscaled before since experiments in our childlike laboratories. We set these up everywhere, in our parents' garages, servants' quarters, and food courts and even in public parks, literally anywhere we can discourse and brainstorm. We become fully aware of each other's capacity and are pragmatic about our assignments.

How much of ourselves do we know and how much of it is self discovery? We seem to almost unhinge from our past. To develop that amount of faith in ourselves when all around us seem to be at odds with us is a tall order that demands an elevated sense of consciousness.

It was common in our youth to hear of children raised by single parents, as orphans, materially disadvantaged or with parents considered negligent. In retrospect, it appears their situations equipped them better to excel in life. Parents were negligent if they didn't obviously appear to reign in on their children in line with societal dictates.

Conceivably, misfortune created need, opportunities, thirst and hunger. They form part of the origins and foundation of creativity. It may start as survivalist but then transcends into a deep desire to out- class and out-smart the haves that showed off and bullied them earlier. Ultimately, it stuck to become a way of life and the driver to become bigger than themselves, than their dreams.

We discover that we need to tap on that which comes naturally to us to be better than the rest. We epitomise our chances in life by capitalising our archetypical gifts and callings from as early as possible.

Unfortunately, things in life come as pairs, dualities in opposing tensions. On the other extreme, some manage to become equally competent capturing troughs of their negative energies. They excel in areas that are self destructive and negate society like dealing in drugs, criminality and creative excellence in scientific discoveries that harm society and weapons of mass destruction.

Communities that developed self discovery cultures competently achieve notoriety in particular fields. We observe that they apprentice their children from infancy to immediate knowledge persons. There exists in place a well developed hierarchy of role models and mentors to emulate and learn from. These lead in opening the eyes of protégés to see further compared to those communities with a strongly edited view of the world and how things work. It is important that we widen our view as much as possible at an early age to counter limitations thrust on us by societal mutilation and mechanistic approaches to our lifestyles.

The process of individuation develops a view reinforced through the emphasis of adherence to our formational processes, the dominance of our cultural views, imposition of personalities and superiority of known disciplines over all others. How then do we expand our horizons to include all that is unknown to us?

Genesis of our self-awareness journeys start with us becoming sensitive to how little we know about ourselves and the meta-knowledge universe. We need to differentiate that which we know and know is unknown. The expansion of the self awareness realm begins with the broadening of our horizons of known-unknowns. The most dangerous and primitive zone to find ourselves in is completely being oblivious of the existence of something. How can we accept its existence if all our senses cannot receive or register signals from the thing? As far as that goes, we argue vehemently of its non-existence when it actually does in reality. Our awareness feeds from our information banks of unknowns. It is this feed we desire to expand continuously.

The pitch dark zone of unknowns is infested with landmines. They detonate if we step on them without recognising their presence negatively unbalancing our lives in ways we cannot counter. We are defenseless against them because it is only their detonation under our feet that warns us of their presence. All of our consciousness fails to identify existence, similarly mysterious causations of our misfortunes. Our total ignorance of the unknown can manifest sin that is detrimental to a life of abundance to a life filled with strife, fundamentalism, ill- health, exclusion, dogmatisation and poverty. How do we re-generate ourselves to infinitely expand our sphere of known-unknowns that taps knowledge archived deep in our sub-conscience?

We can start with familiar contemporary situations whose reality we are more confident of. Are we able to articulate and normatively define our present situations prudently and pragmatically? We apply all the skills at our disposal as we discussed this far. We engage them to help us to originate, found, emerge, emancipate and realise our views as the best truth that we can possibly draw. We journey back into our life histories to extract our life stories, again applying the same principles of relationality, renewal, rationalisation and realisation. The probability of success is much higher as we get closer to our authentic life stories. This is a highly iterative process.

The process deliberately and integratively engages the various known major world cultures, disciplines and personalities to enhance our own views limited to experiential processes of individuation. It is that open mindedness to accept other views and embrace ensuing change coupled with the new that we become at every stage. We expand the content of our unknowns at every rung of our climb towards what we seek.

Not all unknowns will please us at first. Some may reveal things about us that we would rather keep in the dark. We need to deliberately turn around that energy into positive energy that benefits our development towards our objective. On the other hand, our progression along the consciousness continuum towards enlightenment reveals conjectures of beauty, wild imagination, wild imageries, possible hallucinations, and intense meditative moments. It anchors in and borrows from spirituality, contextual cultures and we form our own creative cultures, music, dance, community inclusion, families and friendships, dreams, varied and broad based opinions, love, conviction and the freedom to dare, at times to even fly.

The beautifully blended rainbow of known-unknowns diminishing into the horizon widens and becomes more distinct, enlarging its scope and depth in the process. We begin to see where it was dark with enhanced clarity. Unknowns begin to convert into known unknown. Our simple is another's complex. With time, the complex becomes simple as we become more aware, but a simple of a higher order. Often we appear to struggle with a new elevated simple until we re-tool ourselves to match the new spirally higher position.

Once we achieve a higher level of consciousness, it never regresses. It brings with it its own destruction of the old and the construction of the new. The death of our old consciousness level begets birth in the evolved new. Past consciousness ends here (the world is flat and has an end) to the beginning of the new (the world is a globe that rotates around the sun in 365.25 days). The latter at first sounds complex but to those that are fully aware, it appears ridiculously simple and obvious. How then do we define simple and complex in the context of self enlightenment?

At birth, we could neither define nor identify anything. Inductive and experiential processes commenced immediately upon birth to slowly register everything that we were exposed to. Gradually, we started with recognising our mothers in her gender form. We possibly viewed all women we came across as potential mothers. The process was reduced with time to a familiar, regular and short identification parameter. Any woman that could breast feed it was its mother, simple and straight forward. It quickly escalated as the baby realised that not all women that can breast feed it are its mother. More detail was required. It instantly became inadequate and incomplete to use the old short and neat description. Its reductive view of who mother is had just become longer and irregular. It had just become complex.

As we grew older and more experienced, we started to decipher the differentials between our mothers from other women including her sisters (or even a twin sister). Our journey went around full cycle gathering further detail we needed to zero in on the correct mother. The process continually elevated our awareness to distinct particulars that distinguish our mothers. We eventually came to a point we could easily and regularly identify her every time, even with our eyes closed. Our new simple was now more aware, elevated and sophisticated. It had transcended to the old spirally complex.

We acquire capacities in extracting the simple in the complex and the complex in the simple as we grow. We develop the ability to extract possible chaos areas in our orderly lives. We can equally map out order patterns during chaotic periods. The two exist dichotomously, pulling in opposite directions feeding on each other with paradoxical interdependence. This converges to nexus with our knowledge about everything including ourselves.

We become conscious of what we know-we know, what we know we don't know and that unknown whose existence we are totally oblivious, the unknown-unknown. The sum of what we know- we know and that we know- we don't know is much less than ten percent of what we don't know- we don't know.

The more we are aware about a specific area, the more we can pre-emptively map out matrices of various possible scenarios that can eventually lead us to our desired lifelike existence.

Scenario mapping of our present and future circumstances demands corresponding levels of alertness and consciousness. We require the relevant abilities and fortitude to extract the obvious and that which is not visible to the naked eye. How do we dig deeper into our inner selves to scenario map a true reflection of what is obtaining in the present and future of our lifestyles? How do we ensure with high levels of certainty the desired eventuality?

We are who and where we are today because of the ways we

instantaneously made an infinite number of seemingly inconsequential life decisions in many situations. These decisions pre-destined a particular lifestyle trajectory for us resulting in the contemporary us. We certainly can immediately intervene on the present state of our lifestyles to start effecting that lifestyle we most desire. Again, it starts with our capacity to authentically define who we are and who we wish to be in the present. This demands a very high degree of enlightenment.

We heavily invest in knowing what surrounds us but not what is within us. We learn what love is but are not bothered to learn what it is to enhance that natural capacity to love inherent in all of us. We learn about religion and spirituality but are not religious and spiritual in our core. It is all mostly external and mental, not internalised in application, behaviour and lifestyles.

We commonly hear the saying *believe in yourself*. It probably refers to knowing ourselves first! Successful people, no matter what field they are in, invest the most in knowing themselves; their capacities, capabilities, wants, needs, strengths, weaknesses, breaking points, callings, archetypes, inner most desires, likes and dislikes and so on. They push and over-emphasise their positives to the limit. They work equally tirelessly at minimising to complete healing their negatives. They endeavor to comprehensively answer the *Who am I question*.

It sounds simple when they tell their life stories but it all becomes mighty and complex when we try to simulate their journeys. Each journey is unique and particular to the individual although there are commons we can relevantly borrow from others and re-engineer to suit our own journeys.

Our dreaming, creativity and innovation requires an exceptionally relevant integral design to self–awareness. How do we ensure that our paths are optimally effective to realise the best for us? The meta-philosophy of our unique life integral design does not change but the design itself constantly mutate infinitely. We develop and internalise regular checks and balances as we go along. When we do decide to kick an undesirable habit like talking too loud, making snorting sounds when we eat or a quirky guttural laugh, we put checks and balances to ensure that we are aware when it starts happening. It could be as simple as asking a close friend, a colleague or a partner to give a particular signal when we start doing it again. Or this can be as complex as requiring counseling and therapy.

Some communities managed to enshrine specialised knowledge systems in their people over several centuries to the extent that it has tacitly become part of their culture. These vary from traditions of academia, technical intuitiveness, trading, fabrication, tailoring, shrewdness, provident existence, bravery, spiritual, cultural and communal elevated competence unmatched elsewhere. Individual families with strong filial piety indoctrination have legacies passing on through generations. It appears those that are successful at it remained immersed in their cultural traditions albeit with relatively conservative and pointed modernisation. Excellence at what they do reflects it and has simplified the seemingly complex.

The world society, especially at individual and community level has a lot to learn from those that managed to break barriers. It is conceivable that simplifying the complex may go a long way in creating impetus self-awareness, elevated consciousness, inclusiveness and self sufficiency firstly at those levels. Families create fractals of desired communities, a nation and a global society with specific emphasised views that makes each one unique.

There exists as many views and approaches as the world population today. Even a newly born baby has a view that makes immediate people around it respond in a particular way to its demands. It is not universal to all newly born babies. How can our views help us to optimally enhance our lives as individuals?

We experience an infinite number of deaths and re-births as we progress through life. We are babies at every stage of our development and our old selves die as we are born again in the new. We adopt a view for every situation, some real and useful, others myths and not so useful. Strangely, our minds sponge all experiences only choosing to bring forward those aspects that help to further the next desirable view. We painfully advance at a snail's pace from the time of each re-birth. The journey to present day selves has been continuous and unabated regardless. It cumulatively accounts for the way we acquired the nature of knowledge we have of ourselves and its state of being to make up the basis of who we are.

Impact of the discovery period prior to setting in of what we perceive as our comprehensive level of state of knowing is made up of seemingly trivial and infinite entries. They build on each other to compose our true life stories. It is our responsibility to capture and vividly tell each story in its entirety, deciphering it through our thinking processes, understanding and application abilities buttressed by those of others that can positively contribute. A successful result of this process opens up a vast domain of life choices uniquely available to us with deeper meaning and understanding.

All that inundation and bombardment with a wealth of information progressively form definite patterns and matrices of preference. Over-emphasised and exerted influence from various quarters manifested in us. It could have originated from overbearing grandparents desirous to have their legacies carried forward or a maid who secretly breast fed us to calm us down. Equally, it could be the gardener who lured us into dark corners to molest us in an attempt to fix a boss they viewed as abusive or a rich uncle or aunt who provided us with luxuries our parents could not afford. Either way, their influence impacted positively and negatively on our processes of individuation to last us for the rest of our lives.

The option to transform into what we desire to be from now into the future lies entirely within us. Many lifestyles are pre-disposed and determined by that ability. The discipline we derive from our professions, success limitations, spouse selection processes, sexual preferences, spiritual development and general quality of inter- personal relationships is helpful. How do we revisit them to expose and balance the negative that developed in us and accentuate them into positives that work to our advantage? How do we convert that strong fear of darkness in our shadows into light and a torch to provide us with desirable bearings in more than eighty percent of our decisions?

The paths we take in our education and training, cultural values and ethics formulation, spiritual and meta-physical development and development of general relationships are determined by what we confront and experience. We may have chosen to concentrate on a single meta-philosophy to direct our whole philosophical ecosystem or we might have chosen various sub-ecosystems that feed into each other to form one broad view. Whatever the case maybe, it all amounts to that personified philosophy that takes dominance. It is that primal view that we need to feel, expose and ensure that we heal and balance. Progressively, it transforms into positive aspects that gives us a collective advantage. Its benefits to the collective should always enable the enhancement of individual interests first.

Our different exposures typified our personalities. Superficially, we may appear to have similar traits, but are all different in varying degrees. It is the extraction of the subliminal differences in us and the nature of which we are that creates that luminal edge in our areas of excellence. We could have had indirect and informal styles of orientation whilst others consciously carved their developmental paths. The reverse is equally and competently true. Either way has downsides that are not terminally critical.

Negatives as we perceive them can be remodeled to work to our advantage as long as we identify what they are through concerted conscientisation processes. It is a painful process to come to the realisation of what it is that has been holding us back. Without it, we could have achieved most of our dreams. We could have been enabled to engage our areas of natural ability necessary to develop best performance in real time and in future. The closer we are to our best truths, the better we are at deriving optimally suitable philosophical approaches that take us towards our best.

Our best is unique and most suited to us. It implies that we can all be the Saint Mother Teresas, Jeff Bezos, Nelson Mandelas, Steve Jobs, Elon Musks, Bernard Arnoults and Aliko Dangotes of this world if we engage the best of ourselves. Those bests that are primal and natural to our talent and calling. It can be one small part in a long conveyor belt that moves a massive cogwheel to operate at peak efficiency. Without it, the cogwheel is not the same. It is our duty to bring this out for us to fully realise our spheres of excellence and for the world at large to benefit.

An infinite number of things can influence how we progress on our journeys. How do we as individuals and as communities handle that dialogue when we dogmatically believe in some of them? How do we handle new and possibly strange outcomes, like new knowledge and unprecedented change? Traditionally, our cultures, religions, spirituality and communities define our sense of true consciousness and hence our success toward lifelike existence. How do we metamorphosise that? How do we glocalise immense and unending amounts of global consciousness we experience daily? How do we move from the simple linear to the spiraling global complex?

CHAPTER 6

THE NEW SELF

The rational and the intuitive strive to remain exclusive of the other at the expense of obvious deficiencies. The rational objectifies life existence through foresight, prudence and regularity but emphasises the artistic view less. The intuitive has a contrarian view that minimally emphasises rationality but is subjective to the importance of illusion, imagination, dreaming and beauty. This separation gave birth to the Newtonian atomic thinking that in many respects excluded sociological considerations in most technological innovations. Our thinking needs to be holistically inclusive of the non-physical and intangible to quantum leap our creativity towards re-balancinghumanity's existence into godlike lifestyles.

The world is awakening too slowly to the need for integration of the rational and the intuitive, the spiritual, religious and cultural. It is doing this through dissimilation, de-centring and disavowal of indoctrinated beliefs, forms of truths and meaning enshrined in the narratives, similes and metaphors used to reinforce our processes of intuition. Only very few specially trained and skilled individuals can avowal and simulate their thinking to the complex demands of our world today. Typically, it is those that go through the various tertiary or even terminal degrees and equivalent formal and informal journeys. Very few, very unique individuals manage to circumvent these processes and develop special skills to compensate their need. They manage to achieve or surpass equivalent effect on global integrity, contributing greatly to their advancement and that of all humanity.

Dissimilation, de-centring and disavowal of accepted beliefs, truths and their meaning, society has obligated us to faithfully root us in is essential. In some instances, without questioning their *qualitas occulta*, a few had the brevity to create a sense of notoriety and eccentricism for themselves. They managed to concentrate their thought processes in the liminal crevices of their societal state knowledge and knowing and the state of who they are. This empowers them to push the existing limits of the truths and identity of knowledge of things and its praxis as set by society.

What are our opinions of perceived knowledge in existence from the steady-state system, towards emerging it into a state of dynamism in constant adaptation instead of the statist we experience at times? We cannot be indifferent to this situation for the sake of our survival and that of generations to follow we are totally responsible for. The quality of that future survival in optimal green worlds is imperative if we take responsibility into our hands now. Optimal self awareness mostly domiciles in us through deliberate conscious enlightenment over time. A balancing act of the subjective- objective dialectic!

In this era, we survive in transient cultures constantly evolving parasitically on each other. The dominant preys on the submissive. In Darwinian Theory of Evolution style, the latter eventually atrophies diminishing to insignificance. Some mergers disproportionately manifest in a new culture that totally has no significance to either of the original ones. The impact introduces multi- culturism that has its consequences. How does the emergent transient culture manifest? How do we cope with the inherent evolution it imposes upon us?

The amalgamation of cultures often shows through the creation of a new language system, a new knowledge format that in certain respects has no resemblance to any of the cultures it is born out of. It carries its own value systems, lifestyles, manners of speech and verbosity. A completely new and specific *lingua franca* develops, although it will be intermittent. Corresponding situational behaviour is born out of the new transient culture. Africa appears to have been the greatest victim   of the latter including multi-culturism and *lingua franca* that at times completely disavows the original participants.

Denial is good but proverbially, it is very difficult to conceal a horned head. The head always rears with time. Enculturation from Eastern religions is on the increase in Africa, roping in all and sundry, but concertedly burying local cultures, beliefs and dogma into the sand. Religiopreneurship has created economic, social and political powerhouses. Some are even beginning to steer the direction of the type of leadership we see in politics. Its impact is felt throughout the entire spectrum of societal demographies, be it at family level, community, organisational and national level. The extent of suspicion, lack of transparency, absence of collective and inclusive appointments, fear of the unknown, unitarian democracies and the *either you are with us or you are the enemy* options are gaining ground. Fear of the dark rears its head for all to see. *I am the only one who can do it* is clearly dominant.

How do we harness and convert energies invested in the fear of the dark, that fear of a mighty unconquerable dark power to work for us, to convert into bone-fide positive energy? We must ignite the desire to: authentic self-awareness, enlightenment, true success, luminance, genuine acceptance of the good in who we are, enhancing it with the good from others.

We are experiencing unprecedented dilemma in our comprehension and choice of our positive cultural values. It has become easier for us to abandon and replace them with those of others. Why abandon? Why not leave behind those we view as not good or find irrelevant and borrow from others those that buttress us to be stronger? Are other cultures borrowing from us as much as we are from them? If not, is it because we do not have anything to offer them? Again, the dark side rings loudly. Are we afraid of the unknown that we cannot see? Why are we more accepting of the exogenous over our own knowledge, history and heritage? Are we even fully aware of who we are?

Discussion and discourse on these issues has raged on at scholarly, traditional and political level for decades with very limited success. All else has been blamed but the self. The forces of darkness rendered unfounded suspicions between sisters, brothers, neighbours and differences in traditions reign supreme. Frank and progressive engagements were not possible regardless of the level of commons that exist.

We manipulate situations for personal gain other than for the emancipation of the collective. We push aside our own definitions and understanding of critical issues that impact the self, other and society– love thy neighbor, poverty, hunger and development. We have allowed others to be our proxies and stood on the sidelines only to criticise their perspectives as wholly impregnated with their own biases and beliefs. That fear in us of something out there that can pounce on us anytime and anywhere dominates us to submit to the not so familiar.

The argument of a single generic description of what is an African vehemently rages on globally, generally ignored and unabated by those that are being defined. African communities are as diverse as there are European, Americana and Asian communities put together. Other continents' nationalities at the frontier of modern advancements are clear, bold and articulate of who they are.

It may be impossible to come up with a consensus on these definitions. Their benefits are quantifiable. It provides the affected people with a unitary sense of purpose, a wider range of commons and belongingness. The Americans, British, Indians and Jews are luminary examples.

Origins of the various components of global humanity may differ. We posit the genesis of an inadvertent single epistemology for all else to follow being born out of globalisation. We are contemporarily all forced to learn, know, adopt and adapt the natures of our knowledge to accommodate other cultures of the world as they impact us daily. This is creating a common thread that binds all humanity imposing on us to borrow from each other and share available and existing knowledge. Some regions specialised their knowledge into particular strong views that they became best at. What has Africa at individual, family, community, society or as a continent offered towards global awareness or its enlightenment to contribute towards our desires of Godly lifelike likeness?

At local levels, person to person, community to community, Africa has relationally been successful. Indeed, it is generally accepted that the African continent has a heart, a rhythmic one that beats thunderously like its drums, heard at thanks giving ceremonies throughout. Its strength is in its sense of humanity, its instinctive realisation that survival, power and strength of an individual lies in and is drawn from that of the collective, like a fish in water. This *Ubuntu* thinking resonates throughout Africa inclusive of the Arab north. Foreign enculturation and influences are taking root mostly in urban areas. How does all this relate to who we are as individuals and our advanced tooling towards self-awareness?

Clear understanding of our situations carve into existing cavities to vacillate back and forth as necessary along a three phase continuum that defines the awareness of the operating culture. The primary and inherent tool is the dominant self. The self is fully aware and attempts to stay true to the original culture regardless of the impact of acculturation and enculturation constantly threatening irreversible change, influences and dictates.

An inflexible attitude in this phase results in sticking to traditional tendencies inspite of how undesirable and inappropriate they might be. It can lead to even deeper retrogressive side effects. Negative outcomes born out of over-emphasis on a particular omni-perspective are not conducive to imagined behavior. It is imagined behaviour that results in the creation of new knowledge. What then is more desirable than what is born out of interactions of more than one character, knowledge systems, cultures or contexts that demand change to adapt to the new order? This may result in a middle level situational culture that is reactive. Movement from the dominant to the situational cultural response requires both exposure and the ability to be able to react and change to suit the dictates of what is situational.

The situational self imposes itself on the dominant self capacitating it to cope. It is adaptive to external forces and is open to cross culturation depending on the demands of the dominant social context. It is dynamic and positively responsive. This phase is a higher order phase that demands higher levels of consciousness through learning, processes of knowing, training, exposure, contact and an open system approach to life. The practitioner requires to have developed the necessary skills to adapt almost instantaneously and be able to emerge their self identity in the process. That balance is important. Positive dynamism is instrumental in the survival, success and efficacy of a liminal self driven individual. But in practice, the change demands on the ground when two or more cultures interact are less linear.

The dynamics at play are infinite coming from all societal activists; from the conservatives, the liberals, traditionalists, politicians, business people, civic organizations, academics, scholars, spiritual and religious leaders and just ordinary family interests. The list of variables at play is endless. The levels of emerging interacting complexities require utmost capabilities to be able to bring out positive synergies out of that interaction. Peak performance and much higher levels of skill to decipher patterns, trends, interpretation and order out of this chaotic and complex environment is required.

Interaction of the Western cultural worldview, be it spiritual, religious or an educational initiative like the American styled sense of realism, politics or economics has been both positive and negative on other different cultural worldviews. Specifically those that are more polarized to it are most affected. Its overemphasis on otherwise other dominant cultures has resulted in clashes, from passive resistance to calamities   of world proportion. Those that are liminally empowered with strong fundamental and well developed traditions, philosophies and knowledge systems are in much better positions. They can move to positively contribute towards healing. Preferably, they create pre-emptive frontiers that foster positive energies from their interaction, with minimal compromise and prejudice.

The phase envisaged to deal with the coming together of cultures, contemporarily and continuously evident due to the ever increasing pace of globalization is not so common in the first two phases of cultural frontiers. It is critical that in this time, cultural adaptations, responses and mutations have the capacity to contain the various forms continually at play within the self. It transforms the self into a being with a global culture that continually and positively changes as we move deeper towards less and less unique and distinct dominant cultures. This is termed the complex cultural being.

The complex cultural being implicitly contains many other cultures within them to subconsciously borrow from and switch into as necessary. They developed the capacity to blend to create a new that is contextually relevant at any given time. This becomes part of their   tacit   selves. Those already experiencing part of their self awareness journeys, the transformation to this complex someone is brought about through the intense and rigorous journey this far traversed.

We are marked as marginal and liminal persons comfortable at the frontier of change and knowledge creation. It empowers us to navigate and penetrate global networks cutting across global societies without limitations of the crippling mono-cultural behaviour. Most importantly, the true identity of the authentic self must always emerge.

One may conveniently choose to be recessive as situationally necessary to wisely manage the dictates of given external demands.

Our objective and desire in our lifestyles is to simulate livelihoods as God intended in almost every religious worldview. The desire for Godlike existence makes us strive to be more humane in our approaches to life that attempts to migrate towards the betterment of the condition of all humanity. Each individual, family and community has their own unique view of Godlike living.

Preferably, we need to organically develop Godlike lifestyles we desire for ourselves. They embrace diversity, adaption and rebirth at the end of each feedback loop of every life cycle. Each iteration marginally evolves deeper complexity. Its diversity broadens both horizontally and vertically to include many other enculturations accompanied by their knowledge systems. In this era, it implies that most cultures are constantly in a transient state that is continuously transforming feeding on each other all the time.

The Navajo philosophy posses three postulates that we may need to observe in our journeys of pluralistic development. It considers the dialectic existence of things in nature, most importantly that of the *anima* and *animata,* that of the male and female in its real and metaphorical forms. Positive tensions existing in the dualistic relationships give birth to many other possibilities and dialectics that emerge healthy diversity. It is these births of many others that engender the inevitable constant change we find as the world globalises at an increasing rate. It gives re- birth to other males and females as well, inherent with higher levels of complexity tolerances to more sophisticated levels of multi-culturism, religiosity and spirituality. The cycle starts all over *ad infinitum, sin qua non.* The role of culture gets into constant motion.

How does faith in something that our five senses cannot perceive nor substantiate come to us? We at one point believed in something absolutely abstract and out of our reach. These can be from simple addictions and cravings we cannot shake to passionate dependency on simple things like alcohol, food, medicinal drugs for diabetes or a psychological problem.

We are drawn to these every time we feel a little tension or fail to resolve a challenge. Bigger and more demanding life issues require more formalised interventions like regular consultations with our families, parents, community elders or the local pastor. People from different regions of the world are drawn to different forms of collective philosophical belief they practiced for decades, be they secular or non-secular. The few that easily come to mind are Ubuntuism, Christianity, Islam, Buddhism, Hinduism, Taoism and Confucianism.

Our fascination with some of these is born from regular cultural practice and may develop into active dogmatic commitment. Others elected to partially adopt some of the mysticism throughout their lives. They can manifest through addictive indulgence and dependence in intrinsic wants like music, art, food, the power of meditation and many other subliminal passions we are emotionally and faithfully drawn to. At micro levels, we have some forms of unexplainable vices we cannot shake away. Do we have individual escalating hierarchies of these vices and needs from the primary primitive to the sophisticated tertiary. They inevitably lead us to a meta one recognisable for its abilities to motivate the balancing of our lifestyle challenges?

At some points in our lives, we observed patterns in people who are passionate about their dreams. A musical artist takes a week to alienate everything and everyone around to enable them to withdraw into solitary creative sessions. After a couple of days in an abandoned warehouse somewhere in the middle of nowhere, they emerge with a piece of good work that triggers a short celebratory period of indulgent alcoholism. This is followed by a couple of days of intense melancholic drama that only gets pacified by profuse confessions to the local priest. An enthusiastic participation at the local Baptist Church signals the return to normalcy. A long period of peace and quiet, with low volume Congolese jazz music in the background and junk food caps this episode. It appears these sorts of cycles are the norm in the life of this sixty-one year old artist. How does this pattern feed into the overarching ecosystem of an individual's general transcendent belief? Do we have a peculiar behaviour that blows out in our meditative creative phases?

We notice destructive-constructive religiosity into communities where indigenous religious practices are overwhelmed by the will and mighty of exogenous ones. Broadly, cultural behavioural patterns relate to our dominant forms of religion inspite of the dilemmas born out of the indigenous-exogenous duality. The dominant global religious paradigm appears to vest unquestionable omni-superpower in an outer force to determine paths of our lifestyles. It supposedly gives our lives meaning, faith and reason. Atheists and Gnostics that make up five percent of our populations tend not to want to conform to culturally developed formats. They usually have generic forms of micro belief systems organically developed to motivate and provide them with some form of faith and expected Godly lifestyles. For them, the belief that some omnipotent super power outside them exists is a social construct that runs parallel.

Humans, as the top specie of the animal chain are endowed with capacity to learn from natural phenomena at individual and communal levels. We can simulate it into our real life situations through our ingenuity of dreaming, creativity and ideation up to implementable innovations to solve our human challenges. We achieve this through various elements of our communities, traditions, cultures and knowledge systems, again grounded and originated in nature's ways.

Age old dynamic methodologies of renewing ourselves, transforming us in the process into what we aspire to be are encultured into all obtaining systems that impact us from birth. It inspired and motivated us through our desire to live in Godlike fashion strongly founded in nature. Desirable existence is enabled through most forms of cultural, spiritual and religious practices unique to specific parts and communities of the world.

Dominant global spiritual and religious influences originate and are grounded in the worldview of the east. How then do we rationalise our dreams, creativity and idealisations through our spirituality and religiosity to something that is considered as both locally and globally imported?

Our life objectifies to the fore our want to uniquely transform into brands that are true representatives and true embodiments of lives well lived. We perpetually seek for continual movement that brings us closer all the time towards our sense of reality transcending us to what we perceive as higher levels of existence. To this end, we quest for knowledge and enhanced continuous conscientising processes to enable us to epitomize living Godlike.

We personify ourselves to those characteristics and tenets we desire to be. We empower ourselves with all possible tools that capacitate us to achieve that end. This provides us with far sightedness and visions into the quality of life we intend to live.

Initially, our egos and shallow understanding of those philosophies we base ourselves in route us towards atheism as this is closer to the material, the simple and the simple linear. Further in-depth understanding of the same draws us towards religion as the subjective and objective, the real and arbitrary, reason and emotion, converging into harmony that renews and rejuvenates. The more we are empowered, the greater are our chances to be able to predict what will happen in our lives in future elevating ourselves into unbounded personified prophetic realms. How then do we get to live the lifestyles that we defined for ourselves? How do we awaken ourselves to the reality of that which we desire so much, to help us to live it rather than dwell on the gratification of what could be and what may come as a reward after our deaths?

Four main aspects in our lives we can tacitly engage at any given time need to be objectified and emphasised. These keep our lives in balance by focusing and engaging our daily realities. The processes we engage must result in our optimal consciousness levels, again unique to every individual. They have the capacity to connect with and engage our inner most inexhaustible energies through the inherent inner faith we develop. Our spirituality and religiosity is usually credited with renewal towards this faith. It fuels our enhanced comprehensive self awareness journey that transcends us through to our desired lifestyles. What is it that we must engage for us to practically renew and actualise ourselves into the beings we desire to be?

Mobility towards our desirable lives inevitably brings us less worry, a peace of mind and happiness. These are all a function of our intrinsic setup and are independent of external influences. We totally control them. It is our mindsets, the opinions we form from any given situation, the emotions that manifest and how we resolve them that can be a challenge.

Once we learn to manage and provide ourselves with positive mindsets, we start to attract what we are and manifest a desirable faith mode.

Faith in us can be a lot harder than our faith in God. It is that faith in who we are that gives us strong grounds to want to belong to something bigger, to believe in our dreams, creativity and spirituality. We need well developed and implicit religions like Christianity and Islam. These have evolved hermeneutic knowledge and narratives over centuries that manifest self consciousness necessary for our continual renewal. Our minds get to experience a series of rebirths in a wiser, more informed and self conscious new.

Our transcendence from religiosity to spirituality then faith gradually sprouts like a flower. It boosts our wellness through creation of safe zones around us regardless of any challenges that may be in our lives at that juncture. It alleviates levels of worry, stress and fear that we may have. This may cure any non-communicable diseases like hypertension, diabetes, ulcers, arthritis and nervous breakdowns. Worry precedes fear and results in sinful behaviour detrimental to our wellness mentally, physically and spiritually through our deeds. Our health is sometimes compromised to the extent of incapacitation.

Low faith levels can result in low and finite energy levels inadequate to fight back. Higher levels generate infinite and inexhaustible energy that can conquer most of our challenges including some known scientifically incurable diseases. The beauty is that the requisite energy we need resides in our inner core and simply requires us to draw on it. Without proper and timely intervention, low faith can wreck the quality of lives we lead. Carl Jung observed that elevated religiosity can solve half of our problems. Without it most modern humans cannot gain back fully what they lost.

Highly successful people are religious. They are well researched in their areas of interest, committed and believe wholeheartedly in something bigger than themselves. They submit in prayer, meditation, contemplation and deprivation to develop the necessary elevated consciousness to connect stronger with their higher power. Many of us commit to God through an intermediary. Christians through Jesus Christ and Moslems through Prophet Mohammad. Christians and Moslems each aggregate 31.1% and 24.9% of the world population respectively. However, there are an infinite other regions that the remainder reveres..

Either way, there appears to be a need for us to believe in that ultimate omni-force with infinite wisdom, power, insight, intelligence, creativity, innovation, love, care, forgiveness or something much more superior than our collective power as humanity put together. Growth in our religiosity submits us deeper and more intimately to this higher force that completely takes over from where we start to falter or fail. Our movement as humans from the egoistic physical and material to the metaphysical and emotional, then finally to the spiritual, positively integrates all dualities we experience into one big desirable whole for abundance in our lives.

In the thinking of post-modernism, the spirit that appears to be taking centre stage is of an individual approach to creativity and hence accumulates all benefits that are derived from it. The majority of successful people from the past derived more power from collective creativity. Unlike recent times, most want to go at it individually or in small isolated pockets at best. What has happened for the individual are equally isolated and creatively limited self-awareness innovations.

The collective approach utilising co-creativity results in the advancement of luminaries we enjoy globally today. It is primary that we groom and instill the collective spirit early but keep a close eye on the group and team dynamics without losing ourselves as individuals in the collective. How are we able to manage the dictates of our embodiments and ecosystems and their prevailing enshrined philosophies?

The dynamics of the individual, the dialectics of the individual-collective and the integration of the desires of the collective provide us with the best potential to bring out unique achievements. It canbe for the individual, the collective or the individual-collective combination. This ideally prepares us as individuals or as a whole to engage fully and actively as full participants of a collective. The objective would be to draw the best possible enlightening innovations from our initiatives that right our collective perception of any existing imbalances we may perceive.

Dialectic thinking limits our full potential. We may realise early that it locks up untold creative energy that enhances positive outcomes in our endeavors. The same dialectics exist in nature and brings it much desired balance. If we can simulate nature in our approaches to these dialectics, we benefit from similar synergies existing in nature. We must find best ways to critique and balance weaknesses for our benefit. Dialogical engagement in the discourse that holds us back provides enough fire power to paddle us towards substantive, sustainable and transformative outcomes.

How do we harness the dialectic-dialogical tensions and dynamics of enculturation and acculturation? How can they enhance our senses of latent potential and capacity in the contemporary to become something much bigger and broader than the present? Emancipation and rationalisation of the dictates of our present being versus those of becoming our desirable selves slowly descend into a trough of entrapments riddled with negatives that outweigh the positives. It becomes clear that without proper prior preparation of body, heart, mind, soul and spirit, our emergence from it to the desired new becomes an almost impassable steep ascent. We need all our wits and to ensure that we dig deeper into all available inner energies known or unknown to us. It demands tremendous dexterity of our inner acculturation and the outer enculturation.

Authentic rationalising, culturalising and spiritualising iterative cyclic visitations pragmatically result in our climbing out of this very turbulent trough to a very calm and desirable high. The views from the new altitude are much clearer and gradually draw on our inner sense of beauty. Other secretive knowledge forms hiding from and unknown to us begin to reveal themselves coupled with its related possibilities in unfamiliar consciences. The external and the interior start to converge to a confluence that synergically peaks to a beautiful view. However, the what, why, where, when and how still requires insatiable deciphering. Societal justification of our emerging subjective lifelike lifestyles becomes an outer objective challenge. It shows its relevance as an intelligent participant initially at local practice gradually transcending to global integrity. Its contribution to the healing of our families, our immediate and small surrounding communities must be distinctive.

Personal value systems in this regard and those of the global context converge through re-discovery to a fundamental and sustainable nexus, yielding strategic renewal. We re-interpret the meanings of both what's internal and what's exterior to the needs of our contexts without losing its voice of what is of primary concern to it. Emulation of the exterior without due regard and sensitivity of the voices from within require other skills beyond the traditional rationalising, theorising and pragmatising. Something else that is not obviously there is needed to complete the relevance, inclusion and voices of our contexts.

Mindsets developed over decades need cognisance, convincing and conversion, a difficult task to achieve without trading on many toes. It can be a nag and a drawback not conducive to our self confidence and of all those others around us. Creative and innovative energies take a knock. Other strong doctrines that are more vociferous, more convincing and more demanding can cope with newly emerging unconfident voices. The language of communication is key, verbal, acted or implied. It is critical to communicate whatever it is we want to be heard succinctly if we are to get appropriate contributive reactions. It becomes critical that we are compatibly yoked to our small teams. We regroup and learn to hear the context's challenges as they impact our trajectories rather than blindly impose our narrow views and perceived imbalances.

Understanding of our contexts is through recognising the imbalances in existing dominant perspectives and impoverishing elements in our eco-systems. Context assists in uncovering areas of imbalances and disintegration that lie within the concerns raised by our inner burning desires and issues of our contexts. Contexts uncover for us and activate prospects of equilibrium positions of balance and integration.

Despite the high degree of technological and economic advancement of some societies, many challenges still prevail that need to be addressed not purely by technology or economics, but by social innovations rooted in society. This can be achieved through raising the conscious levels of individuals and families. It is done inclusively, recognising other outer perspectives and disciplinary imbalances, missing depths and evolving impoverished ecosystems.

In essence, context tends to highlight the divides we seek to heal as individuals. Quadrangle considerations can be discussed to define them. We start by considering the transformational terrain that is inductive for us to realise translation towards our intended objectives.

The transformational terrain has four vertical layers, one on top of the other. It typifies the importance of cultural depth inherent in us as individuals. The process involves the progressive transformation of in-depth images into our surface inclinations and attributes. It begins from the core of our particular society. These are its cultural images that are the source of creativity and innovation. We move up to the bedrock of our societies where ideological orientations are represented by its philosophies and policies that are below everyday surface. These stimulate our insights. The subsoil of our societies is next. Our institutional frameworks are represented here by its dominant models and systems, all put together by collective intelligence. These include systems like economic, legal, political, private, public or civic enterprises. We finally get to the top soil of our societies that are made up of personal inclinations dealing with attitudes and behaviours. Everyday transcultural conversations and interactions are carried out in these topsoil arenas.

Clear understanding of social innovation and transformation inherent in our individual integral designs, in-depth appreciation of our own indigenous systems, cultural forces inherent in human society, be they African, Asian American or European is required. It is important to understand the cultural strengths of each of the major perspectives representative of all major societies.

Different meta-cultures resident in cardinal corners of the globe developed certain types of cultural orientations, strong and leading in particular cultural practices and local capacities. This 'mono-cultural' view has its downside. Identified local capacities when effectively activated form the basis for local transformative processes and social innovations. They contribute to global solutions if their existence interacts in balance with other cultural capacities or through a trans- cultural process. This transformation process from mono-cultural to trans-cultural begins with the development of local identity that is grounded in us individually.

Only when there is full understanding of local identity and culture can we as individuals meaningfully contribute to global integrity. Our systems and those within our societies are evaluated in relation to the world at large. Transformation then draws upon individual and local identity, frugal knowledge systems and culture with a view to developing personalised global integrity. Our transcendence links us with the other, the local and the global and our culture with another. Creative interaction between cultural diversities of our different worlds and its core leads to co-creation that benefits us all, each culture contributing, but not a dominating element, evolving transcultural enlightenment in the process.

Movement from over-emphasising only those familiar disciplines we are competent at to include disciplines of others, creating dialogue between knowledge fields result. It engages a wider scope of available formal and informal know-how at our disposal. In order to effect more fulfilling self-awareness, we need to cut across boundaries of regionalised knowledge dwelling and seemingly owned by those societies claiming to have developed it.

Effective contribution towards solving contemporary personal and societal challenges requires our journeys to transform our understanding and marginalised approach to spheres of knowledge. Its success demands a broad based inclusive and embracive approach to disciplines that effectively link nature and community; culture and spirituality; science, systems and technology; politics and economics, and their underlying knowledge systems all set within a particular context.

Modern and global elite knowledge dispensation has been dominated by northern and western worlds where curricula are offered in disciplines most relevant to the two worlds. Typically, these disciplines range from: physics, chemistry, mathematics, biology, social sciences, economics, psychology, sociology, and political science to mention a few. Other regions outside those two were obligated to adopt the western and northern styles of education. However, the social sciences ranging from economics to anthropology and from political science to sociology are all taught in isolation with either majors or minors in sociology or psychology. In business management, finance is taught separately from marketing.

In addition, development of new knowledge is typified in the styles of the dominant. Their view chose to isolate knowledge creation from education. There is a need for us to cross boundary lines between different disciplines in raising our consciousness levels. Boundary crossing is sorely lacking in existing self awareness initiatives.

The suggested trans-disciplinary objectivity results in the fusion of disciplines. The arts, nature, community and humanity encompass human and social ecology, anthropology and psychology all form primary elements in our being. Similarly, spirituality and psychology, philosophy, religion, culture, anthropology and history constitute essential segments of our becoming that we desire to be. Science and technology encompass social systems, political theory, philosophy and natural sciences form primary pillars to our knowing. The practical side to our doing has always been claimed by enterprise and economics since the Newtonian and Smithian eras. But has their doing always resulted in our individual and collective enterprise development? Has it enhanced our structured capacities and their functionality?

The separation of nature and community, as well as culture and spirituality from science and technology impacts negatively on our individual states of being. Organisations and societies well being are equally affected. In addition, the separation between politics and economics stratify individuals, organisations and society into different segments that inhibit our abilities to innovate. We impoverish personal and territorial cohesion, depriving ourselves of collective creativity and knowledge.

The importance of understanding impoverished ecosystems cannot be underestimated. Their relationships shape, map and influence our direction and the quality of outcomes of relations within the ecosystem. According to Jackson, an ecosystem is a complex set of relationships among living resources, habitats and residence of that area whose functional goal is to maintain equilibrium of a self-sustaining state. In contrast, the innovation ecosystem takes into account the economics, dynamics and relevance of complex relationships between those it influences and that influence it.

An impoverished ecosystem is a living organism that expresses our motion as we move throughout societies of the world. Resultant enlightenment ecosystems provide us with innovation processes, mapping out how we can generate knowledge and the different ways of how to go about exposing it. Finally, an impoverished ecosystem establishes a knowledge base on our enterprising or collective development bringing our initiatives to a full transformational cycle, from our grounding up to our abilities to effect.

The relational output from our collective initiatives promotes our grounding, ensuring that transformation is rooted in us as well as the collective. This roots our socialisation deep into the soils of our particular contexts embracing its nature and culture. Our transformation into the lifelike lifestyles we most desire must be politically, economically, socially, culturally and environmentally acceptable and inspirational to those who are impoverished. Renewal abilities we acquire along the way help in building ecosystems and links between us and our ecosystems. We learn to catalyse stimulation of local and global linkages while captivating the imaginary realms of our collective through culture, religion and art to mention a few. Our integral design navigates acquired knowledge, old and new; to ensure that there is a development of an integral theory base and mechanisms to enshrine in ourselves as individuals and in our communities as the collective and representative of society. Finally, we link theory and practice to facilitate the realisation of lifelike living that has tangible impact in us as well as our families, communities and the global village. We need to realise the goals of our life integral design.

Realisation and implementation of our designs require a contextual, integrated and inclusive afrintuneurial approach. It translates our consciousness into usable and realisable knowledge that manifest as technological or social innovations. This immortalizes the inclusion of our context to the centre of enlightenment trajectory. Tom Friedman posits that *we need 100 000 people in 100 000 garages trying 100 000 things in the hope that five of them break through.* The will of dreaming, creativity, rationalising and subsequent realisation of innovations concur with this observation.

Billions of dreams funnel to a handful of plausible creative propositions at best. Success ratios radioactively decay as further processes expose our propositions through more rigorous ideation scrutiny. Marginal success is a reserve for the few that spiritedly engage. Chances of success increase if we dedicate our life journeys to serving our archetypical Callings by simultaneously engaging unique and well integrated innovative approaches.

The whole transformative journey requires intended and elaborate espousal of both the personal and societal definitions of success. They are subsequently interfaced to a common desired meaning in the present and future for a common desirable destiny. In most instances, meaning we derive gets quickly clouded with tangible and specific marginal wealth gain as a primary barometer.

A few of us realise at the beginning of our journeys that wealth always follow true success. Motivation from material greed precipitates to the fore in the early stages of most endeavors for all to see influencing the direction of our desires. It can easily divert us to areas that seemingly maximise our economic visibility in the process to our demise.

Whereas, our economic success or failure is an expression of the effectiveness of creativity. Consistence, sound and well informed decisions result in desirable innovations. It builds on our interior state of being and exterior nature of our historicity, structure of its hierarchies and its level of openness that is ever changing and indeterminate.

Admittedly, material wealth is a true need and a factor of life although most of us exaggerate its importance. Other more urgent needs exist in life we are not conscious of and do not prioritise. We take their latent presence for granted. Our presumption of their guaranteed availability frees us to function at our peak and concentrate on other downstream facets of life. Otherwise makes it difficult to exist as evidenced by our total dependency on them. It is preferable that we let the success of our initiatives result in economic rewards. It becomes important for us to focus more on the deeper meaning of answering to our Callings, our inner glow, espousal and celebration of our archetypes. Fulfillment and the exhilarating feeling of having exhausted our potential to its fullest extent making a difference at self, other and society as a whole ensue.

Once our journeys begin, we start to confront the demands of our inner voices with brevity drawing lessons from our processes of individuation. We notice modest successes within our lives occurring regularly and celebrate them as reflections of a life well lived. We view it as an account and answering to the life choices we made, especially during and after our normative periods responsible for our midlife maneuvers. How can we identify those successes that leave a mark in this world and make us luminaries of our time at our levels of existence?

As we account for our life achievements, especially to ourselves no matter how small they seem, we realise how life has sled past and how short indeed it has been. It is easy to dwell on what could have been and have regrets, missing to focus on recognising and consolidating whatever comes to the fore. It is possible to concentrate on the tangible material at the deprivation of the intangible soft successes, love of family and friends, knowledge we gathered over time and most importantly learning points towards lifelike existence. We want to assess the impact we made to all that we were exposed to.

Did we manage to shake-up any one thing from the static steady state desired by family, peers and society to a level of dynamism that is constantly adapting? Did we manage to take anything, no matter how insignificant it may appear in our eyes, through its life cycle up to its ultimate possible, to the mountain top, so to speak? What are our regrets learnt from our experience? Often, it is performance at the top of the highest mountain that provides maximum view, that extra capacity to impact far and wide outside our families and societies.

Bill Murphy Jnr in *The Intelligent Entrepreneur* postulates four elements he views as critically important to one's work. These are our happiness, achievements, significance and possible legacies. We may achieve any of these singularly but it is great to achieve more than one of the elements for a life well lived. As an example, significance can be realised without the other three. Achievement of desired goals can be realised without intended happiness and without achieving legacies of any consequence.

Over emphasis on any one element hampers and prejudices the development of the other three. Accordingly, Professor Howard Stevenson of Havard Business School suggests jostling of all four at any given time and posits that *"...the most important ball is the ball that's about to fall. It's not the ball in your hand"*. We hasten to preserve the ball secure in our hands, continually polishing and improving it. This comes naturally to us. It may even directly correlate with areas of our natural ability.

We can realise deep inner satisfaction through individual effort, driven and motivated by our burning desire, inclusively engaging the collective and its creativeness to resolve its unique societal objective challenge. It is our unique and unprecedented innovation that comes out of our co-creative effort that considerably rewards us with economic and material benefits. These further manifest our freedom, satisfaction and personal financial security we desire. Sharing this with others provides individual success, glory and legacy.

How do we define our true success? We can evaluate the new transformed us against the comprehensive definitions of who we were as anticipated at the beginning of our journeys. We enabled ourselves to tell our stories, our life histories in detail and became aware of our greatest strengths and weaknesses. At the end of it, we became the best constructive self critics and of everything around us including issues obtaining in our societies. We simultaneously became very keen partners in transformation of others as we transformed ourselves. We are no longer embarrassed to take the initiative to share the little knowledge at hand.

Journeying back into infinite phases of our early lives sets a foundation of who we are. We begin to discover and recognise choices that are available to us. Those that were with us involuntarily throughout become part of the origins of who we are. We developed the courage to embrace our background desires. Wisdom and knowledge we derived from our societies since birth stay with us to influence positively decisions we make in the present and future.

We re-visited our life histories to bring out those significant aspects contributing to who we are at present. We then extended it to the life-stories of our parents and attempted it to be as inclusive of our ecosystems as we possibly could. Our background helped us to realise the importance, major roles and impact of our families, peers, communities and societies play in that respect. Each of them imprinted their best impressions unique to each one of us. In the process, each has played its part on who we become in the end.

Direct influence from every quarter of our external environment is significant and noticeable in each of us. It happens much earlier in some societies and much later or throughout life in others. However, one may never totally divorce themselves from it. Imprinting continues at varying degrees depending on how we impose the dominance of our individual ways we paved through our inspiration. External environment influence continues to solidify already existing positive traits. They are reinforced by our enhanced receptiveness to continual self discovery and development through acquisition of new consciousness all the time. We equally must be accepting of all our faults and weaknesses revealed in the process.

Whoever we become must benefit us and everything around us in a Siphonaptera fashion where humanity benefits throughout its ecosystem. Interrogating and scrutinising every aspect of our histories is not an easy task and can be an uncomfortable one. But it is a pre-requisite to bonefide self-actualisation processes that lead us to lifelike lifestyles.

The journey into consciousness is an infinite journey that never reaches its destination. Its frontier is always in the abyss we hope is buoyed and grounded in the familiar deep onto which we build-on our new. Our continual venturing prepares us to comfortably work in our self discovery zones all the time. We begin to get our adrenalin high in these zones and visit the familiar and regular for relaxation, reconnaissance and long gasps of oxygen so to speak. We learn quickly the processes of discovering knowledge; mastering methodologies that attempt to reveal its secrets; putting as much of its domain within our reach with the least resources at our disposal. Gained ground is consolidated to capitalise on gained knowledge to our advantage. We move the luminal frontier forward, deeper into the abyss all the time. The abyss can be a solitary and lonely place that demands confidence and courage. How do we feel about solitude, independent thinking without primary direction from family, friends and community other than what we got before this stage?

One of the early tale-tells to indicate that we are in the right direction is our enhanced ability to notice differentials existing in our transient environments. We become more observant, curious and ready to indulge with sensitivity to the feedback we get. Our value system becomes more focused and realistic, utilising the best afrintuneurial (contextual, integrated and inclusive form of entrepreneurship) methods exceptionally authentic to us to efficiently achieve our objective. We thirst to commit and dedicate more of ourselves, but only taking that which is adequate for us, empowering others to join us and equally benefit. Lifelike living requires that we carry all others and society with us.

Slowly, less starts to become more. We become interested in the utility orientation of things, but less enthused by blindly collecting what we

185

really do not need. We notice that this frees up more of our time, the most important consumable in our new existence.

As much as solitude slowly ceases to faze us, there is so much to do that is interactive we cannot finish in the lifetime left. Not knowing our death date push-effects further urgency on what we do. Procrastination is a vice we can no longer afford as we start to focus on things that realise maximum results. We become prudent with our choices, activities we partake in, the company we associate with and keep.

We are more expressive and freer to love, compliment and appreciate beauty in most things metaphysical. We become constant dreamers not afraid of rebuff to create and offer ideas to any discourse of interest. We develop an intuition to avoid those that accentuate the negative in us.

Evolving new ideas, behaviours and unfamiliar knowledge is a big challenge. As we interact with people, they appear to notice the difference and enthusiastically want to inquire on what they observe. Interestingly, this comes from people of all walks of life, as long as we do not appear hostile to potential encounters. It can come from a seventy-three year old leather bags sales lady who gets interested in our strange view to things. She is quick to indicate how she had found her Calling in nursing in her late teens but due to societal pressures of the time, she ended up in sales and marketing. She is clear that she is still haunted by her dream of taking up nursing if the opportunity arose in future. The good side we develop exudes an aura attractive to most of our encounters.

Sometimes we will wonder if we became more particular, less patient and less tolerant. We develop exception on how we spend our valuables. It appears those things that are most exciting cost less or nothing. We now watch what we eat, even love to cook, take every opportunity to exercise so that we stay healthy, get to see a doctor regularly and are realistic and not too scared to be told that we have cancer. We now realise that it is more helpful for us to know than blindly hope. We become more faithful to our relationships. We realise the importance of maintaining a quality life to create more time. We now can comfortably walk, cycle or go up a forty storey building to stay healthy. All these used to happen only twenty percent of the time but our desire is to switch the numbers.

Our resumes of life are transient and at times we feel they are obscene and irrelevant. Our past does not hold us down anymore. We do not feel obligated to it except to take from it only that which is relevant and competent in the present and future. The more new items we regularly put under our belts the better we feel. Dynamism allows us the opportunity to continually grow even in those things we felt we had expertise.

We now feel our destinies are within reach. The only inadequate variable is time in the present and future. A bit of regret on wasted resources, especially time, may creep in. We renew our vows to confront all those things that we procrastinated including evolving the list of our peers. They maybe some we feel dragged us down and we were not been able to let them go. There are potential ones we felt were pushy and kept on the periphery.

The time to freely reject, exclude and rebuff becomes now and vice versa. Interestingly we become possessive with those we love and are dear to us. We have the capacity to easily and equally constructively express how we feel. We integratively indulge fully cognisant of how our bodies, hearts, minds, souls and spirits feel about it. We have now fully re-created ourselves. The new self is here.

Who am I? We ask, again!

CHAPTER 7

FUNNELING THE ESSENCE

The responsibility to start this journey and get it going is ours. It begins with us and inclusively envelopes our subjective definition of family and immediate friends. It may all happen within a given community in the beginning. The domain of our communities used to be much simpler to define but have become complex as the world slowly shrinks into one gigantic village. Contemporarily, a community may as well include all its elements that directly impact our daily survival.A strong local influence may trigger it. The ultimate intention is for it to eventually make sense at the global level. Our self consideration has strong local practice and relevance. Its societal considerations require a strong global flare, relevance and recognition.

The grounding of our challenges is addressed through embarking on our self awareness journeys. Some of them are not fully known even to us. They are only revealed through our journeying into our authentic life stories. Through that process, we can fully realise our authentic inner and deep thirst needing to be quenched. Embarking on this long journey draws on our inner core reserves. It must be rooted in something truly habited deep within us for it to have meaning and sustainability. Pacifying it simultaneously satisfies us to levels that we thought of as impossible and non-existent. A deeper draw requires us to connect with our inner sources of creative energies that drive profound creativity, innovation and renewal regardless of our circumstances.

The revelation of our true Calling is a major part of the overarching challenge. Once we do, we can realistically and successfully transcend towards it. We simultaneously start to create and innovate contributions that benefit the greater society.

Iterative processes that dig deeper with every subsequent cycle defines us in collaboration with family, immediate community and peers. We convert the emerging narrative into some formal structure that can be as subjective as we wish it to be. In doing so, we consider the totality of the contents of our habitat to objectify our drive to solve the internal imbalance we perceive. If for an example, our inner impulse is to minimise the suffering of animals, how does this interface with the internal imbalance existing in our societies? Can outcomes from our enlightenment impact on our societies to help in resolving this perceived imbalance and add to existing praxis, no matter how marginally? How can we and our habitats derive maximum benefit from it and still make sense to the rest of the world?

Our habitat is our Context that integratively builds on our Calling and those of society, objectifying it in the process. It is within this realm that the realities of our main challenges are born out of and are subsequently healed.

Self-awareness designs focused on the individual have low success rates of less than one in twenty of those formally embarked on. Adjudicators find it difficult to assign a contributory factor towards measurable attributes of those that are successful. How much do our initiatives directly benefit societies we intend to serve? Can the benefits be quantifiable in social or technological innovations? Are they enshrined in a genuinely derived original challenge that needed addressing and is collective in its outlook?

We must be careful not to embark on high sounding challenges with no relevance in practice whatsoever, especially in the context of transforming our individual lifestyles and those of our immediate communities. Attempting to satisfy other external needs outside our contexts may strongly prejudice our levels of success. If one is fortunate enough not to run out of steam, all they may achieve is to get a pat on the back from those external factors.

It is challenging to find our true way towards our desired enlightenment, let alone disguise a bad one. Hence, grounding and originating processes of our integral design to our self-actualisation campaigns are critical for pure fulfillment node to node. The desired objective infitisimally reveals itself as we collect more and more of those nodes along the way.

We continually and progressively resolve to peel out like an onion gradually exposing the inner core of our being. It activates our in-built radars that enable clarity towards our final self awareness trajectory. Subsequently, the journey emancipates it into implementable *Strategic thinking that is **T**echnologically sound, **I**nnovatively viable, has **P**eople at heart and carries them along, evolving simplified **S**ystems that are **S**ustainable (STIPSS)*. Lack of necessary origination fails to harness enough energy to sustain emerging vulgarities that can be trying, turbulent and bumpy. Investing in a strong base at the beginning hopefully minimises and immensely increases our chances of success to sustain our journeys.

Unlike most narratives we came across before, this is easily the most deeply satisfying and life changing experience we may ever embark on morally, mentally, spiritually, physically and materially. Its inherent transformation is wholesome, holistic and visible for all to see. All those that know us and those whose lives we impacted can give testimony to the insightful and reflective transformation that they notice as we move along our journeys.

The first iteration into our origins and metaphysical initially yields very little. Subsequent ones start to give more as we delve in and gradually intently research on who we truly are. We begin with the history of our parents' ancestors from as far back as we can go. A correlation between our sense of being and that of the two parents begins to converge as we dig deeper. Its manifests clearly relate to the basic drivers of our inner motivations that make up the true tenets of our Calling. Our Calling, whether it precipitates into a social or technological manifest or imbalance, finds its core in the authentic inner and deeper self.

This rooting provides the necessary inner energy referred to as *ntu*. We need to engage it to provide us with lasting energy required for this journey. When revealed, we transcend to our optimal creative and innovative states, a primary tool for this endeavor. This maybe one of the missing links in the present pre-determinates of a potentially successful actualisation practitioner. How do we draw on the manifestation of this resource?

Our first research cluster satisfies the revelation of enabling primal tools within us. These make us function at our best, for optimal outcomes. We compromised it in the past by embarking on projects that do not engage with the best of us. We became farmers instead of doctors, engineers instead of social workers, teachers instead of politicians and practitioners instead of academics performing sub-optimally. This is so because we were unable to engage fully with inherent Energy *ntu* residing in all of us, latent or otherwise.

Some of us consciously or sub-consciously, manage to reveal their archetypes at very early ages in life. Those fortunate enough to do so relentlessly pursued their Callings to realise phenomenal success and satisfaction. We perceive them to have made tremendous contributions towards the betterment of humanity.

The adverse is also true. Equally, fully ignited negative energies resulted in truly spirited and lasting impressions that negated the advancement of humanity.It has produced individuals like Jonathan Savimbi, Idi Amin, Adolf Hitler and others. Notwithstanding, it has happened to a lesser extent.

The revelation of our individual Energy *ntu* is a cyclic process that varies considerably between individuals depending on each of us' process of individuation, socialisation and personification. We must revisit these experiences in their specifity but ensuring that they build on each other to reveal our whole.

The process we engage here is self revealing. It gets into corners that bring out the crest of our best drivers. Throughout various stages of our life cycles, these personified us into the unique individuals that we are. We now want to change the world by contributing something that will disrupt and alter the course of humanity till eternity. Once we exude and glow this belief from deep inside and authentically engage, it becomes inseparable from the self. We couple it with our identified driver, our Calling, that persistent thrust that needs quenching. Our inner voices speak to us when we walk into an operating or arts performing theatre, a children's home, an aeroplane, or into human catastrophe zones.

Inadvertently, we are who we are today because of our historicity, those life experiences and processes of socialisation, individuation and personification. We did not have control over who we are, especially during our critical formative years. We carry most of the responsibility of our contemporary being though. It might be a culmination of numerous coincidences and a series of decisions made on our behalf that has brought us here today. Inevitably, we commonly describe each other with our status and familiar titles in society, for an example professor, civil engineer, medical doctor, architect, accountant, social scientist, musician, artist, businessman and so forth.

When we begin to truly serve our Callings through archetypical professions, our journeys reinforce and exponentiate our *ntu* energies. Our resolve is elevated to a much higher dimension than the one we are operating at. We are enabled to tackle higher order complexities that reflect disorder and chaos in our lives. They take responsibility for the imbalances we contemporarily experience.

We emphasise this phase the most because it creates strong and authentic origination of our journey in the self and that of our family, community, our professional world or organisation and finally society as a whole. As will be discovered later, it impacts on the relevance of our lifestyles and praxis of subsequent philosophical resolutions that may manifest experienced innovations. How do we ground both sides of our parents' life stories and how does all this impact on who we are? Can we establish how our present day reality is influenced by its causalities? How did we come to be and what did this mean to all around us? How did our gender, position in the family, be it first, middle or last born impact on how we were raised, perceived and our evolution up to today? Slowly gaining these insights into our backgrounds prepare us for the now and impending future.

Eventually, the iterative cycles form clusters that go together and make sense to us. The number of cycles depends on various variables and the degree of our imbalance in culture, age, life style, religion, spirituality, learning-education-training styles, value systems, parentage, availability of resources and the spread of family nuclei etcetera. Interestingly, if we tell our revealed stories to people in the know like our grandparents, they are amazed with the preciseness of the minute details that we include. They will have forgotten or had less profound insights on some of the outcomes we emerge. It motivates them to proffer their own detail and versions to things.

Their clear understanding of what it is we intend to achieve and its value is revealed. One of the things that must happen with our main objective or hypothesis is to be understood by the most lay person who necessarily is not at the same level with us. If they can visualise the importance and necessity of what we see, then we are on the right path. We can extend it to our knowledge–people informed by the whole spectrum of the immediate community. We discuss with them the merits and demerits of what is emerging as a very important area of imbalance within us and our societies.

We will find exhilarating moments in most unexpected areas. It is overwhelming how there is an abundance of knowledge informally existing that is available to us. This untapped knowledge strongly impacts on the discourse that unveils in our personal lives with that of our families, friends and society. Our journeys reveal the depth of how ignorant we are of ourselves. We realise the existence of informal knowledge that impacts us outside the realm perceived as formal. The former carries our greatest potential to inform us on what it is that makes a difference and adds value to our status quo.

Some of the information we require is readily accessible and maybe fully catalogued, codified, even available either electronically on the Internet or in various libraries in one form or the other. It is difficult for the self to objectively bring out genuine new knowledge on self and decipher it conclusively to desired levels through these channels only. The process draws out our authentic secrets hidden in both the formal and informal to climax us through to our deep core energy *ntu*. Only the *ntu* draws out motivations that maximally energise creative and innovative juices towards our enlightenment. Clear analysis and articulation of the self lays out the expected trajectory of our journey. It comprehensively brings out both the analytical and transformative trajectories that are intertwined as one. As they unfold, they reveal our inner narrative. How can we ensure that our journeys synergically and integrally build on knowledge that exists on both local and global platforms, formally and informally? We desire our journeys to marginally enhance and improve learning-training-knowing processes, societal and global knowledge bases. Moreover, clarity of this feature is born out of this stage and roots all our future transformative and analytical considerations. How does all this become a reality in practice?

The easiest places to start are the usual analytical channels of discovery. These may cover the objective side of our life stories without going deeper into our socio-cultural elements. It is the story behind the story *ad-infinitum* that we need to keep digging. They objectify and give credence to our present day predicament and equally provide us with the basis necessary to *STIPSS* our integral design. The bottom-up approach reveals abundant higher levels of infinite energy we can harness to carry both our contexts and us through to realising our objective. Preferably, it may root us into both the existing local knowledge and global integrity elevating the quality and sophistication of our outcomes. It minimises dominance of our prior knowledge over the one emerging out of new discoveries from our in- depth authentic journeys into the subjective self.

At first attempt, drawing out the narrative feels quite superficial as we bring ourselves into the right mindset to soul search with the right amount of zeal. We realise that we go out of ourselves and explore possible channels to extract information unknown to us. Another interesting revelation is the espousal of the information our memories hold unconsciously. This does not come to the fore at first iteration. It is uplifting when it begins to build into explaining who we are in the present. It eventually relates to our precipitous Calling and then what it is that we are archetypically best at.

It points at which one of our role models or mentors we became, especially those that were involved with our guardianship in our early formative years. Our strength areas emerge but can only reinforce what we already are. We feel its authenticity when it rings true from deep within us.

We notice exhilaration and inner glow in the faces of those that we carry with us on our journey, particularly those that recognise part of the causalities and the related outcomes that manifest. Collective cohesion develops towards our individual definitions of desired lifestyles that are as many as there are people. This development assists as a vehicle to achieve our end.

Iteration after iteration, it all comes to us. We regret all those years that slid under our feet as if we were in a trance, feeling like we had all the time in the world to chase our dreams. We vertically pile graduation after graduation in ascending order from early childhood to most current, one on top of the other. We regrettably realise how our procrastination and sleeping for long hours distracted us. Others partied, watched television and surfed the internet excessively. We develop the energy to right it all and start to speed towards the life we feel is rightfully ours. We now appreciate that the success of those around us is our own. We are now keen to listen to their life stories and do not feel threatened by it all.

Our paths draw capacity from our unique energy, funneling it into a form of an enabling vehicle that implements it into practice. We actualise differently. We consider four cases here that attempt to reveal the varied transformational routes each of them took. They are particular. Their struggles and approach to experientially transform significantly differed..

As a researcher at one of the finest research institutions in the country, he considered himself a true man of science and rational thinking. That is the image he wanted to portray and had become to all his peers. He felt they expected him to approach his life journey utilising proven known classical methodologies and general principles of reductionism considered rational in natural sciences. This seemed to haunt him constantly. The process he was being asked to engage appeared to be outside his comfort realm of doing things. He limited himself to what he considered as a rational and objective approach compare to what others would consider subjective. Whereas, he probably needed to bring out certain aspects in his subjective and rationalise them into the objective as much as he could.

His resistance to an open approach greatly limited the emergence and engagement of his true inner energy *ntu*. It glaringly reflected on the final derivation of his trajectory towards inner enlightenment most authentic to him. The otherwise enjoyable journey became tedious, burdensome and at times unpleasant. Most aspects of his supporting structures appeared as if they had taken a turn to work against him.

His mind began to wonder aimlessly and his usual focus level was compromised. It was revealed through unprecedented behavioural changes and lack of commitment to chosen paths of action that he was party to. He continued to struggle to find his way and it cost him dearly professionally and socially.

The other three practitioners committed to the dictates of this inspiring journey. They quickly realised that the process added value and enriched them. They embraced and engaged the integral design to their paths whole heartedly from the onset. Their inherent ills and imbalances or challenges that had recessed into dormancy were revealed. Every drop, no matter how minute, quenched that thirst that had stifled them, occasionally at much deeper levels. They did not realise how thirsty they were. It was surprising to realise how this journey correlated and aligned most missing links in their systems.

The second case considered here was a highly relational person with an abundance of energy to share with all those she touched. She viewed herself as a rural girl raised by Pastor parents. The journey explained the level of her faith in people and strength in her spirituality. As short as she was, she towered those that stood next to her. It was was confirmed that she was a people person. Unlike the other guy, abstract concepts and working with machines was not her forte. The human factor and their welfare were critical to her. She could engage with anyone freely. She had always wondered why she had drifted and eventually resigned from a highly lucrative profession in Sales, to start her own enterprise in the social services industry. At the point she started her journey, her enterprise was thriving but she still felt some emptiness, a void that could not be filled with all the excitement that was around her. Our void areas are not always exposed into formal precipitous challenges. Through this process, our beings are conscientised to realise missing links towards our prospering significantly. It includes us in the mainstream of our economic and socio-political societies leaving our senses of individuality intact. We resonate ourselves with real life challenges that exist in our communities.

It was not surprising that her Brigg psychometric test results turned her out to be a strong activist, a trait that is an asset but missing to reflectors, theorists and pragmatists. Others turn out to be one of the other three, rendering them weak in relational tendencies. It makes sense to those of different traits to team up as they can borrow on each other's strengths. It became clear that each needed the other to develop a fully comprehensive holistic integral design. It showed that they lacked skills individually that others had to make them stronger.

Others have approaches we hardly ever emphasised before. In our circles of peers, like the scientist, he possesses traits considered to be for those that are competent at the abstract. In his circles, he is considered as the numbers nerd, lacking in empathy and relevance. We hardly ever consider our peers as incomplete when they lack any of the other three characters.

The third person didn't aspire for anything else other than her career, to successfully go up the ladder of her organisation. She was a self made professional who started at the bottom as a temporary rural teacher. She worked her way into the manufacturing industry. She was familiar with struggling for success and had burnt the midnight candle. She studied privately to achieve credentials to enroll for higher levels of tertiary education and training. She resolutely intended to stay at her place of employment with continual movement up the ladder as she accumulated more certificates on her wall.

She had a very close colleague with a similar life story. The two were clear in their resolve and focused to achieve their objective in the shortest possible time. They were prepared to do whatever it takes. It was not surprising that they immediately embraced the process to bring out their respective strengths and relate them to the fore, but only as far as it could benefit their professional challenge relevantly and employment advancement. Their objective was to keep it simple, clear and targeted. They teamed up and were soon on their journey. Hurried as it looked, they impressed all including their employers who noticed the transformation that was happening in their employees' lives.

How did they cushion themselves against eventual pitfalls and challenges that came with growth and related expansion of horizons? How was their ability to convincingly articulate future challenges through in-depth meditative introspection. It reveals how the coming together of our lives gravitates towards the challenge optimally suited to us. Engaging with our integral designs aligns the contemporary to our desirable present that manifests our foreseeable desirable future.

How do we manage to bring unconscious knowledge we accumulate into the conscious enabling it to benefit us in our transformation? How do we make known the known-unknown that is packed away deep inside us? How can this manifest in our optimal articulation of both our archetype combined with our inner imbalances? We all have them if we dig deep enough. We discover our need to address our ego issues that can easily be confused with our ultimate drive. It is a challenge in the beginning to separate the two. We feel pressure from our environments that includes our individual understanding of what a transformative self-awareness journey needs to be.

Filtration of the essence leaving out the huff evidently becomes primary in our quest to converge to our particular unique strengths. As we become more sensitive and endeavor to listen and hear more, distorting noises become louder as if to intentionally derail our resolve. We subconsciously develop the necessary skills to overcome this peculiarity with each iteration of journeying back into our life stories. The two appear to develop in tandem until we hit that crescendo where they diverge and the distortion begins to diminish.

Earlier on, we intimated the importance of visualising the end at   the beginning into a lived reality we can touch and feel. The stronger we manage to do this, the greater is our chance of realising it. The journey to this juncture has markers that check us in to determine our levels of correctness in relation to the intended trajectory that eventually leads us to our eventual reward. These markers are different for all of us; especially those intended to terminally and optimally bring together our transcendence. This can be through a formal educational, learning or training process.

The doctoral degree in a chosen and challenging area of interest appeals to some as most reflective of an epitome of success. It crystallises their chosen trajectory by holistic engagement of the trinity of learning, education and training. It fully projects and heightens their senses.

Interestingly, when we eventually decide on the route we are going to take, it can be a one hundred and eighty degree turn from what we believed all along. We and everyone around us expected us to be drawn towards engineering, mathematics, physics or some directly related area. Instead, we get wholly inspired and subsequently get absorbed into sociological sciences of creativity, innovation and technology. This, in our minds is a precursor to elevated and sophisticated manifest of the enlightenment we see in the world. It can also be the source to solutions we need contemporarily to heal the imbalances we experience.

We will now go through personal journeys we consider as most enlightening as a reflection of a major approach that we have encountered. We believe that the journeys we individually choose bring us maximum levels of emergence, emancipation and actualisation of our enlightenment. It brings us closest to what we believe to be our destiny, that *who am I* we silently yearn for.

As if the time we took was not long enough, we wait again another agonizingly long period after successfully taking our *viva voce*. The celebrated ceremony of completion to be attended by everyone who mattered in our journey is set and fast approaching. We are ready and impatient. The day we await eventually is right in front of us. It is now a reality and official. Our recognition of effort, sweat and acknowledgement of achievement is here.

The list of those that are fully compliant to attend the scheduled ceremony is now public knowledge. It gradually dawns on us that this journey is coming to its successful conclusion and is going to be uniquely a large part of our lives. Our thinking, our working life practices and the greater part of our meaning to success is coming to its head. This is a validation of our dreams that provides us the recognition and ability to mentor and role- model others.

We vividly imagined the eventuality of this day from the onset of our journeys. We are now at the dawn of death of one journey accompanied by a metamorphic re-birth of another in a form that maybe immediately unrecognizable to us. The vividly imagined and strongly anticipated is now alive and around the corner. It's coming to fruition and soon to be a lived experience. Our mindsets are fast adjusting to come in-tune and be fully motivated, spurring us forward to the ultimate day. The countdown was on, from day one and counting. It is no longer time-minus some arbitrary number in the wind. We are on the home run stretch and cannot imagine anything that can stop it from happening. Maybe except for that which comes out of the powers of darkness?

Shona underestimated the amount of time required to ensure that he met all the demands and requirements for this special day to happen successfully. All administrative issues were met before the deadline without exception. It was and still is a flurry. These were much easier routine and well structured chores to clear. Those mandated for it had done a good job of ensuring compliance. Shona progressively satisfied and ticked the requirements of every stage before embarking on the next one. By the time he satisfied all that was needed of him, there was only one thing outstanding. The ultimate was the celebrated conclusion of this particular phase of his life, its death and its evolved re-birth ready to tackle the next phase.

Shona's latest journey had its own life, especially in this phase where the ceremony was to be held in another country, with different norms and practices from the one he was accustomed to. The administrative side of things continued to pop out issues that kept him extremely busy until the last minute. It was issues from the University Council, the university administration and the national Qualifications Councils. Various forms still needed to be completed and issues to be confirmed.

He was required to confirm his intention to graduate and to attend the graduation ceremony, the University President's dinner, meals he would prefer, dinner dress code, hiring or purchasing the graduation regalia, photographer arrangements, number of his guests to attend the actual capping ceremony theatre and finally the chaperon into the graduation enclosure other than the academic and field supervisors. The onus to ensure that all of these were timely met remained with the graduating designate.

Then there were supporting structures necessary for the actual execution of these items throughout the penultimate and actual graduation day. It was a tighter schedule for those who had taken and passed their *Viva Voce* much closer to the graduation day. They had less than three months to meet all the requirements.

Each stage of the thesis examination received comments to attend to. Some could be fairly extensive enough to delay one's graduation to a later date. It is unusual for one to not succeed at this advanced stage if all processes where done meticulously. The risk of it happening is minimized if liaison between the student, field and academic supervisors remained optimally functional throughout. Sometimes delays to graduate can happen due to an unhealthy relationship between the candidate, the research facilitators or supervisor and the university council. It becomes increasingly paradoxical that the persons that doctoral candidates are supposed to have a cordial working relationship with are the same persons they strongly discourse with and at complete divergence of minds. It gets more difficult as the candidate's own voice awakens.

The tug-of-war in three different directions that can be experienced provides a fractal of what doctoral candidates (or students) lives can be like. As a liminal frontal player, their responsibility, among others is to develop a strong affinity towards fundamental societal challenges. At times, some of the challenges revealed are unbeknown as yet by the intended recipient.

Almost always, a liminal player, the visionary and the self-aware have a responsibility to convince various stakeholders of what they envision. Then they have to reduce that vision into an intelligible inquiry understandable by all. They are required to come up with terms of reference of that vision they see, in essence creating a job for themselves. Their clarity of vision requires and should be able to highlight anticipated outcomes that heal a societal challenge. This may initially appear to be imagined in the first place to everyone else who doesn't see it.

The buy-in can be agonisingly slow. Sometimes, the visionary's intended objectives, eventual transformative and healing processes may take very long to even be realised posthumously. It is a primary need to develop abilities and sensitivities to manage and foster a synergic relationship with those that at first appear to be working from the other side of the table. We are obligated to successfully bridge whatever differences that may occur.

Successful correction of changes suggested by internal examiners advances the thesis to three external examiners who are experts/ academics in those particular main areas addressed by the thesis.

External examiners do not usually have prior exposure to the thesis they examine except for the brief they get when they are appointed.

They must be convinced by the thesis of its worthiness in convincingly articulating and addressing what it purports to resolve. The primary tenets and requisites of this endeavor at the level being examined mustbe met.

Everyone gets a maximum of two opportunities to make suggested corrections before submission of the final thesis to the University. All comments must be addressed to the satisfaction of the examiners and the University. At times one maybe exempted and be allowed to submit with unattended minor diverse comments and recommendations from the three external examiners.

As pointed out earlier, one must prepare themselves for any eventuality during the examination process up to the finalisation of the Viva Voce. There are no absolutes as this area is infested with landmines. An open mind is critical, one that can absorb positively all forms of criticism, instantaneously drawing on the continuous positive energy required to appropriately react to any given negatives.

A significant amount of doctoral candidates are known to give up at this stage. The pressure can be daunting. One must be aware of it and be able to intentionally allow themselves to take all forms of turbulence that may come their way. Fortunately for Shona, he managed to attain a surmountable result. His External Examiners comments and recommendations could be attended to within the timeframe allocated by the University, in time for him to graduate.

Final stages of Shona's thesis left him physically, mentally, spiritually and materially exhausted. Revisions are never enough. Editing and comments from all involved keep coming. Then there are errors in formats and layouts, binding and finally the heavy cost of mailing the requisite number of heavy thesis copies to the university via overnight mail. His biggest hope was there will be no further unexpected demands that draw large amounts of any one resource.

Financial outlays creep upwards at a stage when any amount is too large after four years of continual draw downs. Costs were still there and several of them. Graduating Candidates were required to produce and submit a terminal paper on the highlights, the major learning points and future recommendations of their whole doctoral journey to accompany the final thesis manuscript. The paper is reviewed by an appointed examiner before the dead line set for the seating of the University Approvals Council. As it were, in all the frenzy of finalising and multi-tasking, some candidates are known to leave this for too late. A comprehensive checklist to minute detail came in handy. Shona prepared one that specifically related to his needs. It ensured total compliance on his part.

Then there is the purchasing of the graduating regalia. Hiring is suggested but for most, it might be prudent to purchase one. Unlike gowns for prior degrees, this one maybe required in future for ceremonial occasions.

Penultimately there is the issue of attending the graduation ceremony! Travelling, accommodation and board of one's entourage to the graduating venue require early attention and resolution. In Shona's case, the venue was located in another country.

Ultimately, there is the graduating day logistics, to and from the venue including ensuring that all guests can access the graduating arena or auditorium. Graduation ceremony rehearsals and photo shoots timing before the actual graduation ceremony is quite a huff. Once the rehearsals start, like a bride and groom, one can start to relax and enjoy the view; the wheel is in motion. It now has its own life, a momentum that cannot be stopped until it reaches the bottom of the trough. Shona's entourage agreed to enjoy the process no matter what happened and allowed themselves to be completely led to the pinnacle of the party. The powers of darkness were now totally annihilated!

The duration of a doctoral journey is a very intense and demanding engagement especially for employed part timers with a family. The situation obviates neglect of various unrelated activities particularly those of a social nature. Candidates' wardrobes correspondingly suffered for the four to five years. They were now old and inappropriate for any contemporary occasion. The dress code for is specific and requires candidates to acquire additional items. Resources, particularly financial, are stretched ready to tether. Most adult doctoral students are self sponsored from their savings and current income. Relatives will have been exhausted way before the finishing line. By graduation time, they are at the outer limit of their tolerance of any form of request. Those that still can may grudgingly oblige. Running on empty, they fully draw on all their energies, charisma and put on a brave face to pull it off. They prepare and are determined to harness every resource possible to what they believe is their last sprint to the finishing line. Was it all worth it?

****

Shona's contingent was led by his seventy-two year old mother and his forty-six year old brother. His twenty-four year old daughter, two sisters, two nephews, a niece and two sisters-in-law made the rest of the team. They flew into town on the morning of the dinner day scheduled for the eve of his graduation day. His brother and his wife flew into Johannesburg two days earlier from the United Kingdom. His call to notify us of their arrival came before Shona's departure from home. It triggered the ceremonious mood bottled in everyone. The whistle for the dyeing minutes of the game had been blown. Euphoria, excitement and anticipation set in. Their flight was going to be one hour and forty-five minutes.

His contingent met at the local international airport at 0530hrs for the 0700hrs flight. As all trickled in from their different homes, the discussion was centred on the impending honourous occasion.

Shona was older than the average traditional university graduating age in lower degrees. He took comfort in that his age was lower than the average for doctoral degrees in that part of the world. Airport staff and other travelers were openly impressed when they were informed that Shona was the one graduating, even more so when they heard that it was at doctoral level. Being a relatively small airport, news quickly spread throughout the lobby.

Shona had experienced being the centre of attraction on a minor scale several times before. He had not witnessed genuine respect and admiration in people's eyes and their demeanor at this level. Some even bowed their heads a little and shook his hand with both their hands obligingly. There was so much warmth and deep connectedness between everyone, a couple of times greater than anything he had witnessed. To imagine that most of these people were literally strangers!

His daughter, nephews and niece were quite overwhelmed. What they were witnessing was not common in their peers' world. They glowed and sparkled with pride and anticipation. Shona's desire to mentor others had just experienced a major boost, most importantly, to his primary target group, the youth. By the time the announcement to start checking-in came through, our youngsters were telling anybody who could listen the importance and significance of their trip. Cell phone calls were coming through from long-time friends, acquaintances- old and new, colleagues and other close family members. The unfolding of his dream was actualising right in front of him. The flight boarded and took off on time.

As they sat in flight, Shona's mind reminisced on how these issues had caused him great anxiety. It had immensely contributed towards his procrastination to register and undertake this journey. He had always known from a very young age his desire to get to this ultimate level. He realised there was absolutely no way he could ever have imagined and explicitly known how it was going to unfold.

Getting to this pinnacle of tertiary learning and training was exactly what the doctor ordered towards the healing of his burning quest, thirst and inner desire. It empowered him with the necessary abilities and competent opportunities to confront his many dreams. It skilled him to meet the impetus knowledge demands necessary to advance his enlightenment levels and those of others.

A significant number of people he encountered during his doctoral journey appeared not to fully comprehend what a PhD was all about and the importance of its holders. Most local families had never experienced nor made any contact with a Doctoral Candidate or a doctoral degree holder. Histories of their families were void of any previous attempts. Those that were familiar with it had only heard or casually read about it. Their knowledge of it was in varying degrees and vague, sometimes from complete misinformation to elements of reality. Shona was going to be the first doctorate in the history of his whole extended family. The closest in the clan to this peak of tertiary learning and training he knew first hand was his Medical Doctor brother.

Clearly, PhD awareness and development programs that clearly articulate its purpose, importance, requirements of registration and relevance to self and society were essential. What does it contribute towards high level consciousness and self-awareness? What is the purpose of a doctoral degree? What do they do and study at that level? How different is it from a Masters degree? What is their contribution to the broader society and the world at large, research and pedagogy, creativity and innovation? What is their specific role towards creation and formalization of knowledge, pioneering innovations and initiating life changing holistic transformation in their particular communities and humanity in general?

In the recent past, extensive debate raged in the public, electronic and print media on PhD pre-qualification requirements and processes of obtaining one. Pertinent areas of the various models available at fulltime and part-time engagement for mature and young adults, distance and extended contact learning and supervision or partial contact models as compared to the traditional forms of pedagogy were totally missed. The public further expected elaborate debate and discourse on the capacity of a doctoral graduate in terms of realisable performance that benefits society in the immediate, medium and long- term. Comparison and confusion with medical doctors was common as the function of the latter was known and greatly respected by most in society. Print and electronic media contributions that came through from scribes and various stakeholders supposed to be in the know were superficial, misleading and only scratched the surface. A critical opportunity was lost. The debate was trivialised when issues of concern were raised.

The thirst and demand for information on questions raised vindicate the need to write and publish on this issue. Public debate fizzled out before it had achieved the primary objective of informing, educating and reinforcing its importance to society of training at such a terminal level.

Shona's desired academic path was clear from the onset. He nostalgically retraced his journey this far in flight. There were many negative factors one had to escape to be successful, excluding those from the dark side. Their impact outside the obvious lack of awareness, mentors and role-models in our peers tremendously increased attrition rates of those that qualify compared to those that successfully register at the beginning. Then there is a further sharp convergence of those that register to those that eventually embark on their research journeys after completing all the necessary pre-requisites. Ultimately, we have those that embark on their research journeys referred to as Doctoral or PhD Candidates depending, to those that graduate. Statistics vary widely institution to institution and country to country.

Shona's intake started with two cohorts of 20 students each, three years and ten months earlier. These unprecedented high intakes were deliberate, but not common elsewhere in the world. The intention was to massify the chain and hopefully densify doctoral graduates per capita. The intention was to deliberately counter the high attrition rates that can dwindle to single digits. Only six out of forty on the starting line made it to the finishing line, providing an attrition rate of up to eighty-five percent for our particular intake. This rate is below average for most accrediting institutions, with some doing much worse.

Shona's thoughts were brought back into the cabin when the Captain's voice cracked from the flight deck through the plane's public address system. They were now in cruise at Flight Level 410 when the Captain decided to break protocol and be extremely honourous to announce by name two of his special passengers on board. A name came through the passenger address system to a thunderous applause from all the 120 passengers plus crew. Sheepishly, he unbuckled, rose from his seat and saluted in acknowledgment.

At graduate level, Shona's Masters in Business Administration, MBA class started with 28 students. Only two, equivalent to 7% proceeded to a PhD. The number of graduates at Masters Degree level was significantly boosted by the introduction and densification of distance, electronic and part-time work based intakes. Majority of these intakes are through private institutions. Unfortunately, their data is not readily available and not easy to quantify. It appears the percentage of those that proceed to Masters Degrees from first degrees does not exceed ten percent. The graduation rate at Masters Degree level exceeds seventy-five percent. Attrition rates of one in every hundred from primary education to university undergraduate enrollments are common. The rates of success from those that graduated in High School to those that got their doctorates are dismally under one tenth of a percent.

Most countries outside the technologically advanced world achieve doctorate concentration rates of approximately 1 in every ten thousand. These are five times lower than the one in two thousand recommended for doctorates significant contribution to a country's development. What boggles the mind is why they are so low when this is considered as a direct contributor to increased rates of development? Why is there a *leizzez affair* approach from most of the stakeholders in concerned countries? The domain includes individuals, families and embattled communities all the way to tertiary education institutions, civil society, local leaderships, the private sector, quasi- private organizations and governments amongst.

Emphasis is concentrated on achieving high intakes up to high school graduation and sharply tappers off as we go further up the ladder. Supposedly, training at first degree level produces quick interns that are immediately productive. Vocational training and apprenticeship development after high-school has been the alternative route.

These two areas appear effective in the application of existing knowledge, most of which is probably borrowed from elsewhere. It negates and limits the development of desirable relevant contextual knowledge that is frontally liminal and rich in local application, up- take and utilisation. Formalisation of local knowledge and creation of knowledge is vanguard to any society's development. Without it, considerable continual decay of people and whole cultures emerges.

Majority of indigenous communities are endowed with tacit knowledge. This is passed on from one generation to the next through apprenticing youngsters to the older and experienced folk. In the first world, knowledge has been formalised into explicit knowledge deciphered and developed by experts with long experience. It is thereafter clearly catalogued and codified. Alternatively, this is done through doctoral students, doctorates or equivalent and higher qualifications. They improve existing knowledge or out rightly create new usable knowledge that goes through rigorous theorisation and rationalisation. The ultimate desire is its maximal and optimal effective praxis.

The Captain turned on the sign to fasten seatbelts and announced top of descent for a long approach into OR Tambo Airport. The weather on the ground was a great early autumn day with clear sunny blue skies at fourteen degrees Celsius.

As the descent started to get slightly bumpy on short final, Shona's mind wondered on what his new role was going to be in society after his formal graduation. He peeped through his window on the left (port) side of the plane and could see heavy vehicular traffic congesting well-built Johannesburg concrete spaghetti roads. Cars looked like tiny toys in slow motion. As a single engine pilot and a keen aviator, Shona enjoyed landing sequences the most. He would imagine the few occasions he sat in the jump-seat in-flight a Boeing 737.

How was he going to apply himself most effectively for the good of his people particularly and all humanity in general? Was he going to be of any significance and make an impact at societal and continental level? Maybe even at a global platform? Where would he begin? The quickly globalizing environment felt extremely competitive and promised to be an uphill battle.

Shona expected to create his own space through various initiatives that expose worthwhile societal relevance. The traditional route was to join an established tertiary institution. Was that realistic and was there space there for rookie doctorates? A journey of a thousand miles starts with engagement. The way was to hit the ground running and engage immediately.

The main-gear touched down smoothly on full flaps. The wind sock indicated a fairly strong cross wind directly out of two o'clock, starboard side of the plane if you may. Shona was the only one clapping hands to celebrate the clinical landing. All on board looked at him sheepishly; he presumed they felt he owed the flight deck one. He wondered the same as they embarked onto the bridge into the main terminal gate.

Their entourages mingled naturally at luggage carousel number 14 as they waited for their checked in luggage. They exchanged the usual pleasantries and conversed. We soon departed for our hotels. Courtesy limousines offered by the hotel soon whisked us away.

Shona's limousine was adequate to take all of them. The other limo would take the entire luggage. Shona had visited Johannesburg innumerable before for important business meetings and work seminars on considerably long stays. He had a special fondness for the city and now knew it fairly well. This visit carried a special kind of nostalgic aura and a difference in the familiar surroundings.

Traffic filtered flawlessly in and out of the stacked four-lane spaghetti concrete highways. Each little particle in the conveyor went on its merry way to play its vital role. As infitisimal as their roles appeared, all these mobile particles contributed towards the sustenance of a whole economy and society. Was any of these minute particles conscious of their role in a very complex hierarchy; that without them, the whole system would not function as efficiently? Did they realise that they were genuine representatives of the whole? Collectively, they fully represented and contributed to a formidable force made up of loyal and committed foot soldiers.

There he was, wondering again what his role was in this complex and seemingly chaotic grand machinery. Where was his fit in all of it? His slot was waiting for him to fill in the whole hierarchy and only needed him to find it.

His contingent allowed him to enjoy his thoughts for a moment. The trip from the Airport to the hotel felt much shorter than previous ones. In no time, they were at the hotel check-in counter getting key cards to their rooms pre-checked in by his brother and his wife. The rooms they got were not the best as they had arrived much earlier than the official check in time. Occupants from the night before were still in their rooms. They got rooms that were unoccupied the previous night. The alternative was to wait a few hours until after check out time. They accepted the inferior rooms on the split ground floor level with a promise to upgrade once better rooms became available. Here they all were, all checked in with less than eight hours to the graduation dinner!

The High Schools Shona went to did not have prom nights. A function in their honour the night before graduation was a new experience. He envisioned it to be the same intense fling he witnessed in his daughters on their prom nights. His adrenalin was rising to a hilt. He was experiencing uncontrollable and sporadic shot bursts of shakes from it. He acknowledged it to himself but tried his best to conceal it from everyone else.

The dinner hosted by the President of the Da Vinci Intitute of Technology in honour of doctoral designates is a very popular and prestigious event. The Institute holds it on the eve of graduation day. Invitations to the function are mailed out three weeks before. Preparation for it is hectic and may specify type and colours of preferred dressing considered not offensive to other guests. These tend to require more resources depending on how many of the required items already exist in your wardrobe.

Shona noticed that most had to settle for the same attire for the two occasions. Come to think of it, the graduation regalia envelopes the dressing underneath. In hind sight, there was no need to fuss. The added advantage is that most guests are more fascinated with the main event to notice. Total rookies that they were went all out. It is impossible to adequately prepare for both events. All the excitement is focused on the more glamorous and all important University Council, droned in their much fancier gowns oozing with troves of knowledge and wisdom.

The Dinner started at 1800 hours until late. The venue was the very exclusive and extremely prestigious Johannesburg Country Club. It is located in the old and exclusive part of Johannesburg. The momentum and mood from there was to carry into the following day's graduation ceremony. Its venue was the much bigger and much grander Witwatersrand University Students Centre. It was scheduled to start at 1400hrs and conclude at 1700hrs.

Shona left the hotel at 1600hrs to allow for heavy traffic at knock-off time. He engaged his usual taxi driver on all his previous visits. They now knew each other fairly well. The taxi driver was a strong Christian man who loved his family and people in general. His love for people exuded through his ability to converse happily with anyone he made contact with.

He gave Shona a broad smile of appreciation to see him and for the business. He smiled wider than ever before as he had never seen Shona look this sharp. If he remembers well, the taxi driver clapped his hands as he did a three-sixty degree dance opening the rear door of his taxi for him in the process.

Shona wore a conservative deep navy blue Super 60s double vent

Cambridge blazer, a high thread count snow white shirt with a short folding Chinese-inspired collar, a black Italian bow tie, a charcoal grey trousers, black leather belt and matching lace-up black respiratory shoes. He was feeling a little uncomfortable as, over the years, he had adopted a more informal dress code of short sleeved blue collared shirts with no tie, khaki trousers and all kinds of black or brown shoes adopted from his rookie Engineer days.

They made slow but continuous progress towards the country club. They were on schedule to arrive 15 minutes early. The driver had offered to stay and wait for him in his car to take him back to the hotel when the function finished.

The venue was ideal for this occasion. It was a massive place with a strong colonial presence, undulating thick lawns under very tall and old indigenous deciduous trees. Very old but well maintained, mostly white double story buildings with a Dutch architectural look, sparsely and tastefully located gracing the undulating terrain. Security was strict at the gate. The guards insisted on accompanying every car to its allotted parking bay and to the function check in desk.

A zero cloud cover, blue night sky starded with distant stars rolled into the distant horizon. Shona had hardly ever been that fascinated with early night stars to that extent, but that night he took a moment to take it all in. They were experiencing a South Westerly five knot breeze that dropped the evening temperature to hover around a comfortable twenty five degree Celsius. He could feel every bit of himself as we walked down the slope to the clubhouse. Most of the guests had arrived, escorted by immaculately dressed gentlemen in dark suits, the contrary escorted by the most beautiful and elegant ladies on their arms. Two ladies were graduating out of thirteen designates.

Shona expected to be familiar with most of the guests that were there but realised that he only knew six of them. The other seven designates came from two other cohorts of resident South Africans and a broad mix of international students from India, Germany, the United Kingdom, Nigeria and United States of America. All the same, the jovial spirit around lifted everyone's mood to easily mix and mingle. He maneuvered his way through with the program Director in front of him. He was introduced to everyone that could be reached on both sides.

The four camera persons, three on still and one on motion were all kept busy. They did a great job of making all the guests mingle and comfortable with each other as they arranged them for photo shoots. Shona was immediately whisked away to join one group. They were all talking and laughing with champagne glasses in their hands exchanging pleasantries when the call came through to start walking into the ballroom on a two and half metre wide deep red and cushy carpet. Chaperons at the door escorted them to their spacious tables arranged in a horse shoe with a podium and several microphones at the top middle of the open end. Slowly, the tables filled and the whole room was buzzing with chatter.

The Chancellor's welcoming speech, at 1900hours prompt, called everyone to attention. He passionately welcomed all the guests especially the thirteen graduating designates. He moved to introduce the guest speaker who delivered her speech in ten minutes. She mostly emphasised the importance of PhDs in moving research and development forward. She was soon followed by a senior Academic Supervisor's message that took them into their starters to a phenomenal Durban Opera quartet of young adults in the background. The student representative's message was delivered soon after, leading to the main meal at 2000 hours.

Before dessert, the University Council Chairperson delivered his speech full of humour and satire. Guests were in stitches half the time with his martial arts metaphors. He spoke strongly on the role of Universities in the country, in the region and Diaspora. They had another twenty minute treat to fantastic Opera music during dessert. The wine waiter was the busiest person in the room. At 2100 hours, the President of the University started introducing the designates providing elaborate citations of each one's research journey. They were individually requested to come forward for a photo shoot with the University's Chairperson and his President.

Formal introductions lasted some thirty minutes. The thirteen designates were asked to open the dance floor. Shona could see why they all successfully went through their doctoral journeys. Their heads did most of the dancing. The rest of their bodies' co-ordination required intense choreography. Partners and the Opera quartet joined in to save the beautiful song. The youngsters creatively re-arranged some local genres into opera. It was an ingenious creation that resonated strongly with all the guests. The Quartet was adopted by the University when they were starting out five years earlier.

Shona was back at the hotel lobby sitting with his brother and brother-in-law at 2245 hours, sipping a glass of red wine. The President's Dinner was done and memorably so!

The entourage got out of bed well before 0600hrs the following morning yet the graduation ceremony was scheduled to start at 1400hrs. The night before had stirred considerable excitement and curiosity on what was to come on this great day. Shona had not expected so much. The Doctor in his whole clan was his younger brother, a medical doctor and Anesthetist of repute since he was 25. The rest of the crew, except his mother, held undergraduate degrees from Universities spread around the world.

They were in a foreign country, an enough fit to cause all sorts of anxieties. How was this going to go to the graduating venue? Johannesburg was notorious for its traffic. Were the processes and customs familiar and maybe similar to something they had witnessed before? They agreed to make it an exciting experience for everyone. They were going to celebrate in the best way they know how. It calmed some nerves but Shona's were still dithering at breaking point.

They requested the hotel to arrange a long breakfast table to accommodate at least fifteen people for 0800 but only managed to start at 0830. His two hilarious nephews resident in that country were the last to come in. They apologised and blamed it on traffic. Shona's mother said grace as soon as the little excitement was over. The prayer started off slow but they all knew it will be a long one, as she gained confidence and warmed into it. It gradually peaked to a loud, audible enough for the next few tables to hear. They appeared not to mind. Her prayer was all encompassing. They waited and listened patiently until she finally said the magic word. They all responded with an enthusiastic *Amen* in unison.

One absentee they all strongly felt could have echoed his mother's prayer was her late husband. It was a matter they all skirted around to maintain the excitement.

Conversation was light and easy, touching on everyday contemporary experiences. It was catching up time to reminisce and reflect collectively. Funerals had taken centre stage as the one thing that made families congregate. Otherwise, the traditional sense of an extended family had almost disintegrated. They hardly knew what was happening in each other's lives. This was an opportunity to re- ignite the collective spirit, that *Ubuntu*, the humaneness that allows them to share their successes and failures, the good and bad, the joys and sad. There was so much to catch up on.

Our collective doctrine as a family, drilled into us by our parents used to manifest through important facets of our lives in the past, from eating, parenting, and sharing of happy, as well as our grief moments. It was emphasised as a must and a way of life, not a convenience.

Breakfast progressed as the dining room slowly packed with other hotel guests. The buffet staff was busy but appeared to be managing comfortably. The lady Chef kept an eye on them to ensure they were adequately provided for. It was well after 1030 when they started to file out to their hotel rooms to prepare for the main event of the trip.

Unlike the route his nephews took into town, traffic was exceptionally light. The mini-bus driver maintained close to maximum speed limits without a fuss. The four lane freeways were mostly dotted with delivery vans, highly decorated salespersons vehicles and a few elderly people that looked like retirees not hurrying to anywhere. They asked for directions to the proper venue of the university's three main compasses.

The auditorium was already buzzing with activity when they arrived. They moved around ensuring that they met all the pre- requisites before the 1230 deadline. There was registration to be done, hiring or purchasing of graduating regalia and contracting the official photographer- the only one authorised to take pictures during the graduation ceremony. All private photographing was strictly prohibited. The whole pre-requisites process hardly took 30 minutes at most. By then, graduants were required to proceed to different practice halls depending on the degree being awarded.

Doctoral Candidates shared the practice hall with the Masters Degree graduating class. Shona decided to give the honour of one accompanying chaperon allowed to his daughter. They were issued with two sets of tickets to take with and hand in at two stages of the graduation process. One identified them as they went up the stage when their names were called-out and the other was for the capping photographer.

The Programs Director pointed out that unlike all the other degree programs that needed us to queue, we were required to stay seated until our names were called. Shona's chaperone would escort him up to the base of the podium and return to her seat. His Academic Supervisors received and stood with him on the podium, one on each side as the Chancellor read out the summary of his research work starting with his thesis research inquiry.

This was truly the moment of glory he awaited for a long four years. He was in some kind of a daze throughout as he looked at the pool of eyes and kind faces of the audiences eating in the auditorium. He could not fix his gaze at any one face but finally decided to target the Program guest of honour. She was the South Africa's Public Prosecutor renowned for her fairness, boldness and protection of the marginalised. Her face was kind, welcoming and encouraging.

The little shiver that was with Shona since the ceremony began started to dissipate. At one point when they were filing in, he regretted not having used the bathroom, again. All this completely disappeared to the extent that he managed a genuine smile at her, which she kindly returned. It was at this moment that the official photographer's picture came through. A great portrait indeed! The pinnacle of his PhD journey.

In this final phase of our focused and concentrated self-awareness journeys, we will have acquired considerable experience in working in liminal frontiers. In the beginning, we become effective at the first level of the infinite spectrum ahead of us. This is the individual level. It then radiates to other levels as we grow.

The issue of resources is usually sighted as a pertinent and primary issue. It may have bogged down or even failed some of our initiatives to take off in the past. We occasionally let it overwhelm us to the extent of abandoning our desires and perceived projects. The easiest route is to run to known sponsors to bail us out, if we are fortunate enough to have some.

Outside family and other benevolent financial angels, the common alternatives are government, private corporations, non-governmental organisations, financial institutions and donors scattered throughout the world. There are an infinite number of sustainable avenues to take towards our enlightenment. Each one of us has a preferred model or format that suite them best. The PhD experience route is one of them that epitomized Shona's educational, learning and formal training life journey. Either way, we should not allow limited or total lack of resources outside our inner initiatives and corresponding inner latent energies completely stop us.

As we analyse our various situations, we pragmatically consider existing resources at hand. There are various permutations and combinations of these resources that can achieve different results with varying levels of success. The more exhaustive we are with our scenarios, the more chances we have of achieving different results without adding any new outside resources. It is the derivation of combinations that results in novelty that is truly afrintuneurial. At this point possible outcomes from novelty combinations are a grey area that needs discovery. We must figure out as much as we can how it is going to work out to impact, achieve and surpass desired results on our journeys and those of our meta-ecosystems. Are the perceived outcomes going to be sustainable?

At early stages, it is acceptable if our ill-defined combinations make sense more to us in relation to our given contexts. We will discover that sometimes it is not the availability of new resources that is critical but the need to avail specialised expertise and know-how, to have the relevant knowledge people competent enough to cognize relevant and effective combinations that result in desired innovations. Our lives are a continuous infinite set of combinations we preferably make from most enlightened positions. How do we, as knowledge people, technicians and experts of our situations handle possible outcomes from our new combinations to effectively, continually and consistently reveal the lifelike lifestyles from one cycle to the next?

W. Brian Arthur postulates a few possibilities that we can start with.

We develop further combinations unique to our particular challenges. The optimisation process of the experienced outcomes transcend into the next stage of development. It results in new combinations that yield and enhances previous results, functionaries, activism and even produces tangible products. Up to this stage, we mostly make all efforts to rationalise our combinations. We then move them to sense-making. Does it make sense in relation to our definition of the lives we desire for ourselves? How about our communities, compliance to the original terms of reference we strategized at the beginning and to all stakeholders included in our meta-ecosystems?

Once we are convinced that it is making sense, we consider our skills sets to handle the outcomes we experience including formation of strategic combinations and alliances that further spiral our performance to the next level. Most importantly, we maintain that upward movement no matter how small to avoid stagnation and complacency. That trans capacity fosters the need to constantly adapt to change, a necessary capacity for our initiatives if we are going to sustainably survive.

We soon realise that the enlightenment path we engage here is organic hence it most likely is going to be interrelated, contextual and integrative. We will be answering to process abilities with their related contextual frugal and global technologies. We should be prepared for self-discovery ventures of our systems and abilities to handle complexities that may arise. These require open ended systems with indeterminacy and emergence of perpetual novelty, accepting and giving to the world. Our perpetual challenge is our mindsets, identification and engagement of the impetus philosophy appropriate to implement and actualise our dreams and initiatives. We may cut and paste, simulate, become fully self aware and *kaizen* but it all necessarily needs to be realised for us to actualise the lifestyles we desire.

Our journey is a continuous one that reveals gaps warranting necessity for a contextual form of entrepreneurship more suited to the dictates of our contexts termed *Afrintuneurship*. Its integrated design approach requires a *creative and innovative, an enterprising process that is collective and culturally, ecologically, technologically, economically, politically and socially contextual. It must be implementable with local application and global integrity creating self-determination and socially conscious individuals, communities, organisations, national and global societies.*

Our senses of being is in our self worth born out of what the collective thinks we are worth, the *I am because we are* as posited by Mbiti. It is rooted in our sense of collectivism driven by our individual and collective imbalances and/or opportunities. Exposure to our spirituality enhances our self-awareness. It assists in optimizing the identity of our archetype and calling.

Inclusion of our contexts confluences our archetypical Callings with the context value system through its fundamental and sustainable cycle of re-discovery and strategic renewal. The evolution of balance manifests through balancing of dialogical tensions and dialectic approaches through collective inclusion of familial enterprises. Our mindsets are re-oriented and worthy human wealth unfolds. All these outcomes are rooted in communal imageries and individual-collective dynamics that are authentic derivatives of our past, present and desired future.

These precipitously transform our structural effectiveness and functionality that materializes societal flourishing through living the lifestyles that we most desire. We desire it for others as well. Our success and satisfaction is derived from theirs. Our senses at this point are elevated above our egos to manifest inner development of the soulful and spiritual self. Effectively, our elevated senses of self awareness practically and effectively contribute towards ameliorating identified imbalances within us and our given communities. A eureka at this stage will have funneled the essence.

The way we relate with all the different everyday facets of our lives that make survival possible, no matter how trivial each may individually appear synergically adds up towards our objective. How we connect with family, community, our work engagements and the environment reflects, impacts and founds our humanity and everything else that concerns us intrinsically becoming part of us. To travel far and wide to become that we wish, we need to travel with all the others. Alone, we appear to progress fast but inevitably come short.

We bring to battle all the tools at our disposal to develop a powerful enough thrust for forward movement. A weaker thrust may not be able to go far. How do we reinforce our humanism to develop that dynamism to continually move towards the holistic? How can we have both the humanism and holisticism in adequate critical minimum dosages that bring us the consciousness we need, one that is wholly inspired beyond our imagined capacities? How can we make our journeys personal and prophetic as well as holistic processes that can pretty much tell and develop us towards the quality of our desirable future lifestyles?

Our humanism engages and heightens our sensitivities to relationships with everything that touches us. It starts with us pushing to know ourselves better, to know what we are capable and incapable of, our emotions, our senses of love and jealousy, happy and sad, anger and light heartedness, success and failure, hate, respect, submissiveness, independence, inclusiveness generosity and sharing. We need to know how it engages with others, our immediate communities and the broad society, at our workplaces, the environment and all else.

We add on the view of holisticism that empowers us in its primary tenets of cultural and spiritual inclusiveness. These bring us deeper insights through dialectic engagement of those aspects we mentioned earlier that persistently affect us. We will notice that buoyancy in them provides us the domain and wisdom necessary to merge our dreams as well as our realities. We become capable and enabled to create the impetus knowledge for us to become. But not all desires, wishes and initiatives amount in us realising our lifestyle ambitions. How do we ensure that at least eighty percent of them become successful in the end? How do we critique the brilliance that we envisage to work for us? How do we make our subjective present daily life practices into those whose integrity is widely acceptable?

We become cognisant that nationalised initiatives have lesser chances of success. Most important are those approaches that impact on our persons directly that require our best Afrintuneurial skills informed by related knowledge from the roles of nature and community, cultural practices borrowing from our consciences, available science, systems and technology and finally the impact of enterprise, economics and socio-politics. Our mindsets are experientially developed with dominant

220

particular views at the exclusion or even total absence of other equally important ones.Its compartmentalisation results in exclusive senses of being. Our rationalisation processes need to bring all available related knowledge to the liminal front. Unfortunately not all rationalised knowledge is pragmatic. It requires active application to justify its necessity and levels of success.

As we transform into our true selves, we become ready to accept the new us and develop the ability to let go past assumptions we now find irrelevant. Can the emergent explicit be transcended into the tacit? We now actualise our original prophetic objective through evolution to produce a better us, extincting the lesser, adapting to the new and becoming it in the process.

We incorporate, in enterprising fashions, all the dimensions of our living systems through our personalised integral designs into our interdependent and interrelated lifestyles linking us to everything important to a life worth living.

The chronological series of lifestyles we desire that follow can lead us to our objectified one. It holistically develops, building integratively on the prior lifestyle, giving it birth with an ability to anchor and strongly found itself fully in its origins. From the day of our birth, using it as the lower delineation, nature has provided us with sequential processes that that gave birth to self development from learning to sit, crawl, stand, say our first word, walk and run and so on. Similarly our process of individuation and personification analogously went through the same cycles of learning, education and training to perform elementary tasks up to the present tertiary levels putting us into the professions that we currently enjoy so much.

Society and politics tend to want to safeguard itself against dissent, to maintain its perceived steady-state that is constant and predictable. This is usually achieved by indoctrinating societal mindsets to function in a predetermined manor devoid of behaviors disruptive to the status-quo. Advocates for mind conscientising resumes that effect individual independence, with a sense of absolute freedom are viewed as rebellious to the expected norms of practice. They are considered not desirable. This is characteristic of highly learned or highly self aware people, to an extent that they are looked at as outcasts and can even be ostracized by society. As we awaken this latent being that exists in all of us, we diverge and upset the societal, cultural and institutional fabric that personified us in the first instance.

Our inner awakening manifests in our ultimate desire for self employment that affords us flexi-time to do things that we desire and love the most. The ability to self-determine how we use our time capacitates to dream, ideate and imagine as we please, providing us the freedom and individual distinction to create and innovate to the fullest extent of our being. It capacitates us to operate at much higher levels of complexity required to confront and overcome the dichotomy between our need for cooperation, connection, our individual distinction and absolute freedom. The inadvertent and side effects of pandemics, the COVID-19 lock downs and its intermittent births and re-births of new normals!

In trying to maintain and secure its preferences, society has over time engineered political and socio-economic philosophies that greatly influenced the world we live in today. We enjoyed the glories and suffered the ills of all to varying degrees. Their influence on us widely varied. Cumulatively, we are now the living product of the influences of those structures that fissured and became fully blown volcanoes erupting all over the world. We have all been impacted by them, in some cases helplessly so. It is this sense of helplessness that we need to minimalise at all costs.

Achieving minimalised helplessness requires conscientised and determined effort to skill and equip ourselves effectively in our spirits, souls, minds and bodies. We cannot achieve it effectively without seriously going through a total process of holistic self-awareness that is fully cognisant of the major philosophies born out of the four major worldviews. The South has renowned itself in its collective and relational Ubuntu. In the East we can look at its spiritually, religiously and culturally laden knowledge creating philosophies like the *Kaizen* and *Confucianism*. In the North and West is the pragmatic, theorising and rationally realisable capitalism.

CHAPTER 8

LIFELIKE-SOCIETY SONG AND DANCE

Integral self awareness design, at its pinnacle, places those that realize their full enlightenment in the top one percent of the world's population in understanding their specific areas of enlightenment. This is coupled with a synergic translation of lifestyles as per our defination and desire. At some point, if we keep at it, we can even be *numero uno* in specialised areas related to our archetypified calling. Achievers of this feat place into a category of enabled people least understood by society. These few purposely need to make extra effort to be understood. On first encounter with others not in their realm, they may seem nerdish only to gradually transform into a unique, peculiar and select few.

A sharp decline of those that successfully engage the self-awareness journey reveal the importance of having carried others with throughout their journeys. It can be exhausting and debilitating to be unable to easily articulate and communicate something we consider obviously clear. As self made emissaries of enlightenment, it is of critical importance that we carry those around us with towards making the world a better place. It does not matter how minute we may consider our individual contributions to be.

As our transformation progresses, we become familiar and comfortable with soliloquising, especially in our dreaming and ideation stages. It helps us to concentrate better and draw from both our consciences before we begin to assist others into processes of collective deeper analysis.

At the beginning of our journeys, we tried hard to convince, be understood and carry with us people we otherwise traditionally sideline, both economically and socio-politically. We get better at striking engaging and meaningful conversations with each try. That ability continually develops in us as we grow into a permanent feature to engage at any time. We intentionally and pointedly converse with the taxi driver, the gardener, the barman, the priest and the gym instructor explaining desired accomplishments with our enlightenment as it unfolds. We can now competently encourage others to intentionally embark on their journeys spring boarding from their authentic inner and outer knowledge.

We painstakingly preach to anyone who affords us an ear to listen and hear! We take time to chat, to extend and even show off our discoveries no matter how trivial they maybe. Physical acknowledgment in agreement and reviewed our audience is a good indicator of our emerging eloquence and convergence of minds.

However, some stand there gapping at us wondering if we are going mad. Others choose to politely agree with us even if they don't understand a thing we say. This dialectically indicates who we are against varied perceptions of the social challenge we intend to confront.

We persevere to articulate our dreams, visions and ideas effectively. Our intention, direction and most of our ideation processes gradually become intelligible to our audience. The discussions we now engage regardless of level, from janitors to CEOs are two ways and mutually beneficial. Sometimes they may appear complex using specialised verbose, technical language and intertwined thought processes we picked up along the way. It is an unavoidable side effect we need to work on as we get better. We continually endeavor to adopt simpler ways that effectively communicate our views.

Now that we are getting clearer on what we know for sure and that which we don't, subsequent cycles of our self awakening become more articulate and focused with a refined end objective in mind. We start to eject families, friends and colleagues from their old selves into our emerging realms. The imaginary virtual video of ourselves we made at the beginning of our journeys come in handy at this stage. It reminds us of who we were just before we started and how much progress we are making towards our objective.

The fog around our hunger and thirst lift from the conversations we have, dreams and ideation processes we engage that do not necessarily conform to the everyday discourse around us. Our want becomes more than the eye can see and longer than the reach of our arms. We still feel mutilated and imprisoned to liberally explore those voices making noises from within.

Our sense of time to take all this in and adapt to become part of   the new is relative. It is measured through our transformative ability to become and effect the desired new. It reveals itself in the functional and structural transformation of everything around us. It starts with the self and radiates throughout related functions of our societies. There can be a mis-match in the time frames between the various ecosystems that we need to engage with radical thinking that encourages abrupt reconstruction. Indoctrination to constantly searching for paths that lead to self consciousness with radical forward movement towards a focused sense of reality is the advocacy of most self-awareness initiatives. It provides us with a journey of self and knowledge discovery, an opportunity to reframe our mindsets. These equip us with necessary imaginative reach that has both analytical and transformative power.

Our life processes of individuation empower us to handle structured linear and simple situations. Parental guidance, community involvement, education and learning curricular all work towards our enablement to deal with steady-state domains, those that are contained within the norms of society and institutional settings. Success is measured against our ability to succeed and excel within defined cultural boundaries. Subsequently, individual voices and independent initiatives are muffled to different levels depending on the varied global cultures.

How then do we get to build our unique sense of being onto this culturally laden centeredness? How do we break away from this trodden path but still be able to interface and carry with us the goals and objectives of that cultural path to our desired destination?

It becomes imperative that the linear, the simple and the uni- dimensional does not quench the hunger and thirst our self-awareness trajectories manifest. Our reality now requires us to action and reciprocate, to cyclically move from the simple to the complex and back, from the complex to the chaotic and back, linear to non-linear and back, and finally from uni to multi-dimensional and back.

As we action and reflect through these cyclic processes we are empowered to decipher complexities in our lives to the easily comprehensible simple, linear and one-dimensional that is practical, usable and implementable. This cannot be achieved without moving ourselves in tandem with our various ecosystems through decentring or decentration, temporarily unraveling or unstabilizing societal perceived steady-states.

We impact societal processes; the micro to macro economics at first, possibly expanding and radiating outwards giving birth to a desirable new, hopefully in line with our prophetic view. Sometimes the new may surprise even us, to be something that we never envisaged. We need to be prepared for any eventuality and be restructured to match and adapt to this new.

Our effect may not be felt in the expected period or within our time. How then do we carve all the life activities around us, our businesses, our humanity, our livelihood and our capacities towards any kind of eventuality? How can we include the full participation of all our societal stakeholders from institutional to the civic, private and public communities? How can we create solid foundations for all involved to quantum leap towards a comprehensive and inclusive lifelike existence?

Integrally designed approaches engage most aspects of our lives resulting in specialised awakening in a few and above normal to excellent consciousness of the rest. The transformative philosophies empower us to dig deep into the inner core of challenges we perceive subjectively as individuals and objectively as societies. In the process we are awakened to methods existing in nature's ways. They engage inexhaustible energy for their sustenance, answering to a specific role throughout its ecosystem.

Similarly, we learn to copy nature relevantly to answer to our Callings and Archetypes. We develop the impetus consciousness and engage methodologies that form the basis of our sustainable existence. Our creations and innovations manifest in the technologies existing in nature. We have so far been unable to fathom the necessary energy to engage these nature ways that form our originations and foundations. We learn to skillfully integrate the collective energies inherent in communities and their respective cultures that intimate a specific worldview to bring out our best collaborative effort.

We realise our subjective-objective abilities, capabilities and capacities to zero-in on confronting our varied challenges as we perceive them. We filter those that truly need resolving for our healing and that of our societies in particular and humanity in general. It defines the status of our situation coupled with trans-abilities, dynamics and mobility towards comprehensive cognition processes. How do we learn to stand on our previous platforms and prepare ourselves physically, mentally and spiritually to that which we anticipate to confront us?

We prepare for this moment throughout, to be able to face all our life's adversities as well as its joys. We are naturally equipped with the necessary tools concealed in our bodies, minds, spirits and souls. Certain specific and focused processes only manage to enhance, sharpen and bring to the fore capacities we draw on for appropriate praxis. Without them, the higher order and extremely complex challenges faced by many global societies would remain unresolved. We require continuous evolutionary skills that empower us for the spirally transcending challenges we face now and in the future. We need the ability to renew ourselves constantly, develop the great ability to get up instantly without hesitation when we fall and do so better prepared than before.

Our challenges reconnaissance into a better format each time we fall. We require new thinking, new capacities, evolve energies and knowledge systems to overcome the rejuvenated new form every time we get up from a fall. We strengthen our approaches through engaging our centuries old meditative philosophies, generations of research and development, some of it hidden in latent cultural knowledge. Its frugality creates a renewal platform for us to become that which we desire. It appears, the more we engage our cultural juices, the more creative we become. We also increase our objectivity, rationale and capacities to theorise all that we claim.

The Integral Design we employ here demands that we try to engage all possible views that add value towards our desired quests for elevated consciousness. Views we engage to originate from those that are best at it. In the past, those that were in the know elected to deliberately exclude some of the best views necessary to a wholesome solution. They never gave them a chance. They considered their views as entirely rationale, pragmatic, relevant, applicable and practical. They excluded those they viewed as subjective, incompetent and not relevant to the contemporary. Today, we can agree that this has come back to bite us. We now know that no matter how effective a proposed solution can be to any socio-political innovation, an economic challenge or a technological advancement, as long as it is not inclusive of the other relevant worldviews especially that of the end user, it may not fly.

Sub-Saharan Africans are collective and strongly relational rooted in their centuries old philosophy of *Ubuntu*. Asians cultural approaches are laden with spiritually renewing doctrines. Europeans are emphatic in their pragmatic and reductive Newtonian rational and theorising approach. Finally, Americans seem to love to create and build things in technology, toys to play with and over-emphasise practice. If the rational and theory cannot result in a chair that can comfortably be sat on and watch sun-sets then it is not necessary knowledge and needs to be discarded.

Shrinking of the world through globalisation can now competently borrow from any one of the worldviews to relate local demands with the integrity of the rest of the world. Our Integral Approach becomes richer and richer as it builds on local application and relevance to global integrity, recognition and acceptance. Knowledge creativity and innovation that emerges can now qualify to go through the demands of scrutiny and rationalising rigors from outsiders. Amongst many other integrative worldviews, it finally has to pass the American fundamental question: *Are we enlightened and conscious enough to effect a better lifestyle for ourselves and our peers?*

In our short lives, we had moments we strongly believed in our capacity to create. We sometimes considered it as a sure thing and gave our all only to be terribly disappointed at the very end. Some of our creations, depending on how adventurous we were, failed in dreams, in ideation and some at the design table. Those that made it through formulation had to withstand scrutiny from relevant stakeholders. Others had very limited social success. Similarly, some individuals that were viewed as highly capable in high school and universities failed to find equally luminous relevance in the real world.

Effecting of our creations becomes key in the end. Can they be converted into usable and practical livelihood innovations? Can they solve life challenges and bring about healing to our sores? Can they bring noticeable positive structural changes to those that are directly affected by it? Are the functional behaviors of the concerned areas sophisticated enough to improve or to close existing fissures? Are the affected societies happy with the outcomes of the praxis of our contributions and lifestyle innovations? Are we prepared to positively handle the desired outcomes or are these going to create a higher order challenge we are not ready for? Do the targeted consumers of our contributions really care or want them?

Traditional approaches to awareness are particularly focused to achieve a set of objectives. Contemporarily, there has been a major shift towards addressing individual issues from the liminal zones and frontiers of society. Demand towards traditional areas of engagement are dwindling with a marked increase in self-initiated, self-driven and conscious based approaches that impact on society.

There is an infinite demand and space for front line thinkers, skills and expertise, but function in well defined domains that are vibrant and land mine infested. We thrive in its frontier utilising and capitalising on integrally designed approaches inclusive of all of us. These harnesses transformative energies that are now part of us to draw on wherever and whenever we need them. Our consciousness of their presence is deliberate with an equally developed relative humility necessary for its emergence. This requires us to submit to the dictates of our situations and contexts.

We are what our energies require us to be at any given point and time, to be a volunteer giving back to the communities that serve us, to be philanthropists, motivational speakers that highlight the importance of learning, education and training at the highest level, to be creators, innovators and technocrats that chat the engagement of new knowledge systems and their manifest technologies and cultures, as academics and scholars. Finally to function as business and societal leaders that bring academia, research, civil, private and public sectors closer together in praxis. We transcend to function as the best advisors, best designers, writers, researchers, advocates of success and preferred people to be around when there is a crisis or a deep need.

We are capacitated beings through our highly trained minds empowered with acute perception, analytic enough to conceptualise solutions where most see none, systematic and resolution oriented. Let us open up those liminal spaces through humbling ourselves into practice and application, capitalising on our newly acquired abilities as conscious, self-aware and fundamental purveyors of the hidden truth.

It helps us to manage change with hope, to control our destinies with self-determination and replaces fear with courage to lead and confront our dreams, our ideas and ideals, creations and innovations to solve our daily life challenges. Some of the initial processes we may go through are unrewarding and unbecoming in the initial stages but will definitely and eventually.

We are in to the top one percent of those in the world that are highly capacitated to predetermine the level of success they desire to achieve in any endeavor.

The lifelong and omni-directional discourse towards our desired levels of enlightenment is consistently being defined and redefined. It affirms and expands the same original challenges we perceive at the beginning, but evolving them into higher order and more detailed arguments gradually demanding more with each cycle. It demands more out of us as it reveals itself more. We are taught to strive more to know more of what we don't know on an issue. In the process, we developed the capacity to constantly and persistently interrogate an issue to minute detail. We are now exposed to an unenviable position of having to convince one judge after another and one jury after the other.

From here on, double-jeopardy is acceptable and welcome. We are tried many times over on an issue from all possible perceivable angles by anyone who takes an interest in our stories. Our discourses vary widely in breadth and height. We develop the ability to engage constructively all forms of realities, views and eventualities we perceive. It becomes a comfort zone for us that we increasingly begin to shy away from anything with subliminal discourse. Instead, we focus, cognise, recognise and address topical societal issues that have zero to minimum buy-ins from society in the beginning.

Luminaries who made evolutionary contributions to the world to date had long range visions. They at times led lonely lives but developed comfort with minimum desired company or none at all. This has given them time to concentrate and hear their dreams, ideation and creative processes. They volunteered their time to catalytically activate other external discourse ecosystems that impel their ideation processes forward.

When Steve Jobs started to dream of touch screens, he volunteered advocacy and strong campaigns throughout the world of inventors first and then to other colleagues, users, shareholders, financiers, monopolies commissions and governments.

In Africa, Strive Masiyiwa fought governments to legislate the operation of the first generation cellular networks. There was considerable resistance in opening up African airwaves. Richard Branson, now a prominent aviation entrepreneur convinced Nelson Mandela on his vision to introduce health fitness centres affordable to the black majority with a long view to minimising health bills in future and creating healthy productive nations. This was at a time when South Africa had just gotten its independence and was struggling with other seemingly more pressing problems of crime and poverty.

Bill Gates devoted himself to pioneering research on completely eradicating malaria throughout the world, especially in Africa. Oprah Whinfrey's thinking without the box decided to pursue girls learning centres as an initiative towards empowerment of the girl child and minimising inherent prejudices both in South Africa and Zimbabwe.

Examples cited here are pioneering initiatives that are visionary and did not have any support from local authorities and other stakeholders initially. The four entrepreneurs considered had to aggressively lobby for their visions to see the light of day. They fought from the liminal frontiers of society, where there are constant deaths and rebirths of ideas, constructive-destruction of initiatives and war-zones of conflicting worldviews.

Contemporary and future practitioners of self-awareness infinite journeys require strong tools that create own spaces through innovative identification of a socio-political or economic need sometimes not yet known as an imbalance by the benefactor. Their c reation e ntail massive research into challenges we perceive, lobbying, consciousness and awareness campaigns, dedication to volunteerism, sacrifice and indulgence. It entails ventures out of secure and predictive environments of tenure into green fields of unproven and unknown knowledge and capacities.

It will be through iterative processes of self-discovery, inclusion, building of networks, knowledge creation and continuous fundamental research that one can find relevance. It usually starts from a position of without slowly transcending to within through innovative creations of combinations and recognition, expert identification, professional and competent handling of outcomes. It is from this capacity that our contexts of stakeholders organically co-create and manifest our soft and hard material needs.

The journey towards realising the success we desire can start in the most unexpected places. The energy thus derived can take us into unfamiliar territories like appearances at early child learning centres, high school career days, youth conferences, guest appearances at parties and any other community engagements that enhance our profile. It might appear irrelevant and unrelated to our desired developmental path in the beginning.

It is interesting how enlightening the questions these seemingly unsophisticated engagements pose. They can start from the meaning of every aspect of our exterior demeanor like the regalia we wear, if any, to our whole interior life and educational careers, the challenges we faced and had to overcome. They can interrogate our self-awareness journeys and relevance to society and finally specifics of our desired future. They ask simple questions that may reveal and improve our understanding of the self and related ecosystems in deeper detail.

In-depth understanding of our obtaining status-quo and its related undesirable future outcome; the present day we wish for and its related desired future continually moves towards us. It synergically prepares and creates a strong foundation into our future as prominent leaders, as academics and business practitioners. The new us make our societies much richer. The sum of all its parts becomes that much greater than the whole!

We struggle with finding ourselves; discovering and knowing exactly who we are; recognition of our competences and ranking them in a hierarchy, from the strongest to the weakest. Have we developed ourselves to a level yet where we are fully in charge of our strengths and weaknesses? Are we now able to satisfy our lower order needs to raise our hierarchy of motivations toward actualization of our archetypes and callings? Are we merely surviving and existing without much significance to self, our families and communities? Are we living successful lifestyles of our dreams?

We experience difficulty in impeded upward movement from our present to a more rewarding one whose benefits are universally visible, acceptable, inclusive, intelligent and STIPSS. Our investigations reveal our slots in life and contributions toward positive change in our societies at large. Infitisimal as they may seem, they transform us vertically, resulting in the most rewarding self realisations of consciousness. It concurrently and longitudinally manages to achieve the same in the collective, especially in the immediate family, communities and organisations.

Our hierarchies of motivations converge to considerations unique to us as individuals and our respective societies. Interfacing commons concurrently unfold. We holistically understand our authentic selves. Achievement of that desired vertical movement becomes less elusive. This motion, as it progresses increasingly release higher marginal energy that enhances our capacity to reduce tensions tied up in our lower order motivations. Higher order motivations progressively become more complex and chaotic.

We release marginal energy resources for the pending forward transgression to the next higher rung. A unique sense of beauty, visions, imageries and focused dreaming comes into perspective and becomes alive. Our archetypes are awakened further reinforcing our dreaming to a higher order sense of creativity. Lessem and Schieffer view dreams as originating from critical and inventive imagination exercised in dialogue to create and re-create our world to guide its recreation. The new dreaming order necessitates us to avail and keep on us recording devices constantly, even at our bedsides as we sleep in the event of unprecedented visitations.

On the other hand, our families simultaneously get their eureka moments as we move forward. Their desire to share our experiences and conversations grows stronger and more enthusiastic. Their thirst increases with their reality as they experience self discoveries in ways they had never imagined. The envelope extends to encompass friends and the immediate community.

We sense, feel and share in their vibes alive all around. We can now freely talk, communicate, proffer suggestions or even argue healthily accepting to re-buff or be re-buffed without fear, favour or expectation of any form of retribution. It is an exhilarating and satisfying feeling that is momentous in the beginning but become exponentially more frequent.

The dream is now fully ignited and living within all immediate ecosystems. We transform towards the realisation that we are who we are at any point in life because of our families, friends and communities. We achieved to be who we are inclusively, from our individual merits buoyant in the collective. Continual recognition of the individual is critically important. We are who we are and they make us who we become. We are fish in water. As much as the fish is responsible for its daily survival and decisions that impacts it directly, its livelihood is determined by the water around it.

A bream is considered an intelligent fish. It first bites bait on a hook from the back and yanks it. Quick response from the fisher to reel it in immediately indicates to the bream that this was a dangerous meal and survives the day. Less intelligent fish swallow bait, hook, line and sinker and they are caught from the stomach. Both lives are totally dependent on the water, its presence, quality and behavior, as much as there is significant symbiosis of co- existence.

The pond dreams to exist throughout the worst drought and the fish dreams to survive the fishermen and the fish eagle. The water only needs to change form to live another day, but the fish perish when that happens.

The collective dreaming, ideation and conscientisation process becomes an everyday thing. This is encouraged and acceptable. Through it, further cracks and imbalances in our lifestyles are revealed that require support for us to embark on healing pilgrimages. Our inner burning desires coupled with our outer burning challenge must converge to focus on gaps in our lives that need heeling.

It is through linkage of all these contributing factors and their integration that our local relevance transcends to universal acceptance with intelligence and application that we desperately desire. The final song and dance is the genesis and evolution of a whole new cycle for us as individuals and for the whole of humanity in general. The differential between our life stories and life histories is that the former describe our lives in as an authentic manner as we can, and in most cases as we are told it by others, whereas the latter narrates those life stories in the context of their histories.

We managed to consider both starting with our life stories and then up-scaling them into our life histories that explain the how and why of our past up to a minute ago. Our life histories thread through those of our parents, families, communities and societies making them highly contextual, relevant and practical.

This threading has its challenges that emerge and become more complex as our domain expands. They bring with them conflicts, beliefs, myths, truths, falsehoods, dogmas, dualities and dialectics that can be difficult to explain their source, origins and foundation. It brings us into the dilemma of explaining their authenticity, of filtering what is, what may be and what is not. How do we bring it all into acceptable balance to build stories that can relate to everything that impacts us, considered real, reasonable and can instill in us lifelike lifestyles? How to we move from our mundane life stages towards the best of us, the unblemished us based on the authentic notions of the self? How do we balance them strategically, technologically, innovatively, with people, in a *STIPSS* way and manner?

The application of *STIPSS* is best exemplified by San Tzu's integral approach to the *Art of War*. His integrated approach to military maneuvers can easily be reduced and adapted to our life challenges at individual level that are genuinely authentic to civilians and equally to the military and institutional entities.

Our life journey passes through this world in relative time. We are around for a very short span. We therefore should commit to make the best of it.

It is a true revelation and surprise to most of us that a detailed approach to this depth to know who we really are to fully engage our paths to full enlightenment is necessary. Families, like a pond of water, are usually the first to notice the fish's abilities; how well and nimble it is when swimming, its senses of impending dangers, its sickness, levels   of turbidity and toxicity of the water. They are quick to pick resonance of our adventures with those of the family. They may not have had the opportunity to air their views in the past. They are confident to comment when they see an opportunity to participate in our development, especially after becoming adults. It is a chance they take reservedly and with great caution but become more confident at our invitation. They are touched by our authenticity and deep desire to truly reveal our areas of most strength.

In some areas, they know more about us than they ever profess. It dawns on us how they subtly mentor and role-model us illicitly. We are all fine examples of ourselves from the personhood built out of their commitment. They allowed and desired us to be respectable, develop professional careers second to none and become fine human beings that can fully participate in the development of others.

How does our development to the present carry them with us? What roles do those close to us play, especially families? Our continual self-development with attention to the values of prior knowledge filters through into the contemporary providing us with the background to dream. We can even embark on those highly revered undertakings; those that make seriously brave men stew from within and cower never to be heard from again. We can abundantly unbind our psyche to levels a few traversed before with the buoyancy of our families and networks.

Our definitions of personhood have a direct bearing on the levels of commitment and competence that we achieve. Commitment and competence are a part of primary inputs impetus to our journeys. Through our intended advocacy, these two tenets are exposed to the best of our abilities. They are enhanced by strong influence from dialectical cultural, collective, modernist and traditional tensions to a balanced apprentice like upbringing. How do we rationalise, culturalise and spiritualise these throughout? How do we optimally mix determinant variables consistently at play in our realities with those that help us to self organise towards the realisation of our deep seated inner desires? Sensitivities may differ with gender, place, time and space.

All aspects we routinely deal with are time related. It is never enough lest we be overtaken by absolution. We intermittently manage it efficiently before we lag and are under pressure. We cannot afford to burn out in our lifelong self-awareness journeys. Those consistently around us unwaveringly support, prop and spur us forward whenever we start to falter. They ensure we get to where we are now. Our symbiosis with society propels us into the lifelike.

Our families are a consistent aspect that requires perpetual attention and inclusion for structural and functional evolution of our self- awareness. Familial issues can either stifle or even inhibit our progress if mishandled. Among others, family involves friends, colleagues and networks we associate with on a regular basis and directly influence our lives. The immediate, from siblings to relatives, partners or spouses; with parents and off springs from the inner circle.

The one thing that this journey is jealousy of is time. We must constantly stay cognisant of how finite this resource is. We always have very little of it and its primary relativity tenet does not help very much.

We proffer a daily productive time period of between sixteen and eighteen hours. We count minimum blocks of fifty minute concentration spans coupled with ten minute breaks. Every minute counts. In short, our relationship with time becomes more intense and intimate as we become more self-aware. The trilogy between the time units we spend on those we love, as a productive resource and for recreation inclusive of play and social issues is tensile. Love and recreation time units can be selfishly demanding and not sensitive to processes that our journeys demand. We re-emphasise the need to consciously engage these units fully from the onset.

We may not get it right the first time but then develop avenues of righting it as we go along. It catches up as we become converts. It is important for us to recognise an opportunity when it stares us in the face. Relationships with partners like a spouse demand personal attention and cannot be subordinated. It usually appears as a small issue but its deficiency rear its head as the journey moves everyone forward including our partners. Its rearing can be triggered by anything from lack of attention, missing of special events, anniversaries, visits to family and friends being unavailable. It all hits the fan if, God forbid, it begins to affect intimate relationships. It usually does at some point.

Bedroom issues are clumsy for most people to talk about and address. Denial that a problem exists dominates. It then transcends to over-emphasis of corrective measures that attempt to zero in on the causal factors. We refuse to see obvious commons until there is damage with consequences. Unfortunately, we unnecessarily endure long periods of denial until we finally see the point. What do we do about it from here on?

Half-hearted engagements compromise the rhythms we settle in to a point of sacrificing our relationships. In retrospect, we realise that we trivialised it and did not give it the attention it deserves for no other reason than our egos and half-committed proud approaches. This issue impacts us all, especially those with timelines and are desirous of producing pioneering outcomes. It needs to be addressed formally before we break down or worse, lose our relationships.

The high divorce rate amongst those on their quests of enlightenment journeys is a culmination of similar issues. It is a whopping forty-three percentile! This high statistic coupled with societal divorce rates provides us with a major social problem. We must ensure that it authentically becomes part of our collective journey. The family unit must join in with equal enthusiasm. They encourage and spur us on, protecting us from other demands of our familial social life. They transform with us. And indeed, issues become manageable through their cooperation. Unsolicited successes and opportunities arise. Transformative energies flow unabated.

In conclusion, Stephen Hawkins advises us to *remember to look up at the stars and not down at our feet. Try to make sense of what we see and wonder about what makes the universe exist. Be curious. And however difficult life may seem, there is always something we can do and succeed at. It matters that we don't just give up.*

Bibliography

American Economic Review: *Papers and Proceedings.* 2008. 98:2. Pg. 363-369 Arrighi, G. (2007). *Adams Smith in Beijing: Lineages of the 21ˢᵗ Century.*

Economics and Enterprise. London: Verso of Unilaterism.

Arthur W. B., (2009). *The Nature of Technology: What it is and How it evolves.*

England: Penguin.

Connor, A. M., Karmokar, S. & Walker C., (2014). *Doing Entrepreneurship: Towards an Entrepreneurial Method for Design and creative Technologies.* New Zealand: University of Auckland. 2014 Design Ed. Asia conference. Hong-Kong 2-3 December 2014.

Da Vinci Institute. (2015). *Wise Sayings.* Johannesburg: DaVinci Institute. Goldin, C. & Katz L. F. ( ). Transitions: Career and Family Life Cycles of the Educational Elite.

Hopwood N., (2008). *Doing and Becoming.* London: University of Oxford. July

2008.

Horn J., (2008). *Telling Tales About the PhD.* July 2008.

Kishima, T. (1992). *Political in Japan: Democracy in a Reversible World.*

Princeton, NJ: Princeton University Press.

Kiyosaki, R. T., (2009). *Rich Dad's Conspiracy of the Rich.* New York: Business Plus.

Kurtz-Costes, B., Helmke, L. A. & Ulku-Steiner, B. (2006). *Gender and Doctoral Studies: The perceptions of PhD students in an American University.* University of North Carolina, USA: Gender and Education.

Vol. 18, Issue 2. 2006. Pages 137-155. Published online on 16 August 2006.

Lessem, R. & Schieffer, A., (2010). *Integral Research and Innovation.*

London: Farnham. Gower.

Levinson, D., (1991). *Seasons of a Man's Life.* New York: Ballantine Books. Lewis M., Haviland-Jones, J.M. & Barrett L. F., (2010). *Handbook of Emotions.* Books google.

Merell, F., (2001). 4th Ed. *Simplicity and Complexity: Pondering Literature, Science and Painting.* USA: University of Michigan Press. Amazon.com

Miytaba, Scarff, Cavico, Miytaba. ( ). *Challenges and Joys of Earning a Doctorate Degree: Overcoming the ABD Phenomenon.*

Montefiore, S. S., (2010). *Speeches that Changed the World.* London: QuerusPublishing PLC.

Otto, M., ( ). *Sharia and National Law.*

Perkins, D., (1995). *Theories of Intelligence.* http://www.otec.uoregon.edu/intelligence.htm

Stark, K. & Bainbridge, W. S. (1987). A Theory of Religion. *Toronto Studies in Religion.* Vol 2, New York.

Seelye, H. N. & Wasilewski, J. H. (1996). *Between Cultures: Developing Self Identity in a World of Diversity.* USA, Illinois: NTC Publishing Group.

Smith, A. (1776. *The Wealth of Nations,*

Stonequist E. V. (1937). *The Marginal Man: A Study in Personality and Culture*

Conflict. New York: Charles Scriber.

Thomson, P. & Walker, M. (2010). *The Routledge Doctoral Students Companion: Getting to grips with research.* London: Routledge.

Tyler, B. (1999). *The Philosophical Legacy of Behaviourism.*

Wellington, J. (2003). *Getting Published.* London: Rutledge Falmer.

Wellington, J. J., Marie A., Hunt C., McCullock, G. & Sykes P.(2005). *Succeeding with your Doctorate.* London: Sage Publications Ltd. http://www.jobsontoast.com/after.the.phd/

Humphrey, C. *Life After PhD- * Inspiring post-PhD interview websites.* Accessed on 22.09.2015 http://www.aeaweb.org/articles. php?doi=10.1257/aer.98.2.363 http:// www.guardian.co.uk/ money/2008/may/17/workandcareers

Overell S., (2008). *The Guardian.* Saturday, May 17, 2008.http://www. findaphd.com/advice/phd-types/other

Not just a PhD: Other types of Doctorates. Accessed on 25.06.2015 http://www. fiandaprofessionaldoctrate.com/advice

HYPERLINK "http:// www. fiandaprofessionaldoctrate.com/ adviceProfessional%20Doctorate.%20 Accessed%20on%2025.06.2015"

Professional Doctorate. HYPERLINK "http:// www. fiandaprofessionaldoctrate.com/adviceProfessional%20

Doctorate.%20 Accessed%20on%2025.06.2015"Accessed on 25.06.2015. http://www.psychologydictionary.org

http://www.psychologytoday.com

Index

Social entepreneurship Socrates

Stevenson, H., Josting of 4 Elements of Success

STIPSS   Strategic, Technology, Innovation, People, Systems, Sustainable

Strong Stage Taoism,

Thomson P. & Walker M., Tibetan statements, Transcultural enlightenment Transdisciplinary objectivity Transformational terrain

Tyler, B. (1990), Co-constructed realities, The Philosophical Legacy of Behaviourism.

Wellington J., Worldviews Youthful Stage

Acknowledgements

Reading unedited scripts is an arduous and tedious process that is time consuming and exhausting. Only a few gifted people can commit their minds to such a task. My unreserved gratitude to all who consistently and passionately got involved in the research and writing of this book that took two years. They patiently took the time to read, comment and edit my work in its raw form.

Ronnie *Samanyanga* Lessem, his colleague and friend, Alexander *Mukanya* Schieffer of Trans-4-M Academy for Integral Transformation, Geneva; Bennie Anderson of Da Vinci Institute of Technology, Johannesburg, South Africa; Steve *Wesa* Kada and Paul *Chidhara* Muchineripi of BTD Business Training Centre, Harare, Zimbabwe were instrumental in my journey as a writer. Lessem and Schieffer invited me to be a contributing author to the book *Integral Green Zimbabwe, A Phoenix Rising*.

My eternal source of inspiration and moral support has been from family, especially my late father, my four daughters and my brother, Webster. Special mention goes to my late mother (January 2022), for being such a fantastic Counselor.

To all my friends and colleagues for their immeasurable support.

To Da Vinci Institute of Technology and Innovation, Johannesburg, South-Africa and BTD Business Development, Harare, Zimbabwe.

www.ingramcontent.com/pod-product-compliance
Lightning Source LLC
Chambersburg PA
CBHW021619120626

46545CB00001B/299